The External Dimension of Justice and Home Affairs

This book proposes to cast some theoretical and empirical light upon the external dimension of Justice and Home Affairs (JHA) which has become a priority in the European Union (EU)'s external relations. Counter-terrorism, visa policy, drug trafficking, organized crime or border controls have indeed become daily business in EU's relations with the rest of the world. The external dimension of JHA is a persistent policy objective of the EU and its member states, as the 1999 Tampere summit conclusions, the 2000 Coreper report, the 2005 Strategy for the External Dimension of JHA, and the integration of JHA chapters under the European Neighbourhood Policy testify.

With an interdisciplinary ambition in mind, this book reflects an attempt to draw together theoretical and empirical insights on the external dimension written by academic scholars that take an interest in questions of JHA and European Foreign Policy (EFP). It does so from an issue-oriented perspective (civilian crisis management, the European Neighbourhood Policy, counter-terrorism policy, visa policy, passenger name record) but also from a geographical perspective with in-depth analysis of the situation in the Western Balkans, Georgia, transatlantic relations and of the Mediterranean neighbourhood.

This book was published as a special issue of the *Journal of European Integration*.

Sarah Wolff (MSc London School of Economics and Political Science) is a research fellow in the Clingendael European Studies Programme (CESP) of the Netherlands Institute of International Relations 'Clingendael'. She recently defended her PhD in International Relations at the London School of Economics (The Mediterranean Dimension of the European Union's Internal Security) and was a Fellow of the "European Foreign and Security Policy Studies Programme" of the VolkswagenStiftung, the Compagnia di San Paolo and the Rijksbanken Jubilaeumsfond.

Nicole Wichmann (Master, College of Europe, Bruges) is a Visiting Researcher at the Sussex European Institute. She obtained a MA in European Political and Administrative Studies from the College of Europe, Bruges.

Gregory Mounier (Master, College of Europe, Bruges) is PhD student and teaching assistant in European Politics, University of Reading. He is also a Fellow of the "European Foreign and Security Policy Studies Programme" of the VolkswagenStiftung, the Compagnia di San Paolo and the Rijksbanken Jubilaeumsfond.

The External Dimension of Justice and Home Affairs

A Different Security Agenda for the European Union?

Edited by Sarah Wolff, Nicole Wichmann and Gregory Mounier

Routledge
Taylor & Francis Group
LONDON AND NEW YORK

First published 2010
by Routledge
2 Park Square, Milton Park, Abingdon, Oxon, OX14 4RN

Simultaneously published in the USA and Canada
by Routledge
711 Third Avenue, New York, NY 10017

Routledge is an imprint of the Taylor & Francis Group, an informa business

© 2010 Taylor & Francis

First issued in paperback 2013

Typeset in Sabon by Value Chain, India

All rights reserved. No part of this book may be reprinted or reproduced or utilised in any form or by any electronic, mechanical, or other means, now known or hereafter invented, including photocopying and recording, or in any information storage or retrieval system, without permission in writing from the publishers.

British Library Cataloguing in Publication Data
A catalogue record for this book is available from the British Library

ISBN13: 978-0-415-49719-0 (hbk)
ISBN13: 978-0-415-85112-1 (pbk)

CONTENTS

Researching the External Dimension of Justice and Home Affairs

1. The Justice and Home Affairs Policy Universe: Some Directions for Further Research   1
   KAREN E. SMITH

2. The External Dimension of Justice and Home Affairs: A Different Security Agenda for the EU?   8
   SARAH WOLFF, NICOLE WICHMANN & GREGORY MOUNIER

Institutional Features of the External Dimension of JHA — The Input Dimension

3. The External Dimension of the Area of Freedom, Security and Justice: Hijacker or Hostage of Cross-pillarization?   23
   PATRYK PAWLAK

4. Civilian Crisis Management and the External Dimension of JHA: Inceptive, Functional and Institutional Similarities   43
   GREGORY MOUNIER

Modes of Interaction with the Neighbours — The Output Dimension (1)

5. Deconstructing the EU's Routes of Influence in Justice and Home Affairs in the Western Balkans   63
   FLORIAN TRAUNER

6. The External Governance of EU Internal Security   81
   SANDRA LAVENEX & NICOLE WICHMANN

Opportunities and Limits of the JHA External Dimension — The Output Dimension (2)

7. The Externalization of JHA Policies in Georgia: Partner or Hotbed of Threats?   101
   LILI DI PUPPO

8. When the EU is the 'Norm-taker': The Passenger Name Records Agreement and the EU's Internalization of US Border Security Norms   117
   JAVIER ARGOMANIZ

9. The Mediterranean Dimension of EU Counter-terrorism   135
   SARAH WOLFF

Index   155

The Justice and Home Affairs Policy Universe: Some Directions for Further Research

KAREN E. SMITH

Department of International Relations, London School of Economics, London, UK

The articles grouped together in this special issue are all based on papers that were presented at a workshop at the London School of Economics in October 2007. The workshop was organized by the enterprising and enthusiastic editors of this special issue, and all the papers presented at the workshop were by young scholars working in the area that they have termed 'the external dimension of Justice and Home Affairs'. The workshop was sponsored by the Challenge and EU-Consent research programmes, which are funded by the European Commission under the Sixth Framework Research Programme. Challenge is a research project that looks at issues of internal and external security, and the implications for liberty within the EU; EU-Consent is a network of excellence focusing on issues of deepening and widening within the EU, and has a working group on the link between internal and external security.[1] Both programmes strongly support the work of young scholars, by funding their participation in workshops and conferences, and encouraging them to publish the results of their research.

The subject matter of this special issue is an increasingly popular one; academic interest in the European Union's involvement in 'Justice and Home Affairs' (JHA) has intensified over the past decade and, as JHA issues have been incorporated in its external relations/foreign policy, academic attention has naturally gravitated towards this 'external dimension' as well. Arguably, young scholars have contributed much to this trend, as can be seen also in their intensive and active involvement in networks such as Challenge and EU-Consent.

Justice and Home Affairs is generally held to encompass a wide variety of issues, including immigration and asylum policy, the fight against terrorism and organized crime, and judicial and police cooperation within the EU. These were the issues that originally fell within the purview of the Maastricht Treaty's 'third pillar'.[2] That pillar soon became a very busy one, with numerous meetings at all levels — resulting in what Monica den Boer and William Wallace (2000, 503) termed an 'intense transgovernmental network'.

Such intense activity continues. Each year the Council and/or Commission churn out a bewildering number of ambitious 'strategies', 'comprehensive plans', 'global approaches', 'action plans', and 'action-oriented plans' on various aspects of JHA — all listing measures to be taken in the short and medium term within the EU and outside it; implementing them all is much more of a problem. An increasing amount of money has been devoted to cooperating with third countries on JHA issues: for example, the Commission claimed that between 2000 and 2006, some €934 million from the EC budget and the European Development Fund was programmed for third countries (excluding the Central and East European countries) in the migration field alone (European Commission 2002, 47, 51). JHA issues, such as the fight against international terrorism, organized crime and illegal immigration, are discussed increasingly in the EU's dialogues with third countries and regional organisations; clauses on cooperation in such matters are being included in the EU's agreements with third countries; and sectoral agreements on JHA issues — including readmission agreements — are being negotiated with a growing number of third countries. Clearly, then, there is much activity for academics to analyse.

However, it is no longer a straightforward matter to pin down what JHA or its 'external dimension' means. Justice and Home Affairs is a term that dates from the Maastricht Treaty and denoted the third pillar: the remit of that pillar was set out in the treaty, as were the decision-making procedures and roles of the EU institutions. However, over time, the third pillar has essentially disappeared: the Amsterdam Treaty made provision for moving many JHA issues, particularly those regarding immigration and asylum policy, into the European Community pillar, meaning that those issues would henceforth be decided on according to EC procedures (and, therefore, would be subject to different decision-making and integrative dynamics). The Lisbon Treaty — if ever ratified — would complete this shift (though throughout this process, various opt-outs have been allowed for some member states, notably the UK, and special procedures, some temporary, some not, have still applied to decision-making on JHA issues). As a result, 'JHA' or 'third pillar', indicating a coherent set of issues and procedures, is no longer an accurate label. Likewise, the 'external dimension of JHA' is becoming less and less useful as a descriptive term. Arguably, in fact, it was never appropriately an exclusive label anyway, given that some 'JHA issues', such as terrorism, have long been dealt with by foreign ministers in the 'second pillar' (first European Political Cooperation, then the Common Foreign and Security Policy).[3]

So it may be more useful to consider JHA to be a 'policy universe' — comprising issues that are dealt with at the EU level under a variety of different institutional set-ups (first pillar, second pillar, and remnants of the third pillar) — and across all of them. Those issues can be summarized as immigration and asylum policy, and combating crime (including terrorism, drug-trafficking, currency forgery and so on). They have an 'internal dimension', involving cooperation, coordination and policy-making, which principally relates to within the EU's borders, and an 'external dimension', involving the incorporation of JHA issues in relations with countries outside the EU's borders — though that 'internal–external' distinction can be quite blurry at times.[4]

The creation and evolution of this policy universe raises numerous questions for research and four broad sets of questions are noted here.

1. Why has this policy universe grown so much? What and who are the 'driving forces' (Monar 2001) behind its creation and evolution? Why do the member states cooperate at the EU level (and why within the EU context, and not — or alongside — other institutions such as the Council of Europe, Organization for Security and Cooperation in Europe (OSCE) or UN)? This set of questions is obviously related to larger research questions regarding why states cooperate and what drives integration and cooperation.
2. Why and how has the JHA policy universe developed in the way that it has? Why have the member states agreed to 'communitarize' such a large part of it? How are JHA issues incorporated within the larger EU structure, and how do institutions that act principally within the JHA policy universe interact, cooperate, or do bureaucratic battle with other institutions across the EU? This set of questions refers to larger questions of institutional design and evolution, and the dynamics of bureaucratic politics within the EU.
3. What does the JHA policy universe produce and why? What are the institutions and member states agreeing to do together? Who seems to predominate within the policy-making process — from agenda setting to decision-making and implementation? What are the respective roles, powers and influence of 'supranational' actors such as the European Commission, European Court of Justice and European Parliament, and the member states? How much influence do outsiders (third countries, the UN, and so on) have on EU agenda setting, decision-making and implementation? Does a 'logic of interests', or a 'logic of diversity', or a 'logic of appropriateness' best describe the nature of the policy-making process? Finally, what is the nature of the output produced by the JHA policy universe: is it 'civilian', 'normative', inclusive, exclusive, hegemonic?
4. What is the impact of the policy universe on outsiders? Does the EU successfully export its norms and policy preferences to third countries? What are the limits to EU influence?

The articles in this special issue address several of these broad questions. The emergence and evolution of the 'external dimension of JHA' is covered in the introductory article by the three editors of this special issue, Sarah Wolff,

Nicole Wichmann and Gregory Mounier. They argue in favour of using 'new institutionalism' to try to explain the development of this dimension, but also draw attention to the need to explain those external policies that have been agreed in this area.

Two of the articles also address the evolution of institutions in this field, and their fit — uneasy at times — with other EU institutions. Gregory Mounier notes similarities and overlaps between civilian crisis management and the external dimension of JHA, and draws attention to the 'cross-pillar' nature of both areas. In a similar vein, Patryk Pawlak is interested in the development of cross-pillar coordination and cooperation, and the challenges that arise for policy-making because of the continued existence of separate pillars.

Most of the remaining authors deal in some manner with the way in which the EU tries to export its JHA norms and preferences, or the degree of the EU's influence in so doing. Sandra Lavenex and Nichole Wichmann investigate how the EU tries to export its JHA norms and policies, and find that although the EU tries to engage with outsiders in a 'network' mode of governance, it often ends up resorting to a hierarchical mode of governance or policy transfer. Network governance depends on the existence of compatible administrative structures and expertise in partner countries — not easy to find. Yet Lavenex and Wichmann also point to the limits of hierarchical policy transfer: the EU has a restricted capacity to offer incentives to third countries to adopt its norms, and negative conditionality (sticks rather than carrots) is rarely resorted to or successful.

Florian Trauner also notes the limits to a strategy of policy transfer based on conditionality. He focuses on the EU's ability to influence the Western Balkan countries into adopting the JHA *acquis*, and argues that EU influence exercised via membership conditionality has been limited due to the uncertainties of the accession process. However, he finds that the EU has instead been able to exercise much influence through 'policy conditionality' — offering 'visa facilitation' in exchange for the conclusion of readmission agreements. When a concrete incentive can be put on the table, the EU is more effective at reaching its objectives.

In another exploration of the limits of EU influence, Lili Di Puppo examines EU relations with Georgia. She notes that the EU has lacked strategic vision and policy coherence: its vision (criminal justice reform should come first) does not coincide with the Georgian government's priorities (which wants first and foremost to establish a state monopoly on violence and its territorial integrity). The EU viewed Georgia as both a partner, with whom it can cooperate on certain issues, but also as a threat or source of various problems for the EU's internal security. The EU's extreme reluctance to confront Russia in its neighbourhood has meant that the EU has no vision of how to resolve Georgia's territorial disputes.

Sarah Wolff writes of the evolution of counter-terrorism cooperation between the EU and Mediterranean partners and discovers that even though EU-level action has been increasing, most cooperation with the Mediterranean countries is still driven by individual member states. Their bilateral concerns, interests and relations predominate.

Finally, in an interesting twist, Javier Argomaniz looks at how the US is driving EU policy-making. Much work on 'the external dimension of JHA' has focused on the extent to which the EU influences outsiders and, above all, neighbours (both membership candidates and countries in the European Neighbourhood Policy). Argomaniz's article instead highlights the extent to which the EU has been influenced by the USA on the issue of 'passenger name records' — a case of the US quite successfully exporting its own norms and preferences to the EU.

The articles here thus contribute to the general academic debate about why and how the JHA policy universe has evolved, and what it does. Certain themes appear throughout many of the articles: the challenges of ensuring internal coordination and coherence in policy-making — challenges that have not diminished with successive treaty changes; the limits to the export or transfer of EU norms and policies to third countries; and the dominant role played by the member states — who can easily bypass EU-level mechanisms in favour of their own policies. Incentives are difficult to offer, yet when they can be tied to policies of conditionality, the EU can influence other countries. EU policy may be quite narrow in scope *vis-à-vis* particular countries (such as Georgia) because wider concerns (such as relations with Russia) play a more important role. And, yet, even as it tries to export its own norms to neighbours and beyond, the EU proves extraordinarily susceptible to US influence. Such themes should be familiar to observers of EU policy-making in general, and especially to those researching EU foreign policy-making. The cases discussed in the articles here provide further evidence of the extent to which the EU still struggles to engage in strategic, coherent and effective policy-making — and so should certainly be of interest to those scholars interested in other areas of the EU's foreign relations.

As no special issue can cover all possible avenues of investigation, this one leaves some open questions, including why the member states have chosen to cooperate at the EU level on the issues and in the way that they have, or — perhaps more importantly — what they still insist on keeping out of the EU's grasp, and why. The role of the member states in general, and particular member states such as the UK, France or Germany, in driving the agenda or limiting the EU's remit, is not covered extensively in this special issue, with the exception of Wolff's article. The European Commission's powers, and the evolution of its influence, in the JHA policy universe is another issue that is not discussed at length in the articles published here.

The special issue does point to further avenues to explore, issues that merit further research. The implications of the Amsterdam Treaty and Lisbon Treaty (if ratified ... or if some of the provisions in it are implemented nonetheless) need to be investigated in more depth. What impact do these institutional changes have on the actors involved in policy-making (such as the Council of Justice and Home Affairs ministers)? Are institutional changes leading to changes in the mode of decision-making? Does the increased use of the 'Community method' have an impact on member state preferences, the mode of interaction within the Council, and the output thereby produced?

How have treaty changes affected cross-pillar cooperation and coordination? Will it continue to be difficult? What forms of bureaucratic politics have been spawned by treaty changes? What is the perspective on cross-pillar coordination in the JHA policy universe from the point of view of the foreign policy pillar? What is the impact of the *de facto* extension of the 'Petersberg tasks' (tasks which European security and defence forces can undertake) to include the combating of terrorism in third countries?

The relative importance of the JHA policy universe in EU policy-making in general — and in its relations with other actors (states, international organizations and so on) — could also bear further investigation. How much money, diplomatic resources, European Security and Defence Policy (ESDP) mission mandates and so on does the EU devote to this policy universe in comparison to other areas, and is this proportion changing over time? In a similar vein, is there a danger of 'overstretch', or a 'capabilities–expectations gap' (Hill 1993), here too — just as we have seen in EU foreign relations?

In addition, as several of the articles here have suggested, we still need to learn much more about the EU's impact on outsiders. Evidently, it has little influence on the US (in fact, the direction of influence appears to be rather from west to east in that case), but its influence (and limits to that influence) on other outsiders, both within and beyond the neighbourhood, is still not well known.

Given the extent of the evolution of the JHA policy universe — and the extent to which the 'JHA agenda' has infiltrated the Community and Common Foreign and Security Policy (CFSP) pillars — it is particularly important to guard against the creation of a 'mini-community' of scholars interested only in the JHA policy universe. The boundaries of this universe are fuzzy and ever changing, hence, academic research cannot by definition be conducted within carefully delineated borders. This is an area of research that obviously cries out for cooperation among security experts, foreign policy experts, development policy experts, immigration policy experts, lawyers, integration theorists and so on. As is obvious from the articles published in this special issue, the issues and questions raised, and lessons drawn, by scholars who have been following closely the JHA policy universe are of interest to a wider audience.

Notes

1. Challenge is led by Professor Didier Bigo of Sciences Po, France; EU-Consent by Professor Wolfgang Wessels, University of Cologne, Germany. See the websites: www.libertysecurity.org and www.eu-consent.net.
2. The Maastricht Treaty listed nine issues under the JHA pillar: asylum policy; rules governing the crossing by persons of the external borders of the member states; immigration policy and policy regarding nationals of third countries, including the conditions of their entry and residence, and combating unauthorized immigration; combating drug addiction; combating fraud on an international scale; judicial cooperation in civil matters; customs cooperation; judicial cooperation in criminal matters; and police cooperation for the purposes of preventing and combating terrorism, unlawful drug trafficking and other serious forms of international crime.
3. See, for example, Nuttall (1992, ch. 10) on 'The Grey Area'; and documents such as 'Statement by the Twelve Foreign Ministers on the Combating of International Terrorism, Brussels, 27 January

1986', 'Statement by the Twelve Foreign Ministers on International Terrorism and the Crisis in the Mediterranean, The Hague, 14 April 1986', 'Press Statement by the Presidency on Terrorism, London, 10 November 1986' — all in Hill and Smith (2000).
4. For example, any EU policy on immigration impinges automatically on third countries and their nationals. Many other EU 'internal' policies have external dimensions too (from EMU to agricultural policy), so the JHA policy universe is not unique in that characteristic.

References

Den Boer, M., and W. Wallace. 2000. Justice and Home Affairs: Integration through incrementalism? In *Policy-making in the European Union*, eds. Helen Wallace and William Wallace. Oxford: Oxford Univ. Press.

European Commission. 2002. Integrating migration issues in the European Union's relations with third countries, Dec. 3, COM (2002) 703 final.

Hill, C. 1993. The capability-expectations gap, or conceptualizing Europe's international role. *Journal of Common Market Studies* 31, no. 3: 305–28.

Hill, C., and K.E. Smith, eds. 2000. *European foreign policy: Key documents*. London: Routledge.

Monar, J. 2001. The dynamics of Justice and Home Affairs: Laboratories, driving factors and costs. *Journal of Common Market Studies* 39, no. 4: 747–64.

Nuttall, S. 1992. *European political co-operation*. Oxford: Clarendon Press.

The External Dimension of Justice and Home Affairs: A Different Security Agenda for the EU?

SARAH WOLFF[†], NICOLE WICHMANN* & GREGORY MOUNIER**

[†]Department of International Relations, The London School of Economics and Political Science, London, UK
*Department of Political Science, University of Lucerne, Lucerne, Switzerland
**Politics and International Relations Department, University of Reading, Reading, UK

The provision of peace and security has been at the core of the European integration process since the outset. Yet, the way in which the member states have decided to involve the EU level in the provision of peace and security has changed over time. In the early days, the pooling together of coal and steel resources and the creation of supranational institutions were seen as the main means to build sustainable peace and security between France and Germany. The establishment of European Political Cooperation (EPC) in 1970 marked the beginning of a new era, in which 'external security threats' were discussed in the European setting. In the framework of EPC, the member states decided to coordinate their national foreign policy initiatives (Nuttall 1992; Smith 2004). In contrast to the economic domain, they decided against empowering the supranational institutions; and kept their grip on the formulation of foreign and security policies (Wagner 2003). Cooperation in the domain of justice and home affairs (JHA), or internal security, was added to the EU's competences in the Treaty of Maastricht and completed with the Amsterdam Treaty. Although JHA has experienced a high degree of 'communitarization' over the last two decades, the process will remain incomplete for the foreseeable future.

European policy makers have acknowledged the existence of interlinkages between these various 'elements of security policy making' at different points in time. They realized early on that internal economic integration was going to impact upon the EU's external action, whereas the 'official' discourse has taken longer to acknowledge the relevance of internal security concerns for formulating external policies. Undeniably, if migration and terrorism concerns have often had an impact on EU foreign policy making (Bicchi 2007; Joffe 2008), the explicit acknowledgement of the existence of a linkage between internal and external security is a more recent phenomenon. Critical security scholars working on JHA cooperation, for example, have negated the differentiation between internal and external security from the outset. They claim that security is a crowded policy space, in which numerous actors compete for power and influence and attempt to gain support for their particular threat perceptions (Bigo 1996). Until now, the JHA literature has focused predominantly on the external dimension of specific issue areas, in particular migration and terrorism. Recently, however, more comprehensive analyses of the external dimension have been conducted (Monar 2004; Mitsilegas 2007; Rees 2008).

The external dimension of JHA, the focus of this book, constitutes an attempt to bridge the various divides (internal/external, intergovernmental/supranational, across pillars), and to assess the extent to which this policy field/universe reflects a different EU security agenda.

The European Commission and the Council have produced countless policy documents on the JHA external dimension; however, it remains difficult to understand what it actually is. Gaining a better understanding of the external dimension constitutes another objective of this volume. To achieve this purpose, we have asked contributors to this volume to illustrate what shape the JHA external dimension has in their respective domains of expertise. The results of this exercise provide a panoramic view of how JHA priorities have been inserted into foreign policy initiatives towards third countries (geographically), but also on certain aspects of external action, such as crisis management (policy-wise). The scholars involved in this publication are, for the most part, PhD and post-doctoral students who met during various activities financed by EU research networks launched under the Sixth Framework Programme on Research, mainly Challenge and Securint. In this book, we aim to bring the findings discussed within this restricted 'academic community' to a broader academic audience.

Given that we could not adopt an entirely 'inductive approach' to our project, we needed to start out with a working definition of the JHA external dimension. We have defined it as an attempt to provide an overall strategic orientation to punctual measures adopted in the policy area of JHA, such as border management, the fight against terrorism and the fight against organized crime. In substantive terms, the JHA external dimension describes the contours of a 'policy universe' (Smith, this issue). This policy universe covers the thematic external dimensions of various EU internal security policies in the area of terrorism, migration and organized crime. In institutional terms, the JHA external dimension can be compared to a 'policy space' that encompasses the actors, rules and practices that relate to the EU's efforts to protect its citizens from a wide range of internal and external threats (Boin, Ekengren, and Rhinard 2006).

From the universe of intriguing questions surrounding the JHA external dimension, we have decided to focus on the following: first, we study how the policy space/universe is organized in institutional terms and, in this context, we seek to identify the actors driving the JHA external dimension (Pawlak, Mounier, this issue). Secondly, we investigate the modes of interaction through which the EU interacts with neighbouring countries in the European Neighbourhood Policy (ENP) and in the Western Balkans (Trauner, Wichmann/Lavenex, this issue). Thirdly, two authors consider how and whether the EU's JHA external dimension activities have had an impact on third countries (Di Puppo, Wolff, this issue). The last paper turns the tables and asks how the development of EU norms regarding JHA issues has been influenced by the USA (Argomaniz, this issue). The broad scope of themes featured in this book should attract the attention of scholars working on aspects of the EU's security policy both in its internal and external dimensions.

To analyse these different manifestations of the external dimension of JHA, the authors predominantly draw on two types of academic literature. There is, first, the literature on the external effects of JHA cooperation, which stems from the European public policy research community. It shows that internal cooperation has had both intended and unintended effects on third countries (Lavenex and Uçarer 2002). Authors starting from an analysis of the internal dimension of JHA have also illustrated that JHA priorities have become an integral part of cooperation frameworks with third countries, such as the ENP or the Stabilisation and Association Process (Lavenex 2004; Trauner 2007).

The second type of literature to which the authors refer deals with the EU's foreign policy and is grounded in the international relations narrative. The book starts from the premise that this literature can add value to the analyses conducted from a 'JHA point of view'. Indeed, foreign policy analysts have demonstrated how internal security questions have been tackled with Common Foreign and Security Policy (CFSP) and European Security and Defence Policy (ESDP) instruments (Smith 2003). Foreign policy analysts also provide us with a useful toolbox of approaches, such as bureaucratic politics (Allison 1971), for identifying the actors driving the formulation of the EU's security agenda and the instruments through which the agenda is being realized. From the start, they have pointed to the difficulty of achieving coherence and consistency across the different external policy initiatives (Nuttall 2005). There are three main domains in which these challenges arise: horizontally (i.e. across different policy areas); vertically (i.e. between EU and the member states' actions); and institutionally (across the EU's institutional framework) (Nuttall 2005, 97–8). European foreign policy scholars have highlighted the difficulties arising from the incompatibility of national and European foreign policies, and the emergence of turf wars between European institutions. Moreover, the foreign policy literature has always insisted on the importance of external context variables related to the international environment and the third country in question (Rees 2005).

After providing an overview of the development stages of the JHA external dimension, this introductory chapter highlights some of the challenges facing researchers interested in this issue, in particular the fact that the two literatures described above provide for two different definitions of what is the 'JHA external dimension'. 'New Institutionalism' does not only establish a conceptual connection between this book, but it also complements the two literatures at hand by bridging the gap between the JHA and foreign policy understandings of the phenomenon under investigation.

The Progressive Development of the 'JHA External Dimension'

In the last decade, member states and European institutions have multiplied initiatives aimed at protecting the EU's internal security from outside threats. Many factors may account for this phenomenon, but those most commonly put forward in the academic literature revolve around the changing post-Cold War security environment and the ensuing disappearance of the traditional sharp divide between internal and external security (the so-called 'internal–external security nexus'). For Western governments, the likelihood of being physically invaded by aggressive neighbouring armies decreased relative to the increased fear of seeing their borders submerged by all sorts of 'soft security threats', including organized crime, illegal immigration and terrorism. The prospect of EU enlargement has only strengthened this feeling. Expanding the Union eastwards and southwards implied the importation of insecurity factors inherent to post-communist countries and former war-torn regions into the common Area of Freedom, Security and Justice (AFSJ). Hence, particular attention was given to preparing the candidate countries for EU accession, to ensure they could be integrated into the expanding European internal security area (Monar 2003). The fight against organized crime was the main objective of the Pre-Accession Pact on cooperation against crime, agreed in May 1998, which provided future member states with training in organized crime issues, and enabled cooperation with Europol and the European judicial network (Council of the European Union 1998). This attempt to reinforce the internal security apparatus of candidate countries, in order to reduce potential threats 'on the spot', can be considered as being one of the first concrete demonstrations of the JHA external dimension. However, initiatives to tackle organized crime across the internal/external security divide were preceded by the EU's attempts to build issue-specific external dimensions. In 1987, the Council had adopted a decision on drugs, stipulating that the EU needed to integrate the fight against drugs into external relations (Boekhout van Solinge 2002). The external dimension of the EU's migration policy, launched in the early 1990s, also predates the official inauguration of the JHA external dimension (Boswell 2003, 621).

The multiplication of spontaneous initiatives linking the protection of the EU's internal security to external relations instruments prompted the need to structure this nascent policy space/universe. The matter was put officially on the agenda in 1999, at the Tampere Summit. In the Presidency Conclusions, the member states recognized that the realization of the internal AFSJ also had an external aspect. In point 59 of the Conclusions, the European Council required that 'all competences and instruments at the disposal of the Union, and in particular, in external relations must be used in an integrated and consistent way to build the Area of Freedom, Security and Justice' (European Council 1999, point 59). In other words, the EU's external relations should be used to attain the EU's internal security objectives. The European Council also specified as a priority that cooperation should be developed with candidate countries and neighbouring countries in the Balkans. Outside of the neighbourhood, cooperation should be targeted at countries considered as sources of migrants and illegal trafficking. Accordingly, threats such as international terrorism, transnational organized crime and drug trafficking need to be addressed jointly with third countries. The Council of Ministers and the European Commission were mandated to establish objectives and working structures for this new aspect of the JHA policy domain (European Council 1999, point 61). This initial stocktaking exercise culminated in the adoption of a report at the 2000 Feira European Council (Council of the European Union 2000). Interestingly enough, the report emphasized that the main purpose of the JHA external dimension was to contribute to the establishment of the AFSJ, and not to create an internal security foreign policy in its own right: 'The aim is certainly not to develop a "foreign policy" specific to JHA. Quite the contrary' (Council of the European Union 2000, 5). Under the pretext of mainstreaming the growing number of initiatives in the field, an effort was made to bring JHA activities under the responsibility of the EU's traditional foreign policy machinery and, hence, to assert the diplomats' precedence in this domain. Yet, it was acknowledged that alienating the interior ministries would not be a wise decision, because it might prompt them into launching a parallel 'JHA foreign policy'. This 'demonstration of force' by the diplomats could also be interpreted as an implicit recognition of the progressive 'contamination' of the EU's foreign policy objectives by internal security concerns. From the perspective of realists, there is nothing new about this assertion because, for them, foreign policy has always been about promoting national security interests. It does, however, require scholars working on the EU's external action to envision the EU differently; not just as a normative power active in the area of human rights and good governance promotion, but also taking actions to protect the EU's internal security (Manners 2002).

Parallel with these dynamic developments, the Council decided in 2001 to publish a twice-yearly 'Multi-Presidency Work Programme'[1] on JHA external relations, to direct and manage the legislative work (Council of the European Union 2001). According to most observers, these first attempts at structuring the EU's activities were mainly paper tigers without any effects on policy practice.[2] Following the European Parliament's call for a more strategic approach to the JHA external dimension (European Parliament 2002), the Hague Programme introduced provisions on improving its working structure (Council of the European Union 2004). The programme gave a new impetus to its development, and triggered the production of numerous documents in European institutions. These efforts culminated in the adoption of the Council's JHA External Strategy in 2005 (Council of the European Union 2005; hereafter the 'Strategy').

The Strategy constituted an attempt to achieve a more consistent and coherent policy output and to overcome the predominantly piecemeal approach that had materialized so far.[3] It organized existing instruments around certain key principles and guidelines. One of these is the 'geographical prioritization', whereby all internal security issues should be addressed with countries with whom relations are a priority for the EU (candidate and neighbouring countries). On the other hand, cooperation with other countries should be limited to specific issues, for example drugs in Latin America. The Strategy also introduced the concept of 'partnership' with third countries in the field of JHA. This principle had been established previously as a guideline for the establishment of the external dimension of migration.[4] In the 2005 Strategy, however, partnerships are to be created in the fields of border management, law enforcement cooperation on combating terrorism, organized crime, trafficking of human beings and money laundering, as well as the fight against corruption, judicial cooperation and reform of the judiciary. The last and, perhaps, most important contribution of the Strategy is that it makes JHA a central priority in the EU's external relations, and seeks to ensure a coordinated and coherent approach.

To translate the Strategy into concrete objectives, the Council has elaborated geographical and thematic Action Oriented Papers (AOP). The first one was adopted in 2006, and dealt with ways of improving cooperation between the EU and the Western Balkans on organized crime, corruption, illegal immigration and counter-terrorism (Council of the European Union 2006a). The second AOP proposed concrete EU measures to combat drug production in, and trafficking from, Afghanistan, including transit routes (Council of the European Union 2006b); while a third AOP was agreed the same year, on implementing the common space of freedom, security and justice with Russia (Council of the European Union 2006c). To monitor and evaluate the effective implementation of the Strategy, a report is published every eighteen months. The first one was drafted by the Commission and adopted in December 2006 by the JHA Council (Council of the European Union 2006d).

The active involvement of the three EU institutions in the definition of the external dimension is a sign of its rising saliency and a classic example of 'issue expansion', whereby issues are moved beyond the initial actors in specific venues to a wider set of participants. Although the European Parliament is simply informed of the negotiation of international agreements covering JHA matters, it has shown a constant interest in influencing the course of action in this field, by adopting regular Resolutions (European Parliament 2007) and Recommendations (European Parliament 2004), emphasizing the lack of democratic accountability of the JHA external dimension.

Challenges for Researching the JHA External Dimension

Despite a growing number of policy documents on the topic, one of the main challenges for scholars working on the JHA external dimension is the absence of a recognized definition. First, it is necessary to define the phenomenon from an ontological point of view. Is the 'JHA external dimension' a product of the member states or of the EU institutions? Can it be equated, as JHA analysts argue in their strand of the literature, with the process of 'externalization' of the EU's internal security policies, whereby the EU encourages third countries 'to adopt measures based upon its model of internal security' (Rees 2008, 98). Is it rather, as foreign policy analysts claim, the mere pursuit by the member states of their national foreign policy interests through the EU 'platform'? The appearance of EU-led initiatives at the frontier between internal security and external relations has prompted the mushrooming of new concepts, such as 'the JHA external dimension', the 'security continuum' (Bigo 1994), and the 'internal–external nexus' (Smith 2003, 171). Others have referred to the emergence of a new 'policy space' (Boin, Ekengren, and Rhinard 2006). Inspired by the Bourdieusian concept of 'policy field', a policy space is understood as an 'institutional field of actors, rules and practices associated with governmental efforts to address a particular category of social issues and problems' (Boin, Ekengren, and Rhinard 2006, 407). According to the latter perspective, one has to study the actors and their practices carefully to understand why certain concepts and ideas are included in policy formulation, whereas others are omitted. The counter-argument, which is inspired by intergovernmentalists, states that the JHA external dimension merely reflects the uploading of certain member state security agendas to the EU level in an attempt to rally support behind the pursuit of their national security agendas.

Faced with these definitional uncertainties, we decided to differentiate two aspects of the JHA external dimension, which we have called input and output dimensions. This differentiation is inspired by David Easton's model of political systems (Easton 1965). The input is a fundamental element of politics; it is influenced by the international environment, which generates support for, and makes demands of, a government. An exchange of feedback and transformation brought about by the political representatives results in the system output, which, in turn, affects the general political environment. This toolbox was adapted by Ginsberg to explain European foreign policy. The input/output conceptualization takes into account the specificities of the EU as a foreign policy system, which is the sum of aggregated Community and member states' interests (Ginsberg 1999). On the input side, different sources of demand/support are identified, such as the neofunctionalist concept of 'external stimuli', the logic of collective action or politics of scale, national actors and the existence of European interest *per se*. The output dimension, on the other hand, refers to the policy measures that the EU adopts and the modes of interaction contained in those instruments. This part of the analysis is 'critical to generate the feedback necessary for the initiation of new and improved inputs and for decision-making reforms within the external relations system' (Ginsberg 1999, 445).

A second controversial question concerns the relative power of the actors competing for influence in this crowded policy space. Assessing the power of the various actors requires that we first map them, which is in itself a challenge. From an intergovernmentalist point of view, the member states' representatives are the key drivers of the process, using the EU level to pursue their own domestic interests. The Mediterranean case developed in this volume shows the significant influence that Spain and France still exert upon their ex-colonies, and how those two countries use the EU level to project their national interests (Wolff, this issue). From a bureaucratic politics perspective, certain actors, like the ministries of interior or the European Commission, compete in their attempts to act as norms entrepreneurs in the agenda-setting process (Edwards and Meyer 2008). Thus, national and European actors might 'frame' the threat differently, depending upon their capacity to mobilise specific resources and expertise to advocate a specific answer. In that sense, it is possible to argue that the distinction between internal and external security, or the development of the concept of the 'JHA external dimension', serves specific interests of national and European bureaucracies, enabling them to demand an increase in resources. Although the official discourse on cross-pillar policy making is all about improving coherence and consistency, one can also point to more malign dynamics underlying this process: one contributor describes the 'hijacking' of 'cross-pillarization' by security-orientated policy makers to achieve their own preferences, at the expense of other actors', following a cost/benefit analysis (Pawlak, this issue). Another aspect of relevance to scholars interested in bureaucratic politics is the growing influence of internal security actors (police officers, magistrates) on more traditional aspects of foreign policy, in particular civilian crisis management (Mounier, this issue).

Scholars interested in the 'input' side have also faced the challenge of keeping track of the constant changes in the EU's 'constitutional charter'. As this book goes to print, the EU is giving itself a new 'founding' treaty, the Treaty of Lisbon. From now on, although the pillars have disappeared, any analyses of the JHA external dimension will have to take into account the rules contained in various parts of the new Treaty. They will need to be conducted against the backdrop of titles on the 'Common Foreign and Security Policy' (Title V, Treaty on European Union), the 'Area of Freedom, Security and Justice' (Part Three, Title V) and 'External action by the Union' (Part V). The existence of these three parts, containing different decision-making rules and attracting the attention of different policy makers, indicates that balancing and institutional struggles will remain a challenge in the future. Moreover, as Pawlak argues, institutional fragmentation will increase as a result of the creation of new bureaucratic entities that will have an interest in defending their respective turf. On the face of it, the Treaty has made things easier, since only the CFSP and the Community are subject to different decision-making rules; in reality, however, the AFSJ contains a number of important exceptions to the rule of qualified majority voting and co-decision, which limit the extent of 'communitarization' (Carrera and Geyer 2007).

New Institutionalism as a Conceptual Framework

With these questions and challenges in mind, it seemed to us that a new institutionalist analysis can shed light on some of the questions that we want to investigate. The main reason for choosing new institutionalism is that the EU is, by definition, a 'dense institutional environment' and that it makes sense to explain developments in the EU in terms of 'institutions' (Jupille, Caporaso, and Checkel 2003). As our case studies show, new institutionalism can also explain various aspects of the output dimension, since one of the over-arching objectives of the EU's foreign policy is to institutionalize and, hence, 'domesticate', relations with third countries (Lavenex 2004). As regards the output dimension, however, it is obvious that external factors need to be taken into account to explain the policies adopted with respect to certain countries (Wolff, Lavenex/Wichmann, Di Puppo, this issue).

In our attempt to bridge the gap between the international relations and the European public policy research communities, new institutionalism offers an attractive venue, since it shares its core assumption — that 'institutions matter' — with international relations institutionalists. The international regimes approach developed by Keohane 'argues that institutions represent persistent and connected sets of rules (formal and informal) that prescribe behavioural roles, constrain states, and shape expectations' (Bulmer 1998, 368). In other words, institutions affect outcomes and structure political action. Since the explanatory focus of new institutionalism lies on stability and change of institutions, it is useful for grasping the central question of this volume: whether or not the JHA external dimension reflects a different EU security agenda. Or, to put it differently, does it reflect an instance of continuity or of change?

Endorsing a wide definition of institutions as being a set of rules, but also 'beliefs, paradigms, codes, cultures and knowledge' (Bulmer 1998, 369), the strength of new institutionalism resides in the fact that it does not prescribe a unique recipe for institutionalization; instead it recognizes the diversity of paths that can lead towards the internationalization of cooperation. The various paths find their expression in the three variants of new institutionalism: rational choice, sociological and historical institutionalism, whereby each one is grounded in a different theoretical tradition and hence emphasizes the importance of different explanatory variables. The variants can be used either as rivals to see which variant accounts best for an empirical phenomenon, or in a complementary fashion to elucidate different aspects of a particular phenomenon.

Rational choice institutionalism, with its focus on 'principal–agent' relations, is particularly useful for shedding light on the crucial question of how power is distributed between the intergovernmental and supranational dynamics characterizing the EU. It allows us to assess whether the member states (principals) continue to control the actions of the supranational actors, or whether the latter have been able to 'shirk or slip' the principals' control. Since the JHA external dimension builds, to a great extent, on 'existent cooperation frameworks' (issue and country specific), the legacy of these initiatives has to be included in the analysis. In this context, historical institutionalism, with its emphasis on path-dependencies and lock-ins, provides a useful toolbox. Lastly, sociological institutionalism focuses on the impact of ideas, frames and administrative cultures for explaining paths of institutionalization. These approaches also point to the emergence of new 'roles' or functional frames that are used for legitimizing the EU's actions in a given issue area.

At the internal level of policy making (input), the institution's cultural and societal environment can be perceived as a constraint on the actors (sociological institutionalism). Policy change will occur from the way actors interact with the environment's complexity, stability and competitiveness. These cognitive and ideational elements are strongly present in the EU security agenda, which is based on the notion of 'protecting the security of EU citizens'. The creation of a 'functional frame', whereby the threat to EU's internal security originates from the outside, legitimates the projection of internal security instruments (Mounier, this issue). For others, this shift of the security debate from the national sphere to the EU level is the result of the contest over the new 'policy space' between interior ministers, national law-enforcement agencies, member states' representatives and European bureaucrats (Pawlak, this issue). Alternatively, one could argue that the weight of past decisions has influenced the development of the external dimension of JHA. This case is made in the article on the EU's counter-terrorism policy towards the Mediterranean region. According to historical institutionalism, institutions do persist over time and are not always affected by their environment. Nonetheless, 'critical junctures' may arise and induce some policy change, such as the 1972 Munich Olympic Games or 9/11 in the case of counter-terrorism (Wolff, this issue).

Different variants of institutionalism also allow us to focus on different aspects of the output perspective. In the first instance, Trauner shows how conditionality has been changed through the inclusion of policy-related conditionality linked to the provision of a visa facilitation regime (Trauner, this issue). In particular, he analyses whether the rational institutionalist logic of consequentiality underlying conditionality has been instrumental in bringing about the 'Europeanization' of the countries of the Western Balkans. New institutionalism also brings to the fore the importance of the logics of action underlying the EU's external action. Lavenex and Wichmann engage with the EU's efforts to establish policy networks on JHA cooperation in relations with ENP countries. They argue that, although these networks are expected to unleash dynamics of socialization and learning, in reality they amount to little more than an expression of hegemonic policy transfer (Lavenex/Wichmann, this issue). Hegemony and interdependent asymmetries are also the source of the opposite situation, when the EU becomes a 'norm taker'. As Argomaniz demonstrates in this volume, the EU turned into a receptor of policy by internalizing the USA's security norms in the field of Passenger Name Record (PNR). Partners of the EU can therefore conduct a cost/benefit analysis regarding their cooperation with the EU (rational choice institutionalism).

Perspectives for Further Research

While the book tries to map out the development of the JHA external policy field, it bears limits regarding the impact of the JHA external dimension on third countries. Impact assessment requires in-depth understanding of the legislative environment and the organization of the law-enforcement sector in these countries. We have not aimed to provide detailed case studies for each one of the countries and regions mentioned in this volume; instead, we have limited ourselves to studying the policy initiatives adopted by the EU, which we have called the 'output' of the JHA external dimension. The contributors are intrigued by the question of whether the interaction on JHA questions has changed the nature of the third countries' relationship with the EU. The comparisons are conducted both from an issue area and a geographical perspective. In other words, the contributions analyse how and why interactions vary across policy areas (drugs, organized crime, corruption, terrorism) and across countries covered by one policy framework (ENP, Western Balkans). The study on Georgia comes closest to an impact study; it is interesting in that it shows just how limited the EU's influence in the country has been (Di Puppo, this issue). The case study on the relations with the USA demonstrates that the EU's influence on the USA has been minor and that, on the contrary, the EU has been a receiver of 'US security norms' (Argomaniz, this issue).

Another aspect not tackled in this book is the substance of the decisions produced by the JHA external dimension. This is an issue for future research and, for that matter, foreign policy literature seems to be better equipped (Smith 2003). The latter would allow the analyst to scrutinize the outcome in terms of coherence and consistency: the literature has pointed to the horizontal problems of consistency that arise as a result of contradictions generated by the protectionist Common Agricultural Policy versus the EU's ambition to act as a player in the development area. In addition, they have highlighted the problem of vertical inconsistency, which arises when the member states try to pursue policies on the same questions outside of the framework of the EU, or as part of a limited group within the EU. This kind of behaviour has been witnessed in the CFSP domain, with the creation of a *Directoire* on the question of how to deal with Iran, but also in the counter-terrorism domain, where the big member states have preferred more restricted settings, such as the G5 meetings on terrorism. The question in this context is whether legal provisions or new legal instruments aimed at enhancing 'consistency' can stop the member states from resorting to this type of action.

Lastly, future research shall analyse further the role of the member states in the EU's JHA external dimension. In fact, the 'logic of diversity'

(Hoffmann 1974) is still characteristic of foreign policy making in the EU and is reflected in the development of the 'JHA external dimension'. In an enlarged EU, the member states' preferences differ greatly, which is one reason why they have been able to agree only on lowest common denominator policies. One illustration of these differences hampering the development of the JHA external dimension is that of border management in the Mediterranean: while the Southern member states (Spain, Italy and Malta) want to turn Frontex into an operational border agency, the Nordic countries and Germany are reluctant to support its activities financially (Wolff 2008).

Conclusion

Our investigation of the JHA external dimension against the backdrop of new institutionalism has led to some interesting findings. However, as the preceding section has mentioned, there are still many questions open to further investigation. All we have done in this book is to provide a first snapshot of the state of the art, and to present one way in which the developments can be viewed.

Empirical developments will also have an impact on further academic investigations of the JHA external dimension. A development of considerable importance is the entry into force of the Lisbon Treaty. It is not entirely clear how the new Treaty will influence the organizational aspects of the JHA external dimension. It is, for example, unclear how the role of DG H (the JHA section of the Council Secretariat) will evolve under the new Treaty. Thus far, it has been an important player in shaping JHA policy and the external dimension of JHA, but it is unclear whether its role will change as a result of the disappearance of the pillars. Will DG H function in the same manner as the Community DGs of the Council Secretariat and, hence, lose their influence in terms of policy shaping? Or will it increase its status and become as important a player as the Council Secretariat under CFSP (Christiansen 2001)? It seems that these questions cannot be answered *ex ante*, but that we need to observe what happens in 'policy practice' before writing about it.

Beyond these organizational aspects, the new institutional framework also brings with it a host of other questions that will make a re-assessment of the security agenda necessary in the future. There is, in particular, the question of how the new institutional framework will change the nature of the EU's security agenda; will the disappearance of the pillars bring about a more integrated security policy, or will the pillar 'mentalities and structures' continue to influence the EU's actions? The abolition of the pillars could facilitate the realization of a different security agenda that covers, as proposed in the European Security Strategy, both internal and external security threats. For instance, the creation of a 'Friends of the Presidency group' on the external dimension of JHA at the end of 2008 could suggest the establishment of a permanent JHA/RELEX working group within the Council.

With respect to the overarching question of the book, the editors argue that the JHA external dimension is not a 'different security' agenda in terms of the problems that it addresses. The fight against terrorism, drugs and organized crime has been a constant preoccupation of governments during the last decades. Meanwhile, what has changed in the EU is, first, the explicit mentioning of these internal security preoccupations as objectives of EU foreign policy and, secondly, that police, officials from interior ministries and judicial authorities now have a stake in the formulation and the realization of EU foreign policy, together with diplomats and military officials. Both of these changes are reflected in the JHA external dimension.

Apart from these inward-looking observations, the analysts interested in the JHA external dimension will also have to go and carry out case studies on the effects and the impact that this policy initiative has had on third countries. This will require in-depth studies of legislation and of law-enforcement practice because, as the literature on JHA alignment during enlargement showed, mere legislative alignment with the EU and international standards does not mean that third countries have really changed their practices. There remains a lot of work to be done in this regard.

Acknowledgement

The Editors thank the contributors and, in particular, K. E. Smith, for their active participation in the elaboration of this special issue. The remarks made at the Challenge/Consent workshop and the editorial meetings (one in London on 21 September 2007, followed by a second one at CEPS in Brussels on 17 April 2008) have fed into this introduction. Moreover, the authors would like to thank Challenge for the financial and logistical support received.

Notes

1. The last one (5005/08) was adopted on 7 January 2008.
2. Interview conducted with Council Secretariat official (May 2007).
3. See Duke (1999) for definitions of coherence, consistency.
4. For instance, the Brussels European Council reaffirmed its commitment to 'the use of all appropriate instruments of the EU's external relations ... including strengthened partnerships with the third countries concerned, in pursuit of the EU's strategy to combat illegal migration' (European Council 2003, 10); or the Hague Programme 'EU policy should aim at assisting third countries, in full partnership, ... to improve their capacity for migration management and build border-control capacity' (Council of the European Union 2004, 11).

References

Allison, G. 1971. *Essence of decision*. Boston: Little Brown.
Bicchi, F. 2007. *European foreign policy making towards the Mediterranean*. Basingstoke: Palgrave Macmillan.
Bigo, D. 1994. The European internal security field: Stakes and rivalries in a newly developing area of police intervention. In *Policing across national boundaries*, eds. M. Anderson and M. Den Boer, 161–73. London: Pinter.
Bigo, D. 1996. *Polices en réseaux, l'expérience Européenne*. Paris: Presses de Science Po.
Boekhout van Solinge, T. 2002. *Drugs and decision-making in the European Union*. Amsterdam: Universiteit van Amsterdam.

Boin, A., M. Ekengren, and M. Rhinard. 2006. Protecting the Union: Analysing an emerging policy space. *Journal of European Integration* 28, no. 5: 405–21.

Boswell, C. 2003. The external dimension of EU asylum and immigration policy. *International Affairs* 79, no. 3: 619–38.

Bulmer, S. 1998. New institutionalism and the governance of the Single European Market. *Journal of European Public Policy* 5, no. 3: 365–86.

Carrera, S., and F. Geyer. 2007. *The Reform Treaty & Justice and Home Affairs — Implications for the common Area of Freedom, Security and Justice.* CEPS Policy Brief No. 141/August. Brussels: CEPS.

Christiansen, T. 2001. Inter-institutional politics and inter-institutional relations in the EU: towards coherent governance?. *Journal of European Public Policy* 8, no. 5: 747–69.

Council of the European Union. 1998. Pre-accession pact in organised crime between the member states of the European Union and the applicant countries of Central and Eastern Europe and Cyprus. *Official Journal of the EU* C220 (July 15).

Council of the European Union. 2000. European Union priorities and policy objectives for external relations in the field of justice and home affairs, 7653/00, June 6.

Council of the European Union. 2001. Presidency programme concerning external relations in the JHA field (2001–2002), 5146/01, January 11.

Council of the European Union. 2004. The Hague Programme: strengthening freedom, security and justice in the European Union, 16054/04, December 13.

Council of the European Union. 2005. A strategy for the external dimension of JHA: Global freedom, security and justice, 15446/05, December 6.

Council of the European Union. 2006a. Action Oriented Paper on improving cooperation, on organised crime, corruption, illegal immigration and counter-terrorism, between the EU, Western Balkans and relevant ENP countries, 9272/06, May 12.

Council of the European Union. 2006b. Action Oriented Paper to combat the production of drugs in and trafficking from Afghanistan and along the heroin route, 9370/06, May 15.

Council of the European Union. 2006c. Action Oriented Paper on implementing with Russia the common space of freedom, security and justice, 15706/06, November 28.

Council of the European Union. 2006d. Progress report on the implementation of the strategy for the external dimension of JHA: Global freedom, security and justice, 15363/06, November 20.

Duke, S. 1999. Consistency as an issue in EU external activities. EIPA Working Papers 99/W/06.

Easton, D. 1965. *A systems analysis of political life.* New York: John Wiley & Sons.

Edwards, G., and C. Meyer. 2008. Introduction: Charting a contested transformation. *Journal of Common Market Studies* 46, no. 1: 1–25.

European Council. 1999. Presidency conclusions, Tampere European Council, October 15/16.

European Council. 2003. Presidency conclusions, Brussels European Council, 15188/03, October 16–17.

European Parliament. 2002. Resolution on the progress made in 2001 towards the establishment of the area of freedom, security and justice provided for in Article 2, fourth indent, of the TEU, P5_TA(2002)0048, February 2.

European Parliament. 2004. Recommendation to the Council and the European Council on the future of the area of freedom, security and justice as well as on the measures required to enhance the legitimacy and effectiveness thereof, P6_TA(2004)0022, October 14.

European Parliament. 2007. Resolution on an area of freedom, security and justice: Strategy on the external dimension, Action Plan implementing the Hague programme, P6_TA(2007)0284, June 21.

Ginsberg, R.H. 1999. Conceptualizing the European Union as an international actor: Narrowing the theoretical capability–expectations gap. *Journal of Common Market Studies* 37, no. 3: 429–54.

Hill, C., and M. Smith, eds. 2005. *International relations and the European Union.* Oxford: Oxford Univ. Press.

Hoffmann, S. 1974. *Decline or renewal? France since the 1930s.* New York: Viking.

Joffe, G. 2008. The European Union, democracy and counter-terrorism in the Maghreb. *Journal of Common Market Studies* 46, no. 1: 147–71.

Jupille, J., J.A. Caporaso, and J.T. Checkel. 2003. Integrating institutions — rationalism, constructivism, and the study of the European Union. *Comparative Political Studies* 36, no. 1/2: 7–39.

Lavenex, S. 2004. EU external governance in 'wider Europe'. *Journal of European Public Policy* 11, no. 4: 688–708.

Lavenex, S., and E. Uçarer. 2002. *Migration and the externalities of European integration*. Lanham, MD: Lexington Books.
Manners, I. 2002. Normative power Europe: a contradiction in terms. *Journal of Common Market Studies* 40, no. 2: 235–58.
Mitsilegas, V. 2007. The external dimension of EU action in criminal matters. *European Foreign Affairs Review* 12: 457–97.
Monar, J. 2003. The area of freedom, security and justice after the 2004 enlargement. *International Spectator* 38, no. 1: 32–50.
Monar, J. 2004. The EU as an international actor in the domain of justice and home affairs. *European Foreign Affairs Review* 9, no. 3: 395–415.
Nuttall, S. 1992. *European political cooperation*. Oxford: Clarendon Press.
Nuttall, S. 2005. Coherence and consistency. In Hill and Smith 2005, 91–113.
Rees, W. 2005. The external face of internal security. In Hill and Smith 2005, 205–25.
Rees, W. 2008. Inside out: The external face of EU internal security policy. *Journal of European Integration* 30, no. 1: 97–111.
Smith, K.E. 2003. *European Union foreign policy in a changing world*. Cambridge: Polity Press.
Smith, M.E. 2004. *Europe's foreign and security policy: The institutionalisation of cooperation*. Cambridge: Cambridge Univ. Press.
Trauner, F. 2007. *EU Justice and Home Affairs strategy in the Western Balkans — Conflicting objectives in the pre-accession strategy*. Working Document No. 259/February. Brussels: CEPS.
Wagner, W. 2003. Why the Common Foreign and Security Policy will remain intergovernmental: A rationalist institutional choice analysis of European crisis management policy. *Journal of Common Market Studies* 10, no. 4: 576–95.
Wolff, S. 2008. Border management in the Mediterranean: Internal, external and ethical challenges. *Cambridge Review of International Affairs* 21, no. 2: 253–71.

The External Dimension of the Area of Freedom, Security and Justice: Hijacker or Hostage of Cross-pillarization?

PATRYK PAWLAK

Department of Social and Political Sciences, European University Institute, San Domenico di Fiesole, Italy

ABSTRACT The objective of this article is to investigate the issue of cross-pillarization in the context of the growing interconnection between the EU Justice and Home Affairs and other policies. At the conceptual level, the article traces the development and functioning of cross-pillarization in various contexts: legal and political, internal and international. At the analytical level, it investigates whether cross-pillarization might be used by European institutions in a strategic way in order to promote particular interests. Based on the literature on European inter- and intra-institutional politics, this article makes the case that the process of cross-pillarization has a strong politics component. The Strategy for External Dimension of Area of Freedom, Security and Justice (AFSJ) and the Passenger Name Record Agreement are used to demonstrate how the objective of cross-pillar consistency may be jeopardized by bureaucratic turf wars and conflicts over ideology or resources.

Introduction

The recent debate about the cross-pillar character of EU measures was triggered by the increasing difficulty of distinguishing between 'internal' and 'external' dimensions of European policies.[1] The complexity of security issues has prompted questions about their essence and resulted in discussions about what constitutes an appropriate legal basis and decision-making procedures. Therefore, 'cross-pillar' is a term that points to the blurriness of the EU pillar structure and refers to policies, actors and processes that transcend the artificial borders between Community policies (pillar one), Common Foreign and Security Policy (CFSP; pillar two) and Police and Judicial Cooperation in Criminal Matters (PJCCM; pillar three).

The concept itself, independently of the label we decide to use (i.e. cross-pillar coordination, cross-pillar approach, or cross-pillarization), addresses implications of the pillar structure introduced by the Treaty of Maastricht. The need to reconcile more intense European integration with still strong national sentiments and preoccupation with sovereignty has resulted in the emergence of a hybrid regime trying to combine the intergovernmental and Community methods of integration (Philippart 1998). The Treaty of Maastricht was undoubtedly a big step forward for the European project but its heritage continues to pose several challenges for EU policy makers. The subsequent Treaty revisions in Amsterdam, Nice and Lisbon, in conjunction with external developments (crisis in the Balkans, EU enlargements and the global 'war on terrorism') have further accentuated the complexity of the pillar structure. The Council recognized that the bigger the need for the EU's role, the more difficult it became to maintain a clear line of division between its pillars (Council of the European Union 2001).

This article aims to investigate the issue of cross-pillarization in light of the growing interconnection between the EU Justice and Home Affairs (JHA) and other policies. At the conceptual level, the article traces the development and functioning of cross-pillarization, depending on the context in which it is used. Since the vocabulary used in relation to the 'cross-pillar' bears important policy implications, the differences between the concepts of 'cross-pillar coordination', 'cross-pillar approach' and 'cross-pillarization' are discussed first. Given the diversity of contexts in which cross-pillarization operates, this article identifies its numerous dimensions: micro and macro, internal and external, legal and policy making. At the analytical level, it investigates whether cross-pillarization in practice might be used by European institutions in a strategic way in order to serve particular interests. Based on the literature devoted to the EU as an administrative structure (Stevens and Stevens 2001) and European inter- and intra-institutional politics (Christiansen 2001), this article makes the case that the process of cross-pillarization has a strong politics component and may be jeopardized by bureaucratic turf wars and conflicts over ideology or resources. Finally, this article ponders to what extent the changes introduced by the Treaty of Lisbon may remedy the situation or constitute a missed opportunity.

The following analysis resonates well with the editors' motion that the new institutionalist approach to the study of JHA (i.e. rational choice institutionalism and sociological institutionalism) may provide valuable insights into our understanding of recent developments in the field. The process towards adoption of the Strategy for the External Dimension of JHA (hereafter the Strategy) serves as the setting for the presentation of intra- and inter-institutional politics resulting both from the struggle for power and from ideological differences within and between the EU institutions (Commission services,[2] Council, European Parliament). Intra-institutional politics are elucidated with conflicting positions represented by diplomats and security specialists inside the Council and the Commission. Inter-institutional politics, on the other hand, are illustrated with the conflict between Commission and Council on the one side, and the European Parliament on the other side in the case of the EU–US Passenger Name Record Agreement (PNR).

Cross-pillarization: Some Conceptual Clarifications

The call for more horizontal coherence and coordination inside the EU has translated in reality into 'inter-pillar' or 'cross-pillar' coordination. As such, cross-pillar coordination of policies can be treated as a natural consequence of the legal separation between the pillars and as a tool for ensuring the most effective implementation of policies (Ministry of Justice 2006), as well as achieving the inter-pillar coherence of EU actions (European Council 1999a; European Commission 2005b). Adopting a cross-pillar approach to an issue implies looking for answers across all pillars in order to design the most effective policy and provide the most comprehensive EU response to the matter in question. The goal is not necessarily to ensure the coherence of EU policies but rather to guarantee that all EU resources are used. These subtle differences, however, do not imply any contradiction between the concepts but rather intend to point their complementary nature.

The choice whether to adopt a cross-pillar approach or to employ cross-pillar coordination entails practical implications. Coordination implies frequent communication and exchange of information between the actors involved. The quality of these contacts determines how effective and coherent the EU action finally is. Given the magnitude of European policies, the volume of communication should be significant. Therefore, there is also the need for a body that would undertake the overall coordinating role and ensure that there is not too much 'information noise'. In the case of the external dimension of JHA, this role has been envisaged for the COREPER (Council of the European Union 2005) and for the group of RELEX Counsellors who are responsible for ensuring the inter-pillar consistency and examining the institutional, legal and financial aspects of proposals made within the CFSP.

Taking a cross-pillar approach, on the other hand, seems to imply a more unidirectional process based on gathering information that would allow for designing the most comprehensive EU response to problems in question. This does not necessarily make it easier, since the amount of work depends on the complexity of the issues and the creativity of the body responsible for tailoring such a response. It requires collecting all available information about EU activities in the field from institutions and member states, analysing the information provided and ultimately drafting a response. The body responsible for preparing a draft will have a huge advantage over other actors and may abuse the process, for instance by trying to raise the profile of its organization or the entire policy area. Therefore, whoever drafts a proposal has real power over the issue in question.

The discussion about cross-pillar coordination and cross-pillar approach provides the basis for the introduction of a more encompassing concept of cross-pillarization. Not present in any official EU document, it has been floating in the academic literature for some time now, albeit without any clarification on what it is and what it implies. The definition provided here is one of the possibilities rather than a definite answer. Cross-pillarization throughout this article is understood as the process of constant interaction between actors or policy areas in the search for balance. This balance is context dependent and shaped by the circumstances in which the balancing exercise occurs (i.e. a particular political objective, a preference for one legal basis over others, etc.). The limited knowledge about the external environment and the future does not allow for defining what the 'right' balance would be and when cross-pillarization is over. It could be predefined only with the assumption that actors participating in cross-pillarization have a clear objective in mind and that no external factors can have an impact. More practically, the end of this balancing exercise could be, for instance, the abolition of the pillar structure as such and creation of a European state.

In light of this evolutionary nature of cross-pillarization, this article perceives cross-pillarization as a process without any clearly stated objective, in constant making and shaped by everyday practices. The focus on the process implies that different components of EU activities (i.e. different policies) blend in the search for a certain balance. This leads to changes in particular policies but also causes shifts in the pillar structure or their weight. Such a shift may result from interactions between policy objectives, various actors and from legal debates. Therefore, it is important to see how these processes occur in order to determine and adjust the whole EU construction. This article focuses on three circumstantial aspects of cross-pillarization: legal and policy, micro and macro, internal and external.

Legal and Policy Aspects of Cross-pillarization

From the legal perspective, the major questions regarding cross-pillarization address the issues of legal basis, competencies and consequently the procedures.[3] As a legal concept, cross-pillarization is therefore concerned with ensuring that any policy measures are in agreement with the Treaties. This has important implications for EU decision-making procedures, in particular with regard to the roles that the European Parliament and the European Court of Justice may play. Even more importantly, inappropriate choice of a legal basis may result in invalidity of a concluded international agreement or a policy measure.[4] As argued by Cremona (2006, 9), 'the existence of an appropriate legal base is a necessary basis for the existence of competence' and 'the choice of legal base is relevant in determining procedures to be followed'. This has become a particularly controversial issue in the context of the fight against terrorism and security more generally. One of the fundamental legal issues that need to be addressed concerns the use of Community powers (first pillar) to achieve CFSP or PJCCM objectives (second and third pillars, respectively).[5] Legally, such a move could, for instance, be justified on the basis of art. 308, in conjunction with art. 301 of the EC Treaty, which serves as a bridge between pillars. The Court of First Instance (CFI) solved this dilemma (at least for the time being) in the *Yusuf* and *Kadi* cases (Court of First Instance 2005a, 2005b), where it stated that the fight against terrorism is the objective of the EU Treaty[6] and not of the EC Treaty and, therefore,

> it appears impossible to interpret Article 308 EC as giving the institutions general authority to use that provision as a basis with a view to attaining one of the objectives of the Treaty on European Union ... The coexistence of Union and Community as integrated but separate legal orders, and the constitutional architecture of the pillars ... authorise neither the institutions nor the Member States to rely on the 'flexibility clause' of Article 308 EC in order to mitigate the fact that the Community lacks the competence necessary for achievement of one of the Union's objectives (Court of First Instance 2005b, para 120).

Furthermore, the decision on the legal basis may enhance or limit the supranational character of the EU. It is not difficult to imagine a situation in which member states may prefer to conclude an international agreement on the basis of the third pillar provisions in order to exercise more control in particularly sensitive areas. On the other hand, there are also instances where member states may prefer the first pillar legal basis in order to achieve a universal application of Community law. Therefore, given a number of grey zones in the EU Treaties, the political aspect of cross-pillarization gains in significance and is the primary focus of this article.

Cross-pillarization as a policy concept is concerned with the design of an effective policy response to a given phenomenon (i.e. fight against organized crime, development policy or migration), policy coordination (i.e. between trade, environment, justice and home affairs) and policy-making procedures. Ideally, cross-pillarization should be a win–win situation for all parties participating in the process since it is supposed to guarantee coherence and effectiveness of EU actions. This, however, is not always the case. Cross-pillar coordination is not free from politics and may lead to competition between EU supranational actors and member states, between the institutions themselves, or, even more often, between components of the same institution (i.e. the Commission). Therefore, cross-pillarization is far from a neutral process. Rather, it often creates winners and losers.

Micro and Macro Cross-pillarization

Most of the EU documents and officials avoid the term 'cross-pillarization' and refer rather to 'cross-pillar coordination' or the 'cross-pillar approach'. As one of the interviewees admitted, '... [w]e talk rather about cross-pillar approach and not cross-pillarization. The "process of cross-pillarization" as such does not exist. The ending "-ization" suggests that this is a process, so it still does not exist. It is something you have to push forward. I do not recognise this understanding of cross-pillarization in our reality'.[7]

There is, however, a certain logical fallacy in the assumption that reference to a process must *per se* exclude its existence. By analogy, the whole process of European integration could be questioned or at least stigmatized as an illegitimate term. However, integration as a big project has, indeed, no prescribed end and hardly anyone would risk foreseeing *la finalité* of European integration. This does not mean that integration does not happen. It proceeds every day and, as such, determines what the European project will eventually become. European integration is both a *grand projet* and an everyday practice. Similarly, the differentiation can be made between 'macro' and 'micro' cross-pillarization. Macro cross-pillarization can be understood as an undefined process transcending the formal pillar structure, causing its erosion and eventually creating new structures and balances. Micro cross-pillarization, on the other hand, refers to the processes associated with the daily practice of cross-pillar coordination and cross-pillar approach. As such, micro cross-pillarization influences the advancement of macro cross-pillarization.

Internal and External Cross-pillarization

Another distinction could be drawn based on the internal and external character of cross-pillarization. The distinction is made on the grounds of the political weight and the target of the process. For instance, is cross-pillarization in anticipation of the conclusion of an international agreement the same as in the daily work of the EU? Intuitively, one could argue that cross-pillar coordination in the former will carry more weight and might pose substantial challenges. Daily cross-pillar coordination, on the contrary, is done on the basis of established procedures and informal networks between officials in EU institutions and member states. In a perfect world, the internal cross-pillarization would contribute to the external one in order to build a positive image of the European Union and enhance the effectiveness of European policies. However, in reality, external cross-pillarization may become a hostage of internal cross-pillar politics.

Dimensions of Cross-pillarization: Polity, Policy and Politics

Numerous references to cross-pillarization used in EU documents across several policy areas suggest that the concept is well received among EU officials. However, research on the practice of cross-pillarization has been quite limited, almost non-existent. The focus has been rather on the examination of policy outcomes, mainly by looking at the problem through regional lenses (Lavenex 2004) or case studies focusing on internal security (Pastore 2001; Trauner 2005; Bendiek 2006). Therefore, an investigation of the processes underlying cross-pillarization is still needed. This article suggests looking at this concept through the three related dimensions of polity, policy and politics.

The polity dimension looks at the concept of cross-pillarization through the prism of European integration literature. Questions in the polity realm address the *finalité* of the process. It interprets cross-pillarization in EU policy making as a struggle between supranationalism and intergovernmentalism (Moravcsik 1993, 1995; Sandholtz and Stone Sweet 1998). Authors sceptical about the classification of European policy making according to this logic, argue that 'EU foreign policies are characterised by the evolution of cross-pillar politics settings, which constantly incorporates both European and national actors within an institutionally fragmented, yet functionally unified policy-making framework' (Stetter 2004, 721). This observation is justified mainly in the case of day-to-day cooperation between the EU and member states' institutions. However, there is no doubt that in more extraordinary circumstances, such as the negotiation of international agreements or a treaty revision, all actors will try to maximize their gains (Christiansen 2001, 761). In that context, the question is whether cross-pillarization in the external dimension of JHA (JHAE) serves to strengthen the position of the EU or that of the member states. Such an approach investigates the possibility that cross-pillarization has been introduced to the discussion about the JHAE precisely in order not to allow for the further shift of competences towards the first pillar and to block any further development of JHA beyond the intergovernmental method. Because the number of issues with cross-pillar characteristics is increasing, it would also imply more opportunities for member states to shape measures and decision-making processes.

The policy dimension is concerned with the process of policy design and policy implementation. It assumes that the activities of institutions are motivated by the 'Community interest' in order to 'ensure the consistency of its external activities as a whole in the context of its external relations, security, economic and development policies'.[8] The main concern of this dimension is to what extent cross-pillarization is a genuine instrument aimed at improving the quality of EU policies and whether it is successful. The ultimate challenge for all institutions should be finding the right balance between policies in order to maximize their efficiency. In this case, cross-pillarization could be seen as a positive development and a sign of a learning process occurring among EU institutions. An entity takes into account the views of others, which can be further interpreted as the 'thinking outside the box' approach in any particular organization. Therefore, the analysis of cross-pillarization in the policy realm would focus on its capacities to enhance policy coordination.

The politics dimension views cross-pillarization through the prism of inter- and intra-institutional politics. It asks to what extent the cross-pillar coordination and cross-pillar approach are subjected to inter- and intra-institutional politics. The politics realm assumes that cross-pillarization is used by actors to promote their own interests. For instance, it might mean that the Commission relies on cross-pillarization in order to raise the profile of Justice and Home Affairs, on which it has most control. Such a scenario would possibly result in a growing influence of JHA on other policy areas and would mean the 'hijacking' of the process by the JHA's external dimension.

As a result, we could also speak about its emergence as a foreign policy field that is superior to other components of the EU's external action.

Institutional Politics and the External Dimension of JHA

The importance of bureaucratic politics and inter-institutional factors has been discussed already in the scholarship. Looking at the decision-making processes in the field of foreign policy, Allison demonstrated that decisions might be taken on the basis of institutional interests and concerns rather than following purely policy objectives. Following this logic, bureaucracies may propose policy options that would promote their institutional interests and strengthen their powers (Allison and Halperin 1972; Allison and Zelikow 1999). Nor are the EU institutions immune to internal politics (Radaelli 1999, 38).

Cross-pillarization from the perspective of institutional coherence can be investigated along three dimensions: at the inter-institutional level (i.e. between Commission and Council), between actors at different levels (i.e. national and supranational), and at intra-institutional level (i.e. between Commission services) (Christiansen 2001, 748). The conflict within and between institutions can stem from their striving for influence within policy areas ('turf wars'), ideological differences over policy approaches and solutions and distribution of scarce resources (Stevens and Stevens 2001, 196). Division of organizations into functional units implies that each of them is interested in maintaining their existence, protecting their area of activity and broadening the scope of their responsibilities in new directions (Stevens and Stevens 2001, 196). The investigation of these processes inside the European Commission has revealed that 'Directorates General enjoy a good deal of status and prestige and can be ambitious to increase this' (Cini and McGowan 1998, 52). Intra-organizational competition is also probable in cases where issues spread across several areas of competence and attribution of responsibility to one functional unit is difficult or impossible.[9] Under such circumstances, the actions of institutions risk motivation not only by fights for prestige and status but also by divergent ideologies, beliefs and interpretations[10] (Stevens and Stevens 2001, 199). Such processes are referred to as the politics of cross-pillarization.

In this context, the new institutionalist literature is a powerful approach in the explanation of cross-pillarization practices in the EU. The amalgam of rational choice and sociological institutionalisms, if employed in the study of cross-pillar processes, may reveal its different but genuine facets (Hall and Taylor 1996). While the strengths of rational choice institutionalism are relevant for explaining the struggle for resources and the maximization of institutional preferences through the pursuit of a given strategy (Shepsle and Weingast 1987; Weingast 1996), the sociological approach with its focus on institutional cultures helps to understand how those preferences are formed (Meyer and Rowan 1977; DiMaggio and Powell 1991). In addition, the rational choice perspective sheds some light on institutional politics as a collective action dilemma. As will be demonstrated later, with the example of the European Parliament's actions during the PNR negotiations, individual institutions acting to attain their own preferences may lead to achieving an outcome that is collectively suboptimal[11] (Hall and Taylor 1996). Whereas rational choice institutionalism contributes to our understanding of institutions as rational and strategic actors, sociological institutionalism offers an insight into the process of preference formation. By bringing culture and other cognitive elements into the study of institutions, sociological institutionalism demonstrates how individuals and institutional dynamics are triggered. Tensions between diplomats and security specialists provide several illustrations of this process. The simultaneous recourse to rational choice and sociological approaches may constitute a powerful tool in the analysis of the dynamically developing external dimension of Justice and Home Affairs.

Politics of Cross-pillarization in the External Dimension of JHA

Global challenges such as the fight against international terrorism and transborder organized crime have further accelerated cooperation between member states in the field of JHA. The scope of new threats to the security and freedom of people has strengthened the conviction of European governments that certain issues cannot be fought only from inside but require member states and the EU to undertake joint actions beyond EU territory. Therefore, the development of JHAE seems to be a natural consequence and fits in with general trends in the EU.

Recognizing the growing importance of JHAE, the European Council of June 2005 asked the Commission and Secretary General of the Council to present the Strategy on the External Dimension of the AFSJ. A small group of people in the Directorate General Justice, Liberty and Security (hereafter DG JHA)[12] was in charge of this task. Several other Commission services attempted to join the process in order to ensure that their respective policy area was not neglected in the global picture. In the context of aiming for a cross-pillar approach to EU activities, those attempts should have been welcomed by DG JHA. In practice, however, all other Directorates General were successfully marginalized.[13] This shows that cross-pillarization creates competition between EU institutions or their sub-units and presents a temptation for institutions to abuse the process in order to raise their profile, broaden their competencies or inject more of their own ideology. Consequently, actors aware of the benefits and dangers may perceive cross-pillarization as an opportunity and turn it into a strategic choice.

The possibility of conflict between Directorates in the Commission increased together with institutional growth and higher specialization of individual policy makers (Christiansen 2001). In response to the global character of problems and challenges, an increasing number of policy areas developed their external dimensions (i.e. transport, environment, health). Justice and home affairs was only a part of this general trend. In consequence, an array of new actors emerged for the Commission's external relations and the Directorate General for External Relations began to lose its control over general EU foreign policy. Gradually, most of the Commission Directorates developed their own external relations units responsible for the international dimension of their work. According to Stevens and Stevens (2001), such situations led to conflicts between institutions that compete either for material (i.e. budgets, staffing) or intangible resources (i.e. responsibility for one of the common policies, longevity and reputation of a commissioner in the area).

External Dimension of JHA: From Home Affairs to Foreign Affairs?

The Strategy represents a certain departure from the balance between the field of justice and home affairs and other European policies. When the external dimension of internal security policies started to emerge, the common understanding was that 'Justice and Home Affairs concerns must be integrated in the definition and implementation of other Union policies and activities' while 'all competences and instruments at the disposal of the Union, and in particular, in external relations must be used in an integrated and consistent way to build the area of freedom, security and justice' (European Council 1999b). Furthermore, the European Council in Feira requested that the JHA external priorities be 'incorporated in the Union's overall external strategy as a contribution towards the establishment of the area of freedom, security and justice' (European Council 2000). The subsequent report presented by the Commission and Council in 2000 stressed the need for the Union 'to integrate JHA matters fully in the Union's external policy so that a comprehensive, integrated, cross-pillar action is carried out by the Union as a whole' (Council of the European Union 2000). The report stated very clearly that '[d]eveloping the JHA external dimension is not an objective in itself. Its primary purpose is to contribute to the establishment of an area of freedom, security and justice. The aim is certainly not to develop a "foreign policy" specific to JHA. Quite the contrary'.

This means that the external dimension is not viewed as a separate aspect of the JHA but rather as one of the components of the EU's external actions. It also implies that various aspects of EU external policies are to be coordinated in order to support the European progress towards the Area of Freedom, Security and Justice (AFSJ). This objective can be achieved through the incorporation of a JHA dimension into the Union's external policy 'on the basis of a "cross-pillar" approach and "cross-pillar" measures' (Council of the European Union 2000). The wording of the Strategy, on the other hand, seems to suggest a change in perception of the role that the JHAE is supposed to play. The JHA aspects are not only to be 'integrated' in the EU's external actions but should become their 'central priority' (Council of the European Union 2005). In that sense, the external dimension of JHA is becoming a 'foreign policy specific to JHA' with its own objectives, priorities and instruments.

The Strategy in the version presented by the Commission stated that cross-pillar coordination is one of the main conditions for achieving coherence of the EU's actions — both internally and externally (European Commission

2005b). With regard to internal process in the EU, there is a clear desire for more coordination between EU institutions responsible for external policies, i.e. the Commission and the Council. The role of the European Parliament is not mentioned, although it often plays an important role through the co-decision procedure or assent required on certain international agreements. Another aspect of such cross-pillar coordination refers to Community competences in relations with third countries. Thus, the Strategy already indicates two dimensions for the analysis of cross-pillar coordination: the inter-institutional dimension (relations between EU institutions) and the international dimension (relations between EU and third parties).

In general, the AFSJ has benefited largely from the development of a more strategic cross-pillar approach to issues. Whereas theoretically, there is no hierarchy of issues in EU external policies, in practice one can observe an increasing role and contribution of JHA: 'sometimes it is really a cornerstone of our cooperation with a third country'.[14] A certain turn towards JHA in the EU's relations with third countries can be observed easily. There is a growing expectation among European policy makers that justice and home affairs 'can push things forward'.[15] This reasoning is justified on several counts. First, there is a growing awareness that internal and external aspects of security are linked and, in order to guarantee security 'at home', one needs to address the root causes of those security challenges abroad. Secondly, due to its expertise in provision of internal security, the EU is often requested by third countries to provide assistance and advice on justice and home affairs issues. This also creates additional opportunities for the EU to connect discussions on justice and home affairs with other issues, i.e. human rights. Thirdly, JHA is a rather new policy field itself and there are many more avenues to be explored, as compared to other policies such as trade or agriculture. In addition, leaders are compelled towards the JHA by increased opportunities for deliverables.

JHAE as a Hijacker: Status and Ideology in Internal Cross-pillarization

It is difficult to escape the impression that DG JHA has benefited largely from the process of cross-pillarization. The move from a small Task Force to a whole Unit responsible for external aspects of JHA serves as the best example. Broadening the competencies of DG JHA and gaining more control over EU external relations was high on the political agenda of JHA Commissioner Frattini.[16] On many occasions he called for abolition of the 'artificial divide' created by the pillar structure, which is 'unhelpful in delivering for EU citizens to live in safety, protected from crime and with protected rights' (European Commission 2006). To that end, he argued, decision-making processes need to be improved and the use of veto power of member states in third pillar should be reduced or eliminated (European Commission 2007b). Alternatively, 'bridging clauses'[17] or 'passerelle clauses'[18] should be used increasingly in order to 'shift some decisions to Qualified Majority Voting, enhance the involvement of the European Parliament and enable national Courts to operate in cooperation with the European Court of Justice. The infringement procedure could monitor implementation of legislation by Member States' (European Commission 2007a). Without doubt, such developments would significantly increase the powers of the Commission — and DG JHA, in particular. With reference to the place of JHA policies in EU external actions, Commissioner Frattini called for a significant role of his policies: '... To tackle organised crime all areas of policy must come together. We cannot have artificial borders between different policies nor between internal and external policy. Those who threaten the EU would be the only people to benefit. Rather we must see justice, freedom and security as interlinked to the EU's external action' (Ministry of Foreign Affairs of the Republic of Hungary 2007).

In the opinion of Commission officials, there was a clear intention in DG JHA to 'hijack' the Strategy. This approach can be traced at the sub-unit level of the European Commission. While DG JHA managed quite successfully to limit the access of other services in the drafting process,[19] it still had to deal with them during the inter-service consultation. The Rules of Procedure adopted by the Commission in 2005 prescribe that 'in order to ensure the effectiveness of Commission action, departments shall work in close cooperation and in coordinated fashion from the outset in the preparation or implementation of Commission decisions' (European Commission 2005a). Furthermore, 'before a document is submitted to the Commission, the department responsible shall, in accordance with the implementing rules, consult the departments with a legitimate interest in the draft text in sufficient time' (European Commission 2005a). Such formal procedures and structures intend 'to try to induce consultative and cooperative behaviour within a structure whose organizations, norms and culture do not naturally encourage it' (Stevens and Stevens 2001, 213). Therefore, after other services were denied a voice in the preparation phase, they used the opportunity of inter-service consultation to present their opinions. After a draft of the Strategy was submitted for consultation, a lot of feedback was provided and led to some fierce discussions at cabinet level.[20] At that stage, however, any fixing was difficult. The tactics of circulating the draft at the last minute proved to be successful. Even though other services submitted their amendments, it was too late to prepare a new draft. The deadline provided by the Council was approaching, so Commissioners were left with two options: 'We could have either prepared a new draft and missed the deadline — an option that would be quite embarrassing for the Commission as an institution — or we could have accepted the text that was already on the table'.[21] The second option prevailed and the Communication to the Council was presented in the shape suggested by DG JHA.

Another big challenge for internal cross-pillarization is to overcome ideological differences or particular cultural characteristic. The classical divide is usually between two groups: internal security officials and diplomats, between JHA culture and diplomacy. However, this phenomenon is not only characteristic of the EU but also of national bureaucracies as well.[22] Several examples illustrate the existence of this conflict. In the context of enlargement, two camps emerged in the Council: one group composed of foreign ministry representatives, and another group with officials from ministries of interior. Ministers of Interior established a collective evaluation working group known as the 'Chevenement Group' (Council of the European Union 1998). The group was composed of senior officials and experts concerned with enlargement; it was charged with 'preparing and keeping up-to-date collective evaluations of the situation in the candidate countries on the enactment, application and effective implementation of the *acquis* of the Union in the field of Justice and Home Affairs' (Council of the European Union 1999). Unsurprisingly, the reports prepared by the Chevenement Group and by Ministers of Foreign Affairs diverged in their assessment. In practice, the Chevenement Group was never very successful and, with time, it became sidelined. Different institutional ideologies have also had an impact on the recent debate about readmission agreements concluded by the European Union with third countries. From the Interior Ministers' perspective, such agreements are desired and, therefore, an increasing number of countries is required to sign such agreements.[23] From the foreign relations perspective, such agreements are highly dubious because they may spoil good diplomatic relations with a third country.

JHAE as a Hostage: Politics and Balancing in the External Cross-pillarization

The real test for cross-pillarization came after the 11 September terrorist attacks, when a growing number of EU policies started to develop their own security dimension with international implications. However, the development of a coherent and cross-pillar 'homeland security policy' in the EU posed real challenges (Pawlak 2007). A reconciliation of second and third pillar objectives with mostly first pillar tools was not an easy task. The Passenger Name Record (PNR) Agreements[24] between the EU and the US serve as a good example of how politics of cross-pillarization can impact the external relations of the EU. Their analysis reveals some significant legal and policy issues involved in the process of external cross-pillarization.

First, in advance of negotiations, a decision needed to be taken whether to focus on the objective or on the substance of the agreement. The objective of the PNR Agreements was, on the one hand, to prevent and combat 'terrorism and related crimes and other serious crimes that are transnational in nature' and, on the other hand, to guarantee the protection of fundamental rights, in particular privacy (Council of the European Union 2004). This is clearly the objective articulated in Article 2 of the Treaty of the European Union (TEU), which places this Agreement under the second and third pillars. The substance, however, was related to issues of transportation security and approximation of laws. The focus on substance, therefore, shifts the weight of EU counter-terrorism actions towards the first pillar. The decision had significant legal implications and placed the PNR regime either in the first pillar[25] or, alternatively, in the second and third pillars.[26] More generally, the question was about what constitutes an appropriate framework for conducting EU counter-terrorism policies.

Secondly, as the way towards the conclusion of PNR agreements demonstrates, cross-pillarization is subjected significantly to inter-institutional politics. The behaviour of the European Parliament (EP) is particularly interesting. The Commission was fully aware that the whole issue needed to be placed in a broader context:

> A comprehensive and balanced approach ... needs to give due weight to all of the following considerations: the fight against terrorism and international crime, the right to privacy and the protection of fundamental civil rights, the need for airlines to be able to comply with diverse legal requirements at an acceptable cost, the broader EU–US relationship, the security and convenience of air travellers, border security concerns, the truly international, indeed world-wide, scope of these issues (European Commission 2003).

The EP, however, placed most attention on the problems of data protection. The major objection to the PNR I Agreement was the insufficient level of data protection in the US. This consequently stipulated that any transfer of data to that country should be prohibited. The strong criticism addressed by the EP to the US authorities and the threat of blocking decision making in other areas unless the EP voice was heard, resulted in the emergence of the EP as one of the major actors in the transatlantic debate over the data protection.[27]

This ideological conflict over the protection of privacy was a smoke screen to a more down-to-earth debate about institutional powers. The EP brought the case against the Commission and the Council to the European Court of Justice (ECJ) because it considered the legal basis for the agreement to be inappropriate.[28] The Commission Legal Service had chosen article 95 EC about approximation of laws as the legal basis for the PNR I. The external competence was exercised on the basis of article 300 EC, which, after the modifications introduced in the Treaty of Nice, gave the EP the right to be consulted on international agreements. However, the expectations of the EP were much higher. The EP claimed that since the subject of the agreement falls under the provisions of the European Data Protection Directive of 1995 (DPD), the EU–US agreement on transfer of the passengers' personal data constituted *de facto* broadening of Directive provisions and, as such, should also be subject to the co-decision procedure.[29] It is not difficult to conclude that the behaviour of the EP exhibits elements of a 'turf war' for more power and influence.

The legal proceedings in the ECJ have resulted in annulment of the PNR I Agreement and created a difficult political situation, not only internally but also externally. The position and credibility of the EU *vis-à-vis* its international partners was shaken seriously.[30] In order to avoid similar problems, the third round of PNR negotiations took place on the basis of the second and third pillars and resulted in the conclusion of the PNR III Agreement in

June 2007. Such a move meant a significant decrease in the role that supranational institutions, such as the EP and Commission, play and shifted the cross-pillar balance in direction of the second and third pillars, with an increased role of the Presidency. As the case of PNR demonstrates, there is a clear relationship between internal and external cross-pillarization.

Cross-pillarization in the Treaty of Lisbon

Although the Treaty of Lisbon was welcomed as a remedy to the increasingly cumbersome EU decision-making procedures, its provisions may create more problems than offer solutions with regard to the politics of cross-pillarization. The Treaty does not remedy the problems of turf wars or ideological conflicts between institutions. The maintained fragmentation of the EU's external policies between Community and CFSP pillars suggests that there are still many opportunities for inter- or intra-institutional politics.

First, the Treaty stipulates that a European 'Foreign Minister' will be responsible for external relations and 'for coordinating other aspects of the Union's external action'.[31] However, how his relationship with other Commissioners will develop remains to be seen. It may result in conflicts inside the Commission and between Commission and Council officials. Also, the extensive mandate of the new Foreign Minister raises some questions about his/her capacity to coordinate the overall EU external action. The plate is full enough with pure 'CFSP' issues. If we add to it the external dimension of transport, JHA and customs policies, this task becomes even more intricate. Furthermore, the Treaty prescribes that 'the Union should ensure consistency between the different areas of its external action and between these and its other policies. The Council and the Commission, assisted by the High Representative shall ensure that consistency and shall cooperate to that effect'.[32] However, how this cooperation will be organized is not prescribed. Most probably, it will simply proceed as established by past practices. Finally, in order to fulfil his mandate, the High Representative/Foreign Minister will be assisted by a European External Action Service (EEAS) 'composed of officials from relevant departments of the Council, the Commission and staff seconded from national diplomatic services of the Member States'.[33] Again, it is not clear at all what 'relevant' means and whether the composition of the EEAS will be limited to diplomats or will be extended to specialists in other areas, such as transport, home affairs, etc. Will diplomats dominate it or will they try to strike a balance between diplomats and security specialists? In any case, the establishment of EEAS will either lead to cultural frictions within it or with other Commission services.

Concluding Remarks

As this article has demonstrated, cross-pillarization adds to the ambiguity of the already complicated EU decision making. Because it involves several actors, operating in various areas, often with different institutional objectives, and engaged with each other through a number of procedures, it creates an environment for rivalry and conflict. Such conflict may occur over power and prestige, resources or on ideological grounds. As the case of the Passenger Name Record Agreement shows, the interdependence between internal and external cross-pillarization has significant legal and political consequences. Politically, it may improve or damage the image of the EU in the world. Legally, it may lead to choices that shift the European project more towards intergovernmental cooperation in the framework of second and third pillars, rather than to the Community method.

This article has also shown that the process of cross-pillarization is complex and can be used or abused by European actors. Evidence has been presented in support of the hypothesis that cross-pillarization might be hijacked by security-orientated policy makers to achieve their own preferences at the expense of other actors and overall policy coherence. The interest of justice and home officials in expanding their powers may only enhance this trend. This leads to the conclusion that unless changes are introduced, internal cross-pillarization will remain a hostage of JHA. However, while the tactics of JHA officials may work in the case of internal cross-pillarization, they fail in external cross-pillarization. As the PNR case has demonstrated, the process of cross-pillarization may become a hostage of inter-institutional politics and becomes a problem in cases of international treaty making.

The presented analysis also suggests that European external actions will be exposed increasingly to politics of cross-pillarization due to the growing importance of the external dimension of Justice and Home Affairs. The ability to recognize a proper background to the problem underlying cross-pillarization is extremely important in order to remedy the situation. The difficulty lies in the fact that sometimes actors do not admit openly to their institutional ambitions or political ideologies. Therefore, establishing needs, expectations and intentions of actors participating in the process of cross-pillarization is the first step on the way to designing a cohesive policy. The new institutionalist approach can provide useful tools in enhancing our understanding of those elements.

This article also reconfirms Christiansen's (2001) diagnosis that the Commission and other institutions are seriously fragmented internally and the main division line runs not between institutions but rather between the components that share certain cultural elements, such as security, diplomacy or trade. There is evidence for the growing significance of informal networking taking place across artificial pillar-based cleavages. However, the remedy proposed here is different. While Christiansen (2001) suggested that the EU might be better served by a greater number of smaller self-contained institutions, this article promotes the contrary idea: the creation of a big security-orientated institution that would bring together security specialists from all Commission and Council services. A similar solution has been adopted already in the case of foreign policy, where the European External Action Service is established. The creation of a European Security Service would minimize the risk of inter- and intra-institutional conflicts and would contribute to more coherence in European internal security policies.

Acknowledgement

The author would like to thank the Compagnia di San Paolo, the Riksbankens Jubileumsfond and the Volkswagen Stiftung for their generous support provided in the framework of the European Foreign and Security Policy Studies Programme. In addition, thanks go to Professor Marise Cremona from the European University Institute in Florence for valuable comments on legal aspects of cross-pillarization. Any errors of fact and judgement remain exclusively the author's.

Notes

1. Bendiek (2006) wrote about the 'cross-pillar security regime' in the context of the fight against terrorism, Stetter (2004) focused on 'cross-pillar politics' and functional dynamics in the integration of interior and foreign policies, Trauner (2005) discussed challenges stemming from 'cross-pillarization' and Cremona (2006) provided some legal insights into the 'legal basis and inter-pillar issues'.
2. It needs to be clarified at this point that although theoretically there cannot be any cross-pillarization 'inside' the Commission, the involvement of EU services in a broad array of external action and across pillars means in practice that conflicts inside the Commission will have a cross-pillar aspect to them.
3. For a discussion on the legal aspects of EU's external relations, see Holdgaard (2008), Cremona (2006), Eeckhout (2004), Wessel (2004) and Denza (2002). For literature on the legal aspects of JHA, see Monar (2004), Walker (2004) and Kerchove and Weyembergh (2003).
4. See, for instance, the Opinion 2/00 (European Court of Justice 2001): 'The choice of the appropriate legal basis has constitutional significance. Since the Community has conferred powers only, it must tie the Protocol to a Treaty provision which empowers it to approve such a measure. To proceed on an incorrect legal basis is therefore liable to invalidate the act concluding the agreement and so vitiate the Community's consent to be bound by an agreement it has signed.'
5. How this occurs in practice will be discussed later, on the basis of the EU–US PNR Agreement.
6. Art. 11 Treaty of the European Union.
7. Interview with a Council official, Brussels, March 2007.
8. Art. 3 Treaty of the European Union.
9. Peterson and Bomberg (1999) provided the example of food policy that can be assigned both as a trade and agriculture issue. A policy on energy use as a response to climate change may be seen either as an environmental issue or as energy issue. Cram (1994) on the other hand, exemplified intra-institutional battles with development of the EU policy in the area of Information and Communication Technology.
10. Hooghe and Marks (1999) used the example of structural policies to demonstrate how ideologies influence the development of structural policies in the 1990s. Bulmer (1998), to that end, used the example of ideological discussions surrounding the area of the internal market.
11. An outcome could be found that would make some actors better off without necessarily worsening a position of any other actor.
12. The older abbreviation is preferred in this article because of its closer association with the JHA as a policy area.
13. Interviews with Commission officials, March 2007.
14. Interview with a Commission official, March 2007.
15. *Ibid.*
16. In-depth interview with a Commission official, March 2007.
17. Suggested in Article IV-444 of the Constitutional Treaty.
18. Passarelle provisions in the existing Treaties concern, among others, police and judicial cooperation, as well as immigration and asylum.
19. Such right is provided by the Commission Rules of Procedure: 'The department responsible for preparing an initiative shall ensure from the beginning of the preparatory work that there is effective

coordination between all the departments with a legitimate interest in the initiative by virtue of their powers or responsibilities or the nature of the subject'. See European Commission (2005a).
20. Interview with a Commission official, March 2007.
21. *Ibid.*
22. For a good analysis of how interior ministers try to defend their positions and push forward their approaches, see Lavenex (2006).
23. Interview with a Commission official, March 2007.
24. The plural form is used because the EU and the US have negotiated and signed three PNR Agreements: in 2004, 2006 and 2007. They are further referred to as PNR I, PNR II and PNR III.
25. Art. 300 EC and 95 EC used as a legal basis.
26. Art. 24 TEU and 38 TEU serving as a legal basis.
27. The EP became associated with negotiations of the PNR III, although this agreement was concluded on a third pillar basis, where the role of the EP is very limited. In May 2007 the Homeland Security Secretary Chertoff, for the first time in history, addressed the European Parliament.
28. Case C-317/04 *European Parliament* v *Council*; Case C-318/04 *European Parliament* v *Commission* (European Court of Justice 2006).
29. The DPD was indeed adopted in co-decision procedure. However, article 300 EC, on the basis of which the Agreement was concluded, stipulates that the EP should be only consulted.
30. Interviews with US officials, January–July 2007.
31. Art. 18 TEU (as amended by the Treaty of Lisbon (ToL)).
32. Art. 21 para. 3 TEU (as amended by ToL).
33. Art. 27 para. 3 TEU (as amended by ToL).

References

Allison, G.T., and M. Halperin. 1972. Bureaucratic politics: A paradigm and some policy implications. *World Politics* 24(spring): 40–79.
Allison, G.T., and P. Zelikow. 1999. *Essence of decision: Explaining the Cuban Missile Crisis*. New York: Longman.
Bendiek, A. 2006. Cross-pillar security regime building in the European Union: Effects of the European Security Strategy of December 2003. *European Integration Online Papers*, September 8.
Bulmer, S.J. 1998. New institutionalism and the governance of the Single European Market. *Journal of European Public Policy* 5, no. 3: 365–86.
Christiansen, T. 2001. Intra-institutional politics and inter-institutional relations in the EU: Towards coherent governance?. *Journal of European Public Policy* 8, no. 5: 747–69.
Cini, M., and L. McGowan. 1998. *Competition policy in the European Union*. London: Macmillan.
Council of the European Union. 1998. Joint Action of 29 June 1998 adopted by the Council on the basis of Article K.3 of the Treaty on European Union, establishing a mechanism for collective evaluation of the enactment, application and effective implementation by the applicant countries of the acquis of the European Union in the field of Justice and Home Affairs. *Official Journal of the EU* L191 (July 7): 8–9.
Council of the European Union. 1999. Justice and home affairs 2203rd Council meeting, 11281/99, October 4.
Council of the European Union. 2000. European Union priorities and policy objectives for external relations in the field of justice and home affairs, 7653/00, June 6.
Council of the European Union. 2001. Preparing the Council for the Enlargement, 9518/01, June 7.
Council of the European Union. 2004. Council Decision on the conclusion of an Agreement between the European Community and the United States of America on the processing and transfer of PNR data by air carriers to the United States Department of Homeland Security, Bureau of Customs and Border Protection. *Official Journal of the EU* L183/83 (May 20).
Council of the European Union. 2005. A strategy for the external dimension of JHA: Global freedom, security and justice, 15446/05, December 6.
Court of First Instance. 2005a. Case T 306/01 Ahmed Ali Yusuf and Al Barakaat International Foundation v Council of the European Union and European Commission. *Official Journal of the EU* C281 (November 12).

Court of First Instance. 2005b. Case T-315/01 Yassin Abdullah Kadi v Council of the European Union and European Commission. *Official Journal of the EU* C281 (November 12).
Cram, L. 1994. The European Commission as a multi-organisation: Social policy and IT policy in the EU. *Journal of European Public Policy* 1, no. 2: 195–218.
Cremona, M. 2006. External relations of the EU and the member states: Competence, mixed agreements, international responsibility, and effects of international law. *EUI Working Papers* Law No. 2006/22.
Denza, E. 2002. *The intergovernmental pillars of the European Union*. Oxford: Oxford Univ. Press.
DiMaggio, P.J., and W.W. Powell. 1991. *The new institutionalism in organizational analysis*. Chicago: Univ. of Chicago Press.
Eeckhout, P. 2004. *External relations of the European Union: Legal and constitutional foundations*. Oxford: Oxford Univ. Press.
European Commission. 2003. Communication from the Commission to the Council and the Parliament. Transfer of air Passenger Name Record (PNR) data: A global EU approach, December 16 2003, COM(2003) 826 final.
European Commission. 2005a. Commission decision amending its Rules of Procedure, 2005/960/EC, November 15.
European Commission. 2005b. Communication from the Commission. A strategy on the external dimension of the Area of Freedom, Security and Justice, 12 October 2005, COM (2005) 491 final.
European Commission. 2006. Scoreboard 2006 in Area of Freedom, Security and Justice, Press release of speaking points for Franco Frattini.
European Commission. 2007a. Helping EU citizens seize opportunities: EU's policies and legislation in the Area of Freedom, Security and Justice. Speech by Franco Frattini at the 4th European Jurists Forum, Vienna, 3 May 2007.
European Commission. 2007b. The EU as an area of freedom, security and justice. EU policies in the Area of Freedom, Security and Justice: State of play and future perspectives. Speech by Franco Frattini at Vienna University, Vienna, 3 May 2007.
European Council. 1999a. Presidency conclusions. Helsinki European Council. Annex IV of the Presidency conclusions. *Bulletin of the European Union* 12–1999.
European Council. 1999b. Presidency conclusions. Tampere European Council. *Bulletin of the European Union* 10–1999.
European Council. 2000. Presidency conclusions. Santa Maria Da Feira European Council. *Bulletin of the European Union* 6-2000.
European Court of Justice. 2001. Opinion 2/00 of the Court (regarding the Cartagena Protocol), ECR I-9713, December 6 2001.
European Court of Justice. 2006. Joined Cases C-317/04 and C-318/04 European Parliament v Council of the European Union and Commission of the European Communities. *Official Journal of the EU* C178/02.
Hall, P., and R.C. Taylor. 1996. Political science and the three new institutionalisms. *Political Studies* 44, no. 5: 936–57.
Holdgaard, R. 2008. *External relations law of the European Community: Legal reasoning and legal discourses*. Alphen aan den Rijn: Wolters Kluwer.
Hooghe, L., and G. Marks. 1999. The birth of a polity: The struggle over European integration. In *Continuity and change in contemporary capitalism*, eds. H. Kitschelt, P. Lange, G. Marks and J. Stephens, 70–101. Cambridge: Cambridge Univ. Press.
Kerchove, G. de, and A. Weyembergh, eds. 2003. *Sécurité et justice: Enjeu de la politique extérieure de l'Union européenne*. Brussels: Editions de l'Université de Bruxelles.
Lavenex, S. 2004. EU external governance in 'wider Europe'. *Journal of European Public Policy* 11, no. 4: 680–700.
Lavenex, S. 2006. Shifting up and out: The foreign policy of European immigration control. *Western European Politics* 29, no. 2: 329–50.
Meyer, J.W., and B. Rowan. 1977. Institutionalized organizations: Formal structure as myth and ceremony. *American Journal of Sociology* 83, no. 2: 340–63.
Ministry of Foreign Affairs of the Republic of Hungary. 2007. How the justice, freedom and security policies influence EU's external action. Address by Franco Frattini at the Foreign Ministry Heads of Missions Conference, Budapest, 30 July 2007.

Ministry of Justice. 2006. *National Coordinator for Counterterrorism, Fifth Progress Report on Counterterrorism*. The Hague: Ministry of Justice.

Monar, J. 2004. The EU as an international actor in the domain of justice and home affairs. *European Foreign Affairs Review* 9, no. 4: 395–415.

Moravcsik, A. 1993. Preferences and power in the European Community: A liberal intergovernmentalist approach. *Journal of Common Market Studies* 31, no. 4: 473–523.

Moravcsik, A. 1995. Liberal intergovernmentalism and integration: A rejoinder. *Journal of Common Market Studies* 33, no. 4: 611–28.

Pastore, F. 2001. Reconciling the prince's two 'arms': Internal–external security policy coordination in the European Union. *ISS-EU Occasional Paper* 30.

Pawlak, P. 2007. Transatlantic border and transport security cooperation: Can one swallow make a summer? In *Cooperating against terrorism. EU–US relations post September 11*, eds. D. Hansen and M. Ranstorp, 99–112. Stockholm: National Defence College.

Peterson J., and E. Bomberg. 1999. *Decision-making in the European Union*. New York: Macmillan.

Philippart, E. 1998. Deconstruction and reconstruction of EU pillars: the Euro-Mediterranean Partnership and the Middle East Peace Process Paper presented at the Third Pan-European International Relations Conference ECPR-ISA, Vienna, 16–19 September 1998, 2–3.

Radaelli, C. 1999. *Technocracy in the European Union*. London: Longman.

Sandholtz, W., and A. Stone Sweet. 1998. *European integration and supranational governance*. Oxford: Oxford Univ. Press.

Shepsle K., and B. Weingast. 1987. The institutional foundations of committee power. *American Political Science Review* 81, no. 1: 85–104.

Stetter, S. 2004. Cross-pillar politics: functional unity and institutional fragmentation of EU foreign policies. *Journal of European Public Policy* 11, no. 4: 720–39.

Stevens, A., and H. Stevens. 2001. *Brussels bureaucrats? The administration of the European Union*. New York: Palgrave.

Trauner, F. 2005. *External aspects of internal security: A research agenda, EU-Consent Project: Wider Europe-Deeper Integration?* Constructing Europe Network, EU-Consent.

Walker, N., ed. 2004. *Europe's Area of Freedom, Security and Justice*. Oxford: Oxford Univ. Press.

Weingast, B. 1996. Political institutions: Rational choice perspectives. In *A new handbook of political science*, eds. R.E. Goodin and H.D. Klingemann, 167–90. Oxford: Oxford Univ. Press.

Wessel, R. 2004. Fragmentation in the governance of EU external relations: Legal institutional dilemmas and the new constitution for Europe. *Centre for European Studies Working Paper* No 3/04, Univ. of Twente.

Civilian Crisis Management and the External Dimension of JHA: Inceptive, Functional and Institutional Similarities

GREGORY MOUNIER

Politics and International Relations Department, University of Reading, Reading, UK

ABSTRACT The fragmented European competences in the field of security policy appear increasingly at odds in a context of cross-border and transnational security threats. Discrepancies have initiated a process of adaptation, in particular with regard to external and internal security policies. This article investigates these developments and underlines the growing similarities arising between the European Union civilian crisis management activities and the external dimension of Justice and Home Affairs (JHA). After examining the factors which led to their inception, as well as the respective institutional discourses supporting both fields, the article emphasizes the fact that civilian crisis management and the JHA external dimension not only share 'functional similarities' but also a common 'functional frame'; that of protecting the EU's internal security regime. The sociological institutionalist framework adopted reveals the mechanisms through which the *rapprochement* is taking place, for example by systematic recourse to security sector activities, and the proactive role played by European institutions and the various security actors — police officers, judges and border guards.

Introduction

In the last decade, the member states of the European Union have gradually developed common European security policies in order to address new security challenges. Although these European security policies are spread across the three pillars of the EU, which means that their respective decision-making processes and legal basis are different, recent institutional developments and empirical evidence seem to indicate that their objectives and the actors that implement them share many similarities. This is particularly the case for two of the most recent strands of EU security policies: the civilian crisis management activities and the external dimension of the Justice and Home Affairs (JHA) domain.

EU civilian crisis management activities are conducted mainly within the framework of the second intergovernmental pillar. The major actors are the member states acting through the Council of Ministers and the General Secretariat of the Council (GSC). Based on Joint Actions, the aim of civilian crisis management actions is to complement the military dimension of the European Security and Defence Policy (ESDP) in achieving the so-called Petersberg Tasks: 'humanitarian and rescue tasks, peacekeeping tasks and tasks of combat forces in crisis management, including peacemaking'.[1] Civilian crisis management is part of the general effort of the EU to project stability and peace beyond its borders and address crisis situations in third countries. However, crisis management activities are also conducted under the first community pillar by the European Commission and include a variety of other non-military instruments, such as cooperation and economic development or external assistance programmes.

More recently, EU internal security policies have come to play an increasing part in crisis management. This is because of the development of an external Justice and Home Affairs (JHA) dimension and its potential in security sector reform abroad (Mounier 2007; Monar 2008). Since the Treaty of Amsterdam, the Area of Freedom, Security and Justice (AFSJ) has been embodied by the JHA domain, whose instruments are spread between two pillars. The first community pillar encompasses immigration and asylum, visa, border controls and police and justice cooperation in civil matters,[2] while the third intergovernmental pillar includes police and justice cooperation in criminal matters.[3] The EU has a limited mandate in these fields since it can act only where there is a cross-border dimension and if it brings an added-value to the member states. Therefore, JHA activities have been restricted mostly to information exchange and approximation of national legislations in domains such as organized crime, terrorism and illegal immigration. However, with the development of the external dimension and the creation of external measures, the objective of which is to export norms and standards of internal security by transforming structures and capacities of third countries (Council of the European Union 2005a), the JHA mandate seems to have expanded to the point that the external dimension of EU internal security policies pursue the same objectives as civilian crisis management.

This raises important questions concerning the nature of the JHA external dimension and the extent to which the EU internal security agenda is gradually contaminating the fields of other European policy; the area of civilian crisis management in this case. Is there really a *rapprochement* between the EU internal security domain and crisis management activities? If so, why is it taking place and what is the rationale for such a *rapprochement*? How does this process materialize institutionally and what are the consequences for the future of EU security policies?

This article will take a three-stage approach to addressing these questions. First, looking at the factors which have triggered the inception of both policy domains, the article attempts to explain the reasons why civilian crisis management and the JHA external dimension have come to share more similarities than would at first appear from the formal set of EU rules. Secondly, drawing from sociological institutionalism and in line with the conceptual framework adopted in the introduction of this special issue, this article underlines 'functional similarities' in the official discourses underpinning civilian crisis management and the JHA external dimension. The third stage considers the institutional developments that have occurred recently and examines the behaviour of the actors operating in both fields. The article concludes with some observations on the consequences of this institutional *rapprochement* in light of the new institutional framework brought about by the Lisbon Treaty.

Changing Security Environment as a Triggering Factor for the Inception of Civilian Crisis Management and the External Dimension of JHA

Apart from a few scattered remarks (Hansen 2004; Lutterbeck 2005; Rees 2005; Berenskoetter 2006; Duke and Ojanen 2006), and despite the growing number of indicators pointing in that direction, the academic literature is yet to produce a coherent study addressing the striking similarities between the civilian aspect of ESDP and the external dimension of JHA. One of these similarities is that they were launched at the same time in the history of the European integration and that their inception was triggered by similar factors.

Convergence between Internal and External Security and the Enlargement of the EU to the East

According to Buzan (2000, 5) and others, the ending of the Cold War 'blew away much of the familiar (if not comfortable) security architecture of the previous four decades'. This led international relations academics to reconsider the concept of security in the light of the new features of the post-Cold War. Among the most-cited evolutions is the shift away from purely external and 'hard' security concerns to an almost exclusive focus on transnational and internal security. Western governments no longer fear military attacks involving tanks and missiles but they are concerned with international terrorism, transnational organized crime and uncontrolled immigration. The growing transnationalization of the threats has contributed to blurring the traditional distinction between external and internal security instruments and policies to the point where they have become inextricably intertwined (Katzenstein 1996; Bigo 2001; Pastore 2002). For the EU this 'internal–external security nexus' means that the achievement of internal security objectives is contingent on maintaining international stability and security outside the EU (Council of the European Union 2003). Although this idea is criticized by many (Chandler 2006; Merlingen 2007), the external projection of values and norms underpinning the EU has become essential to safeguard the rule of law, fundamental rights, stability and security inside the EU territory.

The expansion of the EU to include Eastern European countries, whose internal security machinery collapsed together with their respective communist regimes, prompted the member states to develop common policies to tackle security deficiencies in their neighbourhood. Consequently, one of the most important articles that candidate countries have to implement before joining the EU concerns 'cooperation in the field of justice and home affairs'. The objective is to strengthen the security apparatus of candidate countries by exporting technical measures in the field of internal security, in order to reduce potential threats 'on the spot' before these countries join the common Area of Freedom, Security and Justice. The expertise developed by the EU institutions in providing training in the fight against organized crime, border management and police and justice cooperation is one of the factors explaining the development of the JHA external dimension. The EU has responded to the threat of importing insecurity by exporting internal security instruments.

The more assertive role taken by the EU in the building of security institutions in candidate countries within the framework of the 2004 enlargement process also explains its inclination to become more involved in helping third countries in their transition from civil war to democracy by sending civilian crisis management teams. Besides being an appealing idea to Western governments and their citizens, this initiative met the EU's security concerns, based on the assumption that failed and weak states represent a danger to its security. In line with neo-Wilsonian approaches, the EU wants to intervene to strengthen or rebuild security institutions because it feels threatened by these failed states, which are perceived as 'breeding grounds of instability, mass migration, as well as reservoirs and exporters of terror' (Rotberg 2002, 128).

Adaptation of Internal and External Security Policies

To be able to tackle transnational security threats, both internal and external security policies must adapt, cooperate and incorporate tools from each other. Although different driving forces are at work, the adaptation process is perceptible in both internal and external security fields. On the external side there has been the creation of the civilian component of the ESDP crisis management capacity, in particular ESDP police missions, while on the internal side, an external dimension to JHA has gradually developed.

Development of the JHA external dimension. In recent years the EU's perception of internal security has changed dramatically and third countries have been regarded as a source of new security threats, such as organized crime, terrorism or illegal immigration (Trauner 2006). One consequence of this has been the development of an external dimension to the EU internal security regime (Monar 2000; Anderson and Apap 2002; Rees 2005) as a means to address these threats as early as possible. The external dimension of JHA was first mentioned in 1999 in the Conclusions of the Tampere Council, which called for the use of EU external relations to build the area of freedom, security and justice (European Council 1999, Point 59). Concrete policy objectives were then laid down one year later at the European Council of Santa Maria de Feira in 2000. They included an external dimension for migration policy, including common control of the EU's external border and the signature of readmission agreements with the countries of origin of migrants. Europol was given a key role in the fight against organized crime and terrorism and was asked to conclude cooperation agreements with third countries. Lastly, the Council established that the development of the rule of law in countries emerging from wars should be a priority of EU external action. In other words, not only military aspects of ESDP crisis management, but also police and justice cooperation instruments should be used in crisis regions, with a view to securing the internal EU security regime. For Lavenex (2005), these policy objectives amounted to the development of a genuine 'foreign policy agenda' for the AFSJ. As threats to the internal security of the EU were seen increasingly to arise from outside the Union, 'internal security concerns were turned into questions of external security' (Lavenex 2005, 128). Indeed, the Council stressed the need 'to integrate JHA matters fully in the Union's external policy' (European Council 2000a, 2). The external dimension of JHA has gradually become one of the prime concerns of the EU's external relations. The EU seeks to protect its internal security regime by projecting its instruments and policies of internal security (which include migration control, border security and policing) abroad, in particular to areas likely to generate threats. It also attempts to include third countries in the achievement of its internal security objectives, notably by concluding readmission agreements, and judicial and police cooperation treaties with the countries to ensure cooperation in EU security policies.

Development of ESDP civilian crisis management capacities. There have also been adaptations on the external side. The decision to create non-military crisis management capacities within ESDP is explained traditionally by the difficulties in the deployment of a sufficient number of police personnel within the United Nations Interim Administrative Mission in Kosovo (UNMIK) in the aftermath of the NATO-led intervention (Nowak 2006b, 18). This drove the EU to make an inventory of the civilian tools available to respond to emerging crisis situation and adopt an 'Action Plan for non-military crisis management of the EU' at the 1999 Helsinki Council (Rutten 2001, 90). However, reflections upon the changing nature of the threat and the need to improve EU capacities to cope with post-conflict and transnational security challenges are another element that determined the development of the civilian component of ESDP at the end of the 1990s.

The combined effects of the 'movement away from the Cold War approaches to the EU' (Manners 2006, 184) and the growing EU influence in world politics by means of norms diffusion, heightened by the severe limitations imposed by the Petersberg Tasks on the opportunity for military interventions by the common European defence, have led analysts to described the EU as a 'normative' or 'civilian' power (Manners 2004; Sjursen 2007). However, in the context of the internal–external security nexus, being a soft power is not a handicap. On the contrary, 'soft' or 'civilian' capabilities, such as civilian crisis management, are the only long-term instruments to address security threats stemming from failed states and post-conflict situations, which impact directly on the EU's internal security (Rotberg 2002). Hence while the UK, France, Germany and Italy were pressing for the acquisition by the EU of military capabilities, a group of countries led by Sweden wanted to ensure that the EU would also adopt a holistic view in security policy, bringing together military and civilian structures (Bjurner 2001, 12; Merlingen and Ostrauskaité 2006, 41). At the Feira Council of 2000 — the very same European Council where political objectives were laid down for the development of the external dimension of JHA — member states agreed on four priority areas where the EU should become an actor in civilian crisis management: police, strengthening the rule of law, civilian administration and civilian protection (European Council 2000b). The fact that there are more civilian ESDP missions being carried out throughout the world today than purely military operations[4] indicates that, with the emergence of transnational and globalized threats to EU internal security, civilian crisis management has become a central element of EU external security policies. This is particularly true for police missions, which have played an increasing role in the context of multilateral peacekeeping and post-conflict reconstruction operations (Oakley, Dziedzic, and Goldberg 1998; Hansen 2002). Between 1989 and the late 1990s, the number of police officers involved in international peace support increased from 35 to over 10,000.[5] Against this backdrop, EU civilian capacities have quickly taken off, with the adoption of a 'Police Action Plan' in 2001, which set the objective that the EU should have 5,000 police officers ready for international missions of prevention and crisis management by 2003 (European Council 2001).

Adaptation of European external and internal security policies has been necessary to fit the new post-Cold War security environment, characterized by the internal–external security nexus and the increasing complexity of conflicts, where naked military power alone cannot solve complex political and human security problems, but must be coupled with civilian resources. While civilian crisis management has become one of the most dynamic features of the EU's external security policies, simultaneously the JHA external dimension has been integrated in the EU's external actions. Another aspect of the proximity between civilian crisis management and the external dimension of JHA, their 'functional similarities', will be examined in the next section.

Functional Similarities

In a comparative study of the EU's foreign (CFSP) and interior (JHA) policies, Stetter (2007) offered an innovative theoretical framework of analysis. Drawing on sociological institutionalism, he showed that 'functional similarities' have been shaped by substantive and institutional developments in CFSP and JHA, which have, in turn, transcended the pillar structure and 'paved the way for an incremental centralisation of foreign and interior policies at EU level' (Stetter 2007, 6). In earlier work, Wessel (2004) showed that, although the EU's external relations were spread among the three pillars, overlapping competences were linked by an overall 'functional unity'. Building upon this conclusion, Stetter (2007) argued that the numerous substantive and institutional overlaps between CFSP and JHA have led the two policies to share a similar 'functional unity', which creates a political dynamic across pillars. In Stetter's work the 'functional frame' of CFSP and JHA is an 'EU-specific insider/outsider distinction', that is to say that CFSP and JHA both incrementally create an EU external and internal identity (Stetter 2007, 35). Stetter then used this common 'functional frame' as evidence for his claim that CFSP and JHA 'jointly constitute a distinct policy type at the EU level', which he referred to as 'constituent policies', in line with the policy typology established by Lowi (1964). Both authors use the concept of 'functional similarities' as an umbrella, including 'functional frame' (created by institutional discourse and practice) and 'functional unity' (referring to the ensuing process of institutional *rapprochement*). Likewise, the civilian aspect of ESDP and the JHA external dimension have been created not only simultaneously because of similar triggering factors, but they seem to be sharing a similar 'functional frame': protecting the EU's internal security regime. This common frame brought the development of a 'functional unity' discernable in substantive and institutional developments and in overlapping competencies.

A Common 'Functional Frame': Protecting the EU's Internal Security Regime

In line with sociological institutionalist principles, institutions have the capacity 'to mould the preferences, interests and identities of actors in the social world' (Rosamond 2000, 114). They produce 'frameworks of ideas', which shape the political environment and have 'consequences for the interactions of actors' (Jachtenfuchs 1997, 47). If the creation of the JHA external dimension and the civilian aspect of ESDP can be explained partly as a response to changes affecting the security environment, institutional discourses have prepared the ground for these developments. Through the Council, member states have framed a specific understanding of the new post-Cold War security environment whereby the threats to internal security were coming from outside the EU. As an example, Europol's 2006 Organised Crime Threat Assessment makes 17 references to the 'non-indigenous' features of organized crime groups operating inside the EU (van Duyne 2007, 123). The result of this discourse is that projection of values and the externalization of standards of internal security become an essential part of the protection of the EU's internal security regime. Although institutional discourses surrounding both domains mirror their respective institutional settings and therefore differ from each other in some respects, they nonetheless share a common ground and create an identical 'functional frame', which is that in order to protect the EU's internal security regime from external threats, the EU must project its norms and standards of security.

Functional frame in the external dimension of JHA. A study of official EU documents shows that the main rationale for developing an external dimension in various fields of JHA policy was to increase the 'efficiency'[6] of internal security policies, such as the fight against transnational organized crime. For instance, in the 1997 'Action Plan to combat organised crime' (European Council 1997), the Council advocates that the EU should support the efforts of third countries to tackle organized crime and encourage them to enter into cooperative agreements with Europol. The objective here is not only to reduce crime in third countries but also to give member states' law-enforcement agencies more information on crime coming from third countries into the EU. The same logic is behind the 'EU Drugs Action Plan for 2005–2008' (European Council 2005), which provides technical assistance to the judicial and police systems of third countries to aid the fight against drug production and trafficking. The idea is, first and foremost, to reduce the amount of illegal substances reaching the EU. Improving judicial and police systems in Latin America or in the Balkans is only a means to an end. In both cases, institutions have framed the threats as being external to the EU. The external projection of European norms and standards of security to countries likely to generate these threats is perceived as crucial to security inside EU territory. It can be achieved by any of the EU's external actions: development aid, external assistance or trade policy. This is in line with the 2005 Strategy on the external dimension of JHA, which makes it a central priority of the EU's external relations (Council of the European Union 2005a). The European counter-terrorism policy is also very instructive in this regard. In the 2006 revised 'Action Plan on Terrorism' (European Commission 2006c), the EU recommends the use of external assistance programmes, including the support of good governance and the rule of law, as a means to address factors contributing to the support of terrorism. As a result, approximately 400 million worth of technical assistance is provided to help around eighty countries build up their counter-terrorism capacities, which range from border management to terrorist financing (European Commission 2006b, 7).

In order to persuade third countries to cooperate with the EU on internal security issues, the EU signed the 'Vienna Declaration on Security Partnership' with fifty third countries (Council of the European Union 2006b). The concept of 'partnership' is based on the idea that security policies should be beneficial to both parties, and that third countries and the EU share common interests in combating terrorism, organized crime and management of migration flows. This tendency to involve third countries in the EU's security policy is one of the aspects of the externalization of JHA defined by Lavenex (2005). It contributes to the construction of the 'functional frame', whereby third countries are the source of security threats and the EU must project its internal security apparatus and actively engage itself in the reform of their security sector so as to protect its own internal security regime.

Functional frame in civilian crisis management. As far as civil crisis management is concerned, the institutional discourse is misleading because the creation of civilian crisis management capacities is usually justified on humanitarian grounds. However, the link between crisis management and the protection of the EU internal security becomes apparent in the recent recourse by EU institutions to the concepts of 'human security' and 'Security Sector Reform'.

In contrast to 'state security' the concept of 'human security' encapsulates the emergence of a new security agenda in which the point of reference is the individual (Burgess and Owen 2004; Kaldor and Glasius 2006). Although it has been criticized for being either too broad (King and Murray 2001) and/or for reducing the understanding of international security (Paris 2004), it remains a convenient notion to conceptualize the interdependent nature of security, since it postulates that 'the security of one person, one community, one nation rests on the decisions of many others' (Commission on Human Security 2003, 3). In a report commissioned by the Council, Kaldor (2004, 28) argued that the EU 'has a critical interest in developing capabilities to make a contribution to global human security' and recommended that human security should be integrated into the Union's foreign and security policies. However, despite the increasing number of references to the human security lexicon in its strategic narrative (Kaldor 2007), the EU has not yet adopted a genuine human security approach in its external relations. On the contrary, human security has become a 'leitmotif for EU security policies' and it has been emptied of its very substance (Bosold and Werthes 2006). If one deconstructs the institutional discourse underpinning civilian crisis management, where reference is made to human security, a similar 'functional frame' to the one underlined for the JHA external dimension emerges: the main rationale for the ESDP police missions is not only to promote human security in third countries but also to protect the EU's internal security. To find evidence supporting this argument, it is necessary to look at the way in which ESDP police missions perform their task in the field of Security Sector Reform (SSR). The adoption by the EU of the concept of SSR is related closely to the emergence of the human security 'paradigm shift' (Haaland 2006; Sedra 2006). The security sector encompasses all the state institutions that are entrusted with the safety of the state and its citizens, such as the armed forces, the police, border guards and also judicial institutions (Tanner and Hänggi 2005, 13). Reconstructing the security sector after wars or ethnic conflicts is a priority to create the right conditions for sustainable peace. It allows a country to enhance its security, strengthen its governance structures and, in turn, achieve higher economic growth and promote democratization

(Yusufi 2004, 4). In other words, SSR is an instrument to achieve human security objectives. However, in theory, SSR goes beyond the mere notion of 'effectiveness' of the military, the police or the judicial institutions. It should be a holistic process, focusing on the overall functioning of the security structures, with the objective of addressing governance deficits, strengthening transparency and democratic accountability rather than simply improving their 'efficiency'.

Analysis of the EU's strategic documents on civilian crisis management confirms that one of the key objectives of civilian ESDP operations is to reform the security sector of failed states in order to tackle organized crime and trafficking. For instance, the European Security Strategy recognizes that deficits in the security sectors of third countries constitute a challenge for the EU's own security (Council of the European Union 2003, 22). In 2005, the Council adopted an 'EU concept for ESDP support to SSR', where it clearly stated that 'SSR plays an important role in serving the EU's strategic objectives' (Council of the European Union 2005b, 5). This security-orientated understanding of SSR contradicts the official discourse on the promotion of human security by means of civilian instruments. Empirical studies of ESDP police missions have also shown that the efficiency of the security apparatus tends to take precedence over good governance principles (Osland 2004; Merlingen and Ostrauskaité 2005; Sedra 2006; Mounier 2007). Put bluntly, 'SSR activities conducted under JHA as well as those pursued under ESDP, namely conflict prevention and crisis management, almost exclusively focus on the restructuring of security institutions ..., rather than on the strengthening of their democratic accountability' (Tanner and Hänggi 2005, 40). This idea of civilian crisis management being an instrument that serves the EU's internal security objectives is also supported by Hansen (2004, 173), who stated that 'as a central crisis management mechanism, civilian police operations are a means for protecting Europe — by providing instruments to uphold the law — and thus counter the potential security risks from for example organised crime and refugee flows'.

The Role of Actors: Functional Unity and Transnational Security Networks

New institutionalism allows us to underline the role of institutions in the implementation of policies. Not only do they frame a specific cognitive frame but they also influence the manner in which the implementing actors behave. The functional similarities between civilian crisis management and the JHA external dimension are strengthened further by overlapping competences at supranational level and growing inter-pillar implementation.

Supranational Actors

The power struggle opposing the Commission against the Council over their respective competences in the field of civilian crisis management is well documented. The novelty resides in the emergence of the JHA external dimension as a tool of crisis management, which has increased the institutional overlaps and reinforced 'functional dynamics' between the two institutions. Efforts to coordinate actions across the three pillars have induced the development of some sort of 'functional unity' and a process of cross-pillarisation. However, as underlined by new institutionalism, institutional change is incremental and only small decisions can show the logic of change.

Inter-pillar cooperation between the Council and the Commission is the 'Achilles heel' (Marquina and Xira 2005) of civilian crisis management. As for JHA, competences are spread across the pillar structure and not confined only to the second pillar. In fact, first pillar instruments provide the main bulk of EU assistance for conflict prevention and crisis management (Gourlay 2006). Within the EU external relations budget, 5 billion per annum is dedicated to regional programmes directly relevant to crisis management activities, such as police training in the Balkans, law and order projects in Asia and training in human right standards for judges and police officers in Afghanistan, Iraq and the Palestinian Territories. The scale of the Community funds available and the capacity to coordinate policies as diverse as trade, development, enlargement and humanitarian assistance, while relying on a vast network of delegations, makes the Commission an extremely important player in this field. Yet, civilian crisis management is associated with the Council, whereas training programmes for local police forces in Guatemala, Algeria or Albania, financed by the Commission, receive less attention than the highly visible ESDP police missions in Afghanistan or Kosovo. In the past, activities of both actors were complementary. For the Council, it was a short-term activity to be applied as an immediate reaction to a crisis, while for the Commission it was a long-term activity. This balance was altered in 2001 when the Council started to develop its own civilian crisis management capacities. Schroeder (2006) has shown that as the Council widened its mandate, taking over more activities in the post-conflict reconstruction sphere, the Commission altered its existing competences in order to reorientate them towards security sector reform. This led to strained relations between the two institutions.

Nevertheless, the need for 'Comprehensive crisis management',[7] has led the two institutions to coordinate their actions and create institutional synergies. While the Council-led ESDP operations focus increasingly on SSR using JHA instruments (Duffield 2001), the long-term activities of the Commission cover a range of functions from the police to the judiciary. In its 'Concept for European Community support for SSR', the Commission emphasized the JHA external dimension as a key instrument for SSR activities (European Commission 2006a, 3). As a result, the grey area that emerged between the two fields (Emerson et al. 2007, 11) encourages an institutional *rapprochement*. Although problems remain (Duke 2006), concrete efforts have been made to increase the coordination between not only first and second pillar, but also third pillar policies. For instance, in May 2006 the Council invited the General Secretariat and the Commission to work together on a common concept of SSR across the three pillars.

The tendency towards 'functional unity' is perceptible in the recent endeavours to coordinate civilian and military capabilities. In 2003 the Council adopted a Civil-military coordination concept (CMCO; European Council 2003), which stresses the need for integration between the different pillars of EU activities and promotes the idea of a 'culture of coordination' based on 'shared political objectives' (Khol 2006). It was given institutional expression through the establishment of the Civ/Mil Cell in 2005, within the Council Secretariat. Staffed at parity with military and civilian planners, it also encompasses two Commission officials, further linking the two institutions. In parallel, Crisis Response Coordination Teams (CRCTs) were created to enhance Commission–Council coordination in the planning phase of crisis management operations. They bring together all concerned services, including the one dealing with JHA, to ensure inter-institutional coherence. Despite their limited success (Schroeder 2007, 27), these initiatives point to a beginning of cross-pillarisation (Pawlak 2009, this issue, 25–44). The same philosophy prevailed during the creation of the new 'Stability Instrument' for crisis responses, which is aimed at strengthening the coherence between EC assistance and EU's foreign policy response using CFSP instruments. The other rationale is to address 'transborder challenges affecting civilian security such as the fight against trafficking, organised crime and terrorism' (Dewaele and Gourlay 2005).[8]

The institutional *rapprochement* also had an impact on the ground. In 2004 the Council adopted an 'Action Plan for Civilian Aspects of ESDP', which recognized the need to link crisis management with JHA instruments, and proposed the involvement of key JHA stakeholders, such as the EU's Police Chief Task Force in ESDP police missions planning (European Council 2004). Interviews[9] have confirmed that the Council's main JHA policy-making working groups, such as the Article 36 Committee or the Police Cooperation Working Party, are currently involved in the decision-making process of EU crisis management policy. For instance, the Amended Operation Plan (OPLAN) for the Police mission in Bosnia (EUPM) was drafted by the Police Unit of the Council in February 2006, and then circulated to and discussed with the Article 36 Committee several times before its adoption in April 2006 (Council of the European Union 2006a). Likewise, regional and thematic task forces across the pillar structure, such as the 'Working Group on Organised Crime for Bosnia and Herzegovina', have been created within the Council, enabling greater cross-fertilization among experts.

More recently, the institutional *rapprochement* reached a new level with the EU Border Assistance Mission to Moldova and Ukraine (EUBAM). EUBAM is not formally an ESDP mission but a community mission financed[10] and managed mostly by the European Commission. The legal basis is a Memorandum of Understanding between the Commission, the Government of the Republic of Moldova and the Government of Ukraine and not a Council Joint Action. In addition, the Political and Security Committee (PSC) is not included in the chain of command. However, the Head of EUBAM is a senior political advisor and team leader of the EU Special Representative (EUSR) in Moldova, who represents Solana and the

Council Secretariat in the region. This last example shows two things: first, that the Commission and the Council are not only coordinating their efforts in the planning phase of missions but are now jointly running some missions and, secondly, that a new, powerful supranational actor has emerged in the form of the GSC (Christiansen 2002, 35). The role of the GSC as an interface between crisis management and the JHA external dimension was strengthened in 2005 when a cooperation arrangement between Europol and the GSC became operational. It allows for regular exchange of strategic and classified information between Europol and SitCen, the body in charge of intelligence gathering for second pillar activities.[11] The same pattern is applied currently for the negotiations of an information exchange agreement between Europol and ESDP civilian police missions.[12]

Transnational Security Networks in Crisis Management and Internal Security: Ubiquitous Actors?

One of the important aspects of the internal–external security nexus in the JHA policy field is the increasing role given to national police forces at the external level. Lutterbeck (2005, 236) noted that, confronted with growing concerns of transnational security issues, police forces have come to view their tasks as being orientated more externally. International cooperation between law-enforcement agencies has increased many fold with the development of liaison officers (Bigo 1994). In parallel, the size of gendarmerie-type forces has expanded sharply, while purely military forces were downsized. The popularity of paramilitary police forces is related to their intermediary status; they combine features of both the police and the military, which makes them extremely flexible and deployable under civilian and military command, in and outside of national territory. This trend toward the externalization of national police forces in JHA is paralleled by an increasing role of civilian police forces in peacekeeping and crisis management operations. Because they are ideally suited to tackle internal security threats outside the borders, they have come to play a growing function in counter-terrorism, riot control, border control and peace support operations (Hansen 2002). Consequently, as described in the first part of this article, civilian police have rapidly become the cornerstone of the EU's crisis management capacities, with a larger number of civilian operations than military ones. The functional dynamics between the external dimension of JHA and civilian crisis management have thus contributed to the progressive merging of internal and external national security actors' tasks.

These actors are identical across both fields. They operate alternatively under one or the other policy domain and the official division of tasks between civilian crisis management and the JHA external dimension (i.e. humanitarian intervention and protection of the EU's internal security regime) is, in fact, often unclear to the actors themselves. Police officers, judges and border guards from the member states are 'national' actors rooted in local systems. They are trained and employed by the member states to work in a domestic context. In the framework of the third pillar, they cooperate with other member states' law enforcement and justice officials and, therefore, constitute the main 'workforce' of the EU internal security regime. Simultaneously, they are the same individuals who implement the external dimension of JHA, for instance by conducting police and justice training programmes in third countries financed by the European Commission, or by exchanging information via Europol or Eurojust agreements with third countries. However, in the context of second pillar crisis management operations, these very same police officers, border guards and judges are sent abroad to reform security sector systems and enhance the capacity of third countries to tackle security threats that put the EU's internal security regime at risk. The fact that the same individuals participate in both policy fields reinforces their socialization and contributes to frame a common understanding of their mission, regardless of the framework under which they operate.[13]

The phenomenon is strengthened by the fact that these actors belong to closely interwoven national and transnational security networks, which are characterized by their fluidity. This makes the distinction between theoretically different objectives very difficult to sustain. The first of these networks is the national security network. In the Balkans, for example, most member states have established an extended security network composed of police liaison officers (P-LO), custom liaison officers (C-LO) and various intelligence cells disseminated throughout the countries of the region. They are usually located in their embassies, but an important part of the intelligence community in the Balkans is based in the *Butmir* military camp of the EU military mission in Bosnia and Herzegovina (EUFOR) on the outskirt of Sarajevo. All these security officers constitute the national security network whose task is to protect the internal security of member states abroad. Security actors also belong to a second network, which is transnational. Judges and police officers who speak foreign languages tend to be sent on missions abroad. They might work for some time in an embassy, then serve in an ESDP police mission and, later, work for Europol or Eurojust as liaison officers. In the case of the Balkans, most countries have security personnel active in UNMIK working in the fields of policing, justice and the fight against organized crime. They also have police officers and border guards working for the ESDP police missions in Bosnia (EUPM), or for the Community police mission in Albania (PAMECA). Working together with colleagues from other countries, being used to exchanging information and intelligence, knowing the ins and outs of international police and justice cooperation, these transnational security actors end up using the same methods and work with the same objectives in mind when serving in an ESDP civilian crisis management mission, working for a Community-financed SSR project or for their national embassy. For example, police officers working for EUPM in Bosnia are undertaking an SSR mission within the ESDP institutional framework. Their mandate is to monitor, mentor and advise the local police in performing their duty according to best European practices. While doing so, they come across information on local organized crime activities. In theory, they should ensure that the local police themselves make good use of this information. However, when the information is relevant for the internal security of the EU or for their country of origin, it is systematically transmitted to the relevant national administration.[14] The future agreement between Europol and ESDP police missions will reinforce this practice further.

This is a crucial aspect of the functional unity between civilian crisis management and the external dimension of JHA. In this second part of the article, we have demonstrated that despite the different institutional discourses, they share a similar 'functional frame'. This argument is confirmed by the fact that actors implementing both policies behave in the same way and work with the same objectives in mind, regardless of the context in which they work, whether in civilian crisis management missions or the external dimension of JHA.

Conclusion

The more the European Union is developing into an international actor, the more the artificial division between pillars becomes unsustainable. External competences are spread inefficiently among various actors and legal frameworks, hindering the ability of the EU to act on the international scene. The new post-Cold War security environment and the ensuing internal–external security nexus have raised the saliency of this issue. The EU's internal security is increasingly dependent on two elements: its capacity to foster peace and stability in third countries, and its ability to project security instruments abroad in order to address threats as early as possible. These competences should be considered not as two separate unrelated elements, but as complementary policies. This article has shown that there is a progression towards this approach, and that a *rapprochement* is taking place between the external and internal side of EU security policies.

Not only do the inception of ESDP civilian crisis management and the external dimension of internal security seem to be rooted in the same factors, but they also share significant functional similarities; they are both intended to protect the EU's internal security regime from external threats, mainly by a systematic recourse to security sector reform activities. Despite ongoing institutional fragmentation, supranational actors are in the process of overcoming their rivalries. They are using functional dynamics to establish coordination mechanisms and exploit various linkages between the two fields of activities. This leads to a gradual 'functional unity', whereby supranational actors active in both fields act in a coordinated manner to conduct a global policy in line with their functional frame: protecting the EU's internal security. Furthermore, at implementation level, actors are the same in both policy fields. Their networks are fluid and interconnected, which leads to a process of socialization across the pillars.

The coming into force of the Lisbon Treaty is expected to increase the functional similarities between civilian crisis management and the external dimension of JHA. What will be important will not be the communitarization of the third pillar, as notable exceptions will remain intergovernmental,[15] but initiatives such as the creation of the Standing Committee on Internal Security (COSI) within the Council,[16] the aim of which will be to promote operational cooperation between member states' internal security authorities. This new structure is an opportunity to redesign the current segmented pattern of Council working groups. It has the potential to become a forum for actors in both fields to meet and discuss common actions, such as security sector reform activities.

The changes brought forward by the Lisbon Treaty in the ESDP/CFSP domain will also increase the *rapprochement* process. The extension of the Petersberg Tasks to the fight against terrorism, including the support of third countries in combating terrorism in their countries[17] or the creation within the Council of a 'High Representative of the Union for Foreign Affairs and Security Policy', who will also be one of the Vice-Presidents of the Commission,[18] will encourage the diffusion of common views and practices between civilian crisis management and JHA communities. Indeed, the High Representative will simultaneously exercise the political control and strategic direction of the crisis management operations,[19] take part in the discussions of JHA external dimension initiatives in the Council, while supervising all the Commission's financial instruments in crisis management and security sector reform activities. This new position in the EU institutional architecture will bridge the gap between internal and external security and will strengthen the functional similarities between both fields.

In the preface to this special issue, Smith stressed 'the extent to which the "JHA agenda" has infiltrated the Community and CFSP pillars' (Smith 2009). Accordingly, Pawlak (2009) pointed out, that cross-pillarization processes have benefited EU internal security bureaucracies, who have gained more control over EU external relations, despite attempts by diplomats to secure their competences in this domain.[20] In line with this argument, one of the lessons to be drawn from the functional *rapprochement* between civilian crisis management and the JHA external dimension is that the internal security agenda of Ministers of the interior is, to some extent, determining the EU's crisis management objectives. This is because security sector reform activities are mostly implemented by actors of the JHA external dimension and are therefore inspired by the EU internal security objectives. The provisions of the Lisbon Treaty will undoubtedly further the 'contamination' process[21] of the EU civilian crisis management by the JHA external dimension.

Notes

1. Article 17.2 of the Treaty of the European Union (TEU).
2. Title IV of the Treaty of the European Community (TEC).
3. Title VI of the TEU.
4. As of writing there have been 20 operations launched as part of ESDP, among which 16 are/were of a civilian nature.
5. Figures taken from the UN Department of Peacekeeping Operations (UNDPKO; http://www.un.org/Depts/dpko/dpko/contributors/).
6. The author is aware of the ambiguity of the term 'efficiency' when applied to internal security policies. Here it simply conveys the idea of the police and judicial system being able to disrupt criminal activities and try criminals more effectively but in accordance with human rights and fundamental principles.

7. A concept often put forward by the Commission and the Council and which refers to the ability to provide complete responses to complex problems of weak states and civil conflicts.
8. See http://europa.eu.int/comm./external_relations/reform/intro/ip04_1151.htm.
9. Confidential interviews, General Secretariat of the Council, Brussels, 12 June 2006.
10. The EC budget finances the core of the 24 million mission, mainly through the European Neighbourhood Policy Instrument (ENPI).
11. Cooperation arrangement between Europol and the General Secretariat of the Council, 27/09/2005, doc. 12332/1/05.
12. The agreement between Europol and ESDP police missions was discussed for the first time at the CATS on 3 April 2008. *Possible cooperation mechanisms between ESDP Missions and Europol as regards exchange of information*, 22/01/2008, doc. 5466/08.
13. Interview with Europol's officials, The Hague, November 2007.
14. Personal interviews with EUPM officials from France and the UK, Sarajevo and London, 2006–2007. Some officers denied the practice; however, it was confirmed by several other sources.
15. The maintenance of law and order and the safeguarding of internal security.
16. New Article 71 of the Treaty on the Functioning of the European Union (TFEU).
17. New Article 43(1) of the TEU.
18. New Article 18 TEU.
19. New Article 38 TEU and new Article 43 TEU.
20. See the description of the 2000 European Union priorities and policy objectives for external relations in the field of Justice and Home Affairs, in the introductory article to this special issue (Wolff, Wichmann, and Mounier 2009).
21. Missiroli (2008) also spoke about 'contamination' with regards to civilian crisis management.

References

Anderson, M., and J. Apap. 2002. *Changing conceptions of security and their implications for EU Justice and Home Affairs cooperation.* CEPS Policy Brief No. 26, October 2002. Brussels: CEPS.

Berenskoetter, F. 2006. *Under construction: ESDP and the 'fight against organised crime'.* Challenge Working Paper London.

Bigo, D. 1994. The European internal security field: Stakes and rivalries in a newly developing area of police intervention. In *Policing across national boundaries*, eds. M. Anderson and M. Den Boer, 161–73. London: Pinter.

Bigo, D. 2001. The Möbius ribbon of internal and external security(ies). In *Identities, borders, orders – rethinking IR theory, borderlines*, eds. M. Albert, D. Jacobson and Y. Lapid, 91–116. Minneapolis: Univ. Minnesota Press.

Bjurner, A. 2001. *Vision and achievements of the Swedish Presidency in developing a civilian crisis management capability.* Stockholm: EU Civilian Crisis Management Capability.

Bosold, D., and S. Werthes. 2006. Caught between pretension and substantiveness: ambiguities of Human Security as a political leitmotif. In *Human Security on foreign policy agendas, changes, concepts and cases*, eds. T. Debiel and S. Werthes, 21–31. Duisburg: Eigenverlag.

Burgess, J.P., and T. Owen. 2004. What is human security? *Security Dialogue* 35, no. 3: 345–70.

Buzan, B. 2000. 'Change and insecurity' reconsidered. In *Critical reflections on security and change*, eds. S. Croft and T. Terriff, 1–18. London: Frank Cass.

Chandler, D. 2006. Back to the future? The limits of neo-Wilsonian ideals of exporting democracy. *Review of International Studies* 32: 475–94.

Christiansen, T. 2002. The role of supranational actors in EU Treaty reform. *Journal of European Public Policy* 9, no. 1: 33–53.

Commission on Human Security. 2003. *Human security now.* New York: United Nations.

Council of the European Union. 2003. A secure Europe in a better world. European Security Strategy, 15895/03, December 8.

Council of the European Union. 2005a. A strategy for the external dimension of the Area JHA: Global freedom, security and justice, 15446/05, December 6.

Council of the European Union. 2005b. EU concept for ESDP support to Security Sector Reform (SSR), 12566/4/05, October 13.

Council of the European Union. 2006a. Draft Operation Plan (OPLAN) for the EU Police Mission (EUPM) in Bosnia and Herzegovina (BiH), 8025/06, April 4.
Council of the European Union. 2006b. Vienna declaration on security partnership, 8501/06, May 8.
Dewaele, A., and C. Gourlay. 2005. *The stability instrument: defining the Commission's role in crisis response*. European Security Review, June. Brussels: ISIS.
Duffield, M. 2001. *Global governance and the new wars: The merging of development and security*. London: Zed Books.
Duke, S. 2006. *Areas of grey: Tensions in EU external relations competences*. EIPAscope. Maastricht: EIPA.
Duke, S., and H. Ojanen. 2006. Bridging internal and external security: Lessons from the European Security and Defence Policy. *European Integration* 28, no. 5: 477–94.
Emerson, M., E. Gross, I. Ioannides, A.E. Juncos, and U.C. Schroeder. 2007. *Evaluating the EU's crisis missions in the Balkans*. Brussels: CEPS.
European Commission. 2006a. A concept for European Community support for security sector, May 24 2006, COM(2006) 253 final.
European Commission. 2006b. Progress report on the implementation of the strategy for the external dimension of JHA: Global freedom, security and justice, SEC(2006) 1498, November 16.
European Commission. 2006c. Revised action plan on terrorism, SEC(2006) 686, May 25.
European Council. 1997. Action plan to combat organized crime. *Official Journal of the EU* C251 (August 15).
European Council. 1999. Presidency conclusions, Tampere European Council, October 15–16.
European Council. 2000a. European Union priorities and policy objectives for external relations in the field of Justice and Home Affairs, 7653/00, June 6.
European Council. 2000b. Presidency conclusions, Santa Maria da Feira European Council, June 19–20.
European Council. 2001. Presidency conclusions Annex I, Göteborg European Council, June 15–16.
European Council. 2003. Civil–military co-ordination (CMCO), 14457/03, November 7.
European Council. 2004. Action plan for civilian aspects of ESDP, June 17–18.
European Council. 2005. EU drugs action plan (2005–2008), July 8.
Gourlay, C. 2006. Community instruments for civilian crisis management. In Nowak 2006a, 49–69.
Haaland, M.J. 2006. When soft power turns hard: Is an EU strategic culture possible? *Security Dialogue* 37, no. 1: 105–21.
Hansen, A.S. 2002. *From Congo to Kosovo: Civilian police in peace operations*. Oxford: Oxford Univ. Press.
Hansen, A.S. 2004. Security and defence: The EU police mission in Bosnia-Herzegovina. In *Contemporary European foreign policy*, eds. W. Carlsnaes, H. Sjursen and B. White, 173–85. London: SAGE.
Jachtenfuchs, M. 1997. Conceptualizing European governance. In *Reflective approaches to European governance*, ed. K.E. Jorgensen, 39–50. Basingstoke: Macmillan.
Kaldor, M. 2004. *A human security doctrine for Europe. The Barcelona Report of the study group on Europe's security capabilities*. Barcelona: CIDOB.
Kaldor, M. 2007. Human security: a new strategic narrative for Europe. *International Affairs* 83, no. 2: 273–88.
Kaldor, M., and M. Glasius. 2006. *A human security doctrine for Europe: Project, principles, practicalities*. London: Routledge.
Katzenstein, P.J. 1996. *The culture of national security. Norms and identity in world politics*. New York: Columbia Univ. Press.
Khol, R. 2006. Civil–military co-ordination in EU crisis management. In Nowak 2006a, 123–39.
King, G., and C. Murray. 2001. Rethinking human security. *Political Science Quarterly* 116, no. 4: 585–610.
Lavenex, S. 2005. Politics of exclusion and inclusion in 'wider Europe'. In *Soft or hard borders? Managing the divide in an enlarged Europe*, ed. J. DeBardeleben, 123–45. Aldershot: Ashgate.
Lowi, T. 1964. American business, public policy, case-studies, and political theory. *World Politics* 16: 677–715.
Lutterbeck, D. 2005. Blurring the dividing line: The convergence of internal and external security in Western Europe. *European Security* 14, no. 2: 231–53.
Manners, I. 2004. Normative power Europe reconsidered. From civilian to military power: the European Union at a crossroads? CIDEL Workshop Oslo, October 22–23.

Manners, I. 2006. Normative power Europe reconsidered: beyond the crossroads. *Journal of European Public Policy* 13, no. 2: 182–99.
Marquina, A., and R. Xira. 2005. A European competitive advantage? Civilian instruments for conflict prevention and crisis management. *Journal of Transatlantic Studies* 3, no. 1: 71–87.
Merlingen, M. 2007. Everything is dangerous: A critique of 'normative power Europe'. *Security Dialogue* 38, no. 4: 435–53.
Merlingen, M., and R. Ostrauskaité. 2005. The EU and the democratisation of policing in countries in transition: the case of BiH. *Populaçao e Sociedade* 00: 131–48.
Merlingen, M., and R. Ostrauskaité. 2006. *European Union peacebuilding and policing.* Oxford: Routledge.
Missiroli, A. 2008. *The impact of the Lisbon Treaty on ESDP.* Briefing Paper, January. Brussels: European Parliament.
Monar, J. 2000. *Justice and Home Affairs in a wider Europe: The dynamics of inclusion and exclusion.* Working Paper 7, ESRC One Europe or Several? Univ. Sussex.
Monar, J. 2008. Justice and Home Affairs: Security sector reform measures as instruments of EU internal security objectives. In *The European Union and security sector reform,* eds. D. Spence and P.H. Fluri, 126–41. London: John Harper.
Mounier, G. 2007. European police missions: From security sector reform to externalization of internal security beyond the borders. *HUMSEC* 1, no. 1.
Nowak, A., ed. 2006a. *Civilian crisis management: the EU way.* Paris: EUISS.
Nowak, A. 2006b. Civilian crisis management within ESDP. In Nowak 2006a, 37.
Oakley, R., M. Dziedzic, and E. Goldberg. 1998. *Policing the new world disorder: peace operations and public security.* Washington D.C.: National Defence Univ.
Osland, K.M. 2004. The EU police mission in Bosnia and Herzegovina. *International Peacekeeping* 11, no. 3: 544–560.
Paris, R. 2004. Still an inscrutable concept. *Security Dialogue* 35, no. 3: 370–72.
Pastore, F. 2002. The asymmetrical fortress: The problem of relations between internal and external security policies in the European Union. In *Police and justice cooperation and the new European borders,* eds. M. Anderson and J. Apap, 59–80. The Hague: Kluwer Law International.
Pawlak, P. 2009. The external dimension of the Area of Freedom, Security and Justice: Hijacker or hostage of cross-pillarization? *Journal of European Integration* 31, no. 1: 25–44.
Rees, W. 2005. The external faces of internal security. In *International relations and the European Union,* eds. C. Hill and M. Smith, 205–24. Oxford: Oxford Univ. Press.
Rosamond, B. 2000. *Theories of the European integration.* Basingstoke: Macmillan.
Rotberg, R.I. 2002. Failed states in a world of terror. *Foreign Affairs* 81: 127–35.
Rutten, M. 2001. *From Saint-Malo to Nice. European defence: Core documents.* Chaillot Paper 47. Paris: EUISS.
Schroeder, U.C. 2006. Converging problems — compartmentalised solutions: The security–development interface in EU crisis management. *CFSP Forum* 4, no. 3: 1–4.
Schroeder, U.C. 2007. Governance of EU crisis management. In Emerson et al. 2007, 17–46.
Sedra, M. 2006. European approaches to security sector reform: Examining trends through the lens of Afghanistan. *European Security* 15, no. 3: 323–38.
Sjursen, H. 2007. *Civilian or military power? European foreign policy in perspective.* London: Routledge.
Smith, K.E. 2009. The Justice and Home Affairs policy universe: Some directions for further research. *Journal of European Integration* 31, no. 1: 1–7.
Stetter, S. 2007. *EU foreign and interior policies. Cross-pillar politics and the social constructions of sovereignty.* London: Routledge.
Tanner, F., and H. Hänggi. 2005. *Promoting security sector governance in the EU's neighbourhood.* Chaillot Paper 80. Paris: EUISS.
Trauner, F. 2006. External aspects of internal security: A research agenda. *Consent Deliverable.*
van Duyne, P.C. 2007. OCTA 2006: the unfulfilled promise. *Trends in Organized Crime* 10, no. 3: 120–8.
Wessel, R. 2004. Fragmentation in the governance of the EU external relations: Legal institutional dilemmas and the new Constitution for Europe. In *The European Union: An ongoing process of integration,* eds. J.W. de Zwaan, J.H. Jans, F.A. Nelissen and S. Blockmans, 371. The Hague: T.M.C. Asser Press.

Wolff, S., N. Wichmann, and G. Mounier. 2009. The external dimension of Justice and Home Affairs: A different security agenda for the EU? *Journal of European Integration* 31, no. 1: 9–23.

Yusufi, I. 2004. Understanding the process of security reform in southeastern Europe. *Journal of Security Sector Management* 2, no. 2: 18.

Deconstructing the EU's Routes of Influence in Justice and Home Affairs in the Western Balkans

FLORIAN TRAUNER

Institute for European Integration Research, Austrian Academy of Sciences, Vienna, Austria

ABSTRACT   What routes of influence could the European Union use to bring the Western Balkan states closer to EU standards in Justice and Home Affairs (JHA)? The paper argues that although the mechanisms of Europeanization identified for the Central and Eastern European countries are useful for understanding the EU's external influence, they are not sufficient for fully deconstructing the avenues of external leverage. The key to understanding the Europeanization of the Western Balkans is to take policy-related conditionality into account, in addition to membership conditionality. In offering more relaxed travel conditions in exchange for the signing of an EC readmission agreement and reforming domestic JHA, the EU could counterbalance the shortcomings of the pre-accession strategy and establish an additional avenue of external leverage. The paper suggests understanding the EU's use of policy-related conditionality in the Western Balkans as exemplary for the European Neighbourhood Policy.

Introduction

The present discussion concerns how the EU has exercised influence under the external dimension of Justice and Home Affairs (JHA) in the regional setting of the Western Balkans.[1] The countries aspiring for EU membership in South-Eastern Europe have been of particular concern for the EU in terms of security links. Following the Dayton peace accords, organized crime networks took advantage of these countries' porous borders, missing regional cooperation links and ill-functioning institutions. The traditional Balkan smuggling route was revitalized and the region became a major gateway for illegal drugs, commodities and migrants into the EU (see Schelter 2003, 7; Hill 2004, 12). Not surprisingly, the gradual development of the JHA external dimension has always made close cooperation with the Western Balkan countries a priority (see also Wolff, Wichmann, and Mounier 2009, this issue, 9–23).

This situation has ameliorated in recent years,[2] also due to the countries' efforts to strengthen their border control and law enforcement capacities. Regardless of their status of real or potential candidates, all Western Balkan countries have initiated a reform process aimed at coming closer to EU standards in JHA. The Commission acknowledged the Western Balkans' efforts in its communiqué, 'The Western Balkans on the road to the EU: consolidating stability and raising prosperity', by stating that

> progress in the area of Justice, Freedom and Security has been significant and includes action to combat organized crime, building up institutional capacity in the judiciary, improved police and prosecutor cooperation, an Action Plan for drug trafficking, measures for combating money laundering and illegal migration, as well as implementation of commitments made at the Ohrid Conference on border security and management (Commission of the European Communities 2006c, 4).

This paper aims to analyse the actual routes of influence through which the EU could bring the Western Balkan states closer to EU standards in JHA. By focusing on the EU's 'mechanisms of change' (Radaelli 2000, 15ff.), the study seeks to complement a research project which empirically proved that the Western Balkan states have shown strong compliance efforts in JHA (Trauner 2007). Building on the same argument, this paper provides a detailed analysis of the other actor-level, namely the EU. It deconstructs the EU's routes of influence in JHA in the Western Balkans by intersecting the studies on the use of conditionality from previous enlargement rounds (see, for example, Grabbe 2001, 2003; Pridham 2005; Schimmelfennig and Sedelmeier 2005a; Vachudova 2005) with the current enlargement strategy for South-Eastern Europe. The comparisons across enlargement rounds make it possible to identify the differences in the Europeanization processes of candidate countries, a subject hitherto largely neglected in the literature (for this claim, see Sedelmeier 2006, 20).

The research proceeds in three steps: first, it looks at how the EU may exercise external influence in candidate countries by discussing the Europeanization literature identified for the Central and Eastern European countries. In a second step, the 'mechanisms of Europeanization' (Grabbe 2001) are adapted to the specific circumstances of the Western Balkans' pre-accession strategy. The argument the paper advances is that they are useful for understanding the EU's influence in this regional setting in South-Eastern Europe, but they are insufficient for fully deconstructing the avenues of external leverage. The key to understanding the Europeanization of the

Western Balkans is to focus not only on the obligations associated with an eventual EU membership (understood as membership conditionality), but also on an additional avenue of external leverage. The EU developed policy-related conditionality by offering the reward of a more relaxed visa regime in exchange for the signing of an EC readmission agreement and reforming domestic JHA. Finally, the analysis considers the broader implications of these findings and concludes that policy-related conditionality may become an important instrument for the external dimension of JHA within the context of the European Neighbourhood Policy (ENP; see also Di Puppo 2009, this issue, 103–118).

The Europeanization of the Western Balkans

Why should the Western Balkan states accept the EU's influence on their national patterns of governance? Most literature interested in the Europeanization of candidate countries sets the analytical framework within an institutionalist perspective (for an overview, see Sedelmeier 2006).

Sociological institutionalists suggest that candidate countries accept the EU's influence due to socialization and persuasion processes in which domestic actors internalize identities, values and norms. For intrinsic reasons, political actors choose in a given situation what they consider good and appropriate. The EU's impact is therefore expected to stem from a 'logic of appropriateness' rather than from a 'logic of consequences' (March and Olsen 1998). By contrast, rational institutionalists maintain that adherence to EU rules prior to accession is driven mainly by rational cost–benefit calculations and actors in pursuit of maximizing their own power. The crucial mechanism employed by the EU to make candidate countries accept its rules is the use of conditionality, meaning that the EU sets its rules as conditions which the applicant country has to fulfil in order to receive rewards (see Schimmelfennig, Engert, and Knobel 2003, 496ff). The strongest rewards relate to the progressive improvement of institutional ties with the EU, with the ultimate goal of full membership.

Research on the Eastern enlargement made a strong argument for the rational institutionalist argument (see, for example, Kelley 2004; Schimmelfennig and Sedelmeier 2005a; Vachudova 2005). As Heather Grabbe (2002: 93) noted, 'membership conditionality gives the EU significant leverage in transferring to the applicant countries its principles, norms, and rules, as well as in shaping their institutional and administrative structures'. She set out a typology of five conditionality instruments with which the EU managed to change governance patterns in Central and Eastern Europe (Grabbe 2003, 312ff). The 'mechanisms of Europeanization' referred to

- 'models: provisions of legislative and institutional templates' corresponding with the legal downloading of the *acquis communautaire* and the harmonization with EU regulations;
- 'money: aid and technical assistance' that had 'an important role in reinforcing the transfer of EU models' (Grabbe 2003, 314);

- 'benchmarking and monitoring', meaning to rank candidates, benchmark in particular policy areas and provide examples that the applicant seeks to emulate;
- 'advice and twinning', which involved the direct secondment of civil servants from EU member states to work as advisers in domestic institution-building programmes;
- 'gate-keeping: accession to negotiations and further stages in the accession process', which was the 'EU's most powerful conditionality tool' and related to 'access to different stages in the accession process, particularly achieving candidate status and starting negotiations' (Grabbe 2003, 316).

Although these five Europeanization mechanisms were powerful instruments for the EU, they did not automatically result in strong external influence. Scholars showed in the Eastern enlargement that the EU's conditionality approach was dependent on several mediating factors (see, for example, Grabbe 2003; Schimmelfennig and Sedelmeier 2005b). The credibility of EU conditionality was a central factor. As Ulrich Sedelmeier (2006, 12) noted, 'credibility has two sides. The candidates have to be certain that they will receive the promised rewards after meeting the EU's demands. Yet they also have to believe that they will only receive the reward if they indeed fully meet the requirements'.

The credibility of EU conditionality represents a major difference between the Eastern enlargement and the enlargement strategy used for the Western Balkans. The current candidates are less certain when or even if they will receive the ultimate reward of EU accession. In view of a European public opinion increasingly opposed to further enlargement, European political actors are unwilling to specify a possible accession date for the Western Balkan countries. Instead of presenting the current enlargement round as a major political project, the political debates increasingly emphasized that not only should the candidate country be prepared to be absorbed, the other side must also be prepared to absorb it. The EU's 'absorption' or, more recently, 'integration capacity', has moved into the centre of discussions, meaning that the capacity to absorb new member states must be taken into account when deciding on further enlargement (see Emerson et al. 2006). As a result, some scholars assumed that the changed circumstances of the Western Balkans' EU integration and the questionable credibility of the membership perspective would affect the candidate countries' calculation of the non-adaptation costs (Lavenex and Uçarer 2004, 432–3). Othon Anastasakis and Dimitar Bechev (2003, 15–16) even stated that the EU's regional strategy would suffer from a 'commitment deficit' resulting in, among others, a decrease in 'the chances of success for domestic reforms'.

So how can we explain the comparatively successful reform efforts in the Western Balkans' JHA sector? This article suggests that the EU's external leverage in JHA proved to be strong, as the EU relied not only on membership conditionality, but also on policy-related conditionality that derived from the prospect of visa-free travel. The EU used this issue of high political salience in the Western Balkans as a threat and main incentive for cooperation. By defining visa liberalization as a gradual process to be achieved through the signing of a readmission agreement with the European Community and other reform steps in domestic JHA, the EU managed to fill its conditionality approach with more substance and to establish a clearer relationship between demand and reward. EC visa facilitation and readmission agreements became the most important intermediary reward in the process towards visa liberalization. Even though these agreements were not concluded for the first time with the Western Balkan states, but rather with the Russian Federation and Ukraine, this regional setting in South-Eastern Europe provided the EU with a model case that will now be used in several neighbouring states.

How EU Influence Works: Deconstructing the EU's Routes of Influence

This section deconstructs the EU's routes of influence by assessing the EU's JHA strategy within the framework of the Stabilisation and Association Process, and by presenting a second avenue of external leverage, namely policy-related conditionality.

The EU's JHA Strategy in the Stabilisation and Association Process: Dismantling Membership Conditionality

Launched in May 1999, the Stabilisation and Association Process (SAP) 'is an ambitious strategy that helps the region to secure political and economic stabilization and to develop a closer association with the EU, opening a road towards EU membership once the relevant conditions have been met' (Commission of the European Communities 2001b, 2).

The prospect of the Western Balkan states joining the EU was first expressed at the European Council in Feira in 2000. The conclusions stated that all of the countries in the region were 'potential candidates for EU membership' (European Council 2000, Point 67). After first being announced, the prospect for membership was reiterated several times, most notably at the European Council of Thessaloniki, which was largely dedicated to EU–Western Balkans relations (see European Council 2003). At the summit, the Council endorsed the so-called 'Thessaloniki Agenda for the Western Balkans: moving towards European integration', which enriched the SAP process and bolstered it by methods based on the experiences of the Eastern Enlargement. Moreover, the improvement of regional cooperation links among the Western Balkan states was defined as an additional measurement for judging their qualification for EU integration (see Council of the European Union 2003b).

As mentioned earlier, conditionality, or as the Council understands it, 'the cement of the Stabilisation and Association process' (Council of the European Union 2001b, Point III), pervades the EU's strategy for the region and has to be viewed as its decisive cornerstone. In its pre-accession strategy for the Western Balkans, the EU has refined the conditionality approach applied in the Eastern Enlargement. An unusually broad range of political and economic conditions is linked to the coveted perspective of EU membership. In addition to the 1993 Copenhagen Criteria, the aspiring candidate countries are also expected to meet country-specific conditions stemming from different peace agreements (e.g. UN Resolution 1244 and the Dayton, Ohrid and Belgrade agreements). If the EU chooses, it can also invoke 'programme conditionality' and 'project level conditionality', threatening to freeze financial means if the country concerned fails to meet the objectives set by the EU (Commission of the European Communities 2001a, 25).

To understand how EU membership conditionality is translated into concrete output, the five Europeanization mechanisms, as defined by Heather Grabbe (2003, 321ff.) for the Eastern Enlargement, are adjusted to the Western Balkan setting.

'Gate-keeping: accession to negotiations and further stages in the accession process'. The most powerful mechanism for inducing changes is 'gate-keeping', that is, to allow (or not) a country to proceed on the step-by-step road towards EU membership (see table 1). In each case, the SAP is a bilateral affair between the EU and the applicant country. The EU takes the initiative in the sense that it first has to judge if the country in question is ready to proceed with the step-by-step process. This phased strategy ranges from the establishment of a consultative taskforce and a feasibility study on a Stabilisation and Association Agreement (SAA), to the beginning, conclusion and finally the ratification of this agreement. SAAs are seen as the most important cornerstone in achieving candidate status for EU accession. SAAs are legally binding international agreements that institutionalize the relationship between the contracting parties on a higher level. In the wake of such an agreement, several institutions and sub-institutions are installed. The most visible one is the Stabilisation and Association Council, where ministers of the EU meet their SAP counterparts. Although this meeting has high symbolic significance (namely, belonging to the 'European family' of nation states), the content is 'precooked and rather low in substance', as one Commission official noticed.[3] The Stabilisation and Association Council usually takes place in side-talks at a Foreign Affairs Council and lasts for around two hours. The real work takes place at the different Stabilisation and Association committees (high official level) and at several sub-committees (technical level) installed hierarchically below the former. Each SAA involves a specific title on justice and home affairs, which provides for intense cooperation on issues such as reinforcing the rule of law, migration and asylum, money laundering and illicit drugs. A salient aspect of the title is dedicated to the field of 'prevention and control of illegal immigration', whereby the contracting parties agree to readmit any of their own nationals illegally residing in the other parties' territories. In addition, the EU reserves the right of the 'Stabilisation and Association Council [to recommend] additional subjects for cooperation under this Article' (see, for instance, Art. 77 of Croatia's SAA) (Council of the European Union 2005).

The proper implementation of the SAA opens the way for the next step of the *rapprochement* process — the application for membership. Following the application, and based on the Commission's *avis* (opinion), the EU may decide to grant the applicant country real candidate status. This approval is an important political gesture and implies, in practical terms, that the now-to-be applicant country can use EU assistance 'in all areas relevant to the ability of the country to assume the obligation of membership, such as the preparation for the implementation of the structural funds' (Commission of the European Communities 2005b, 11). The candidate status is a necessary but insufficient precondition for opening the concrete accession negotiations — the next step on the road into the EU. Before the negotiations for EU accession can start, the applicant country is supposed to reach a sufficient degree of general compliance with the Copenhagen Criteria and full cooperation with the International Criminal Tribunal for the former Yugoslavia (ICTY). Until the Commission is satisfied with the country's performance in complying with these conditions, the European Council will not agree to open the negotiations.

In brief, the entire SAP, with its manifold *rapprochement* steps, is quite tedious — one scholar called it the 'rocky road to Europe' (Pippan 2004). Therefore, as one observer noted, it is very important for the EU 'to keep up the momentum'.[4] This exhortation refers to the need to provide the right incentives at the right time in order to prevent doubts concerning the EU's sincerity about the regions' integration. Rewards in terms of advancing in the step-by-step process can be given to one country, but may be seen as a signal to all SAP countries. For instance, when Croatia was granted the status of a candidate, the EU intended to give a positive sign and incentive to all of the other countries in the region as well.[5]

'Models: provisions of legislative and institutional templates'. Under the 1993 Copenhagen Criteria, membership requires that a candidate be capable of fulfilling the obligations of membership, which entails the implementation of the entire EU *acquis* as it evolves. The legal downloading of the *acquis* was not defined as a top priority for the Western Balkans, given the comparatively low level of European integration and institutional stability. Rather, the SAP was constructed in such a way as to link the agenda of European integration with the stabilization and transformation of these countries on a more fundamental level.

Within the policy field of JHA, this means that the EU is focusing on four main priority areas: (1) police, public order and organized crime; (2) integrated border management; (3) judicial reform; and (4) asylum and migration. In doing so, two strategies — a regional one and a country-by-country one — are to complement each other. The regional strategy aims at improving regional cooperation through the establishment of contractual relationships in the policy fields of border management, visa policy, migration issues and organized crime. The EU's efforts in this respect have been complemented by the Stability Pact for South-Eastern Europe, which has taken the lead role in promoting regional co-operation in South-Eastern Europe.[6] Working Table III of the Stability Pact, dealing with both internal and external security, has launched regional initiatives in the areas of police cooperation, mine clearance, organized crime, anti-corruption and migration, asylum and refugee return. In February 2008, the phased evolution of the Stability Pact into a regionally owned framework called the Regional Co-operation Council (RCC) came to an end. The South-Eastern European countries are now themselves in charge of setting the agenda and providing money and personnel.[7]

The specific JHA priorities for each of the Western Balkan countries are outlined in the 'justice, freedom and security' chapter of the European Partnerships. These partnerships, which were introduced in the 2003 Thessaloniki agenda, define the short-, medium-, and long-term priorities in the policy field and provide guidance for the EU's financial assistance. Although JHA is defined in each of these countries as a key area of cooperation, the individual priority areas of action depend on the domestic conditions in JHA. In Croatia, for instance, the EU and their Croatian counterparts have begun focusing relatively early on the transposition of the EU *acquis*, whereas the EU's main objective in Albania is to enhance the capacities of law enforcement institutions on a much more basic level.

'Money: aid and technical assistance'. Financial assistance is offered within the framework of the Instrument for Pre-Accession-Assistance (IPA). IPA was established in 2006 to streamline the EU's financial efforts and to achieve a higher impact with the resources available (Council of the European Union 2006). Funded with 11.5 billion between 2007 and 2013 (including pre-accession support for Turkey), IPA consists of five components: transition assistance and institution building; cross-border cooperation; regional development; human resources development; and rural development. Whereas 'potential candidates' receive funding under the first two components only, candidate countries have access to all components. IPA is based on multi-annual planning cycles outlined by the Commission in the so-called Multi-Annual Indicative Financial Framework (MIFF). This document delineates the forthcoming financial support for a period of three years and breaks down the IPA envelope by country and component (Commission of the European Communities 2006a).

In the last financial perspective (2000–2006), the EU offered 4.6 billion in pre-accession funding within the framework of the Community Assistance for Reconstruction, Development and Stabilisation (CARDS) (Council of the European Union 2000). In line with the framework established by the SAP, the CARDS programme was based upon a regional strategy and country-specific strategies. The priority of JHA in the SAP has been reflected further by the allocations under the CARDS programme — roughly 1 in 6 has been devoted to this heading. In Albania, for instance, about forty per cent of the CARDS funding between 2000 and 2006 targeted reform priorities in JHA, turning the field into the most prominent area of cooperation (Commission of the European Communities 2007a, 8). The bulk of the financial resources was spent on national CARDS programmes, whereas the regional component accounted for around ten per cent of the total CARDS programme. In relation to JHA, assistance has been granted typically for projects such as infrastructure support, improvement for asylum procedures, institution and capacity building, including the training of staff, judges and lawyers, improvement of reception conditions for asylum seekers, and upgrading national legislative standards in line with the European and international asylum *acquis* (see UNHCR 2003, 160ff.).

'Benchmarking and monitoring'. In its annual Progress Reports, the European Commission regularly assesses the performance of the Western Balkan states. First introduced in April 2002, these annual reports carefully list achievements, enervations and things to do and monitor the implementation of the priorities set out in the European Partnerships. Each country report contains a chapter on cooperation in JHA, in which the Commission assesses the progress of the target country in coming closer to the EU's JHA priorities as defined. A very particular and highly important aspect of monitoring is the European Commission's opinion on a country's application for membership (also known as the *avis*). So far, the Commission has expressed its opinion in two cases — Croatia (Commission of the European Communities 2004) and Macedonia (Commission of the European Communities 2005a). These reports are very powerful because they form the basis on which the Council decides whether or not to grant an applicant country candidate status.

The instrument of benchmarking becomes very important after a Western Balkan country has shifted its status from a potential to a real candidate country and, thus, is able to start accession talks with the EU. When the EU member states decide, upon a Commission recommendation, whether or not to open a chapter of the *acquis* for negotiations, they may include benchmarks to be met by the candidate country before the concrete negotiations can be opened. Benchmarking is a new tool of the sixth enlargement round, and its purpose is to 'improve the quality of negotiations, by providing incentives for the candidate country to undertake necessary reforms *at an early stage*' (Commission of the European Communities 2006b, 6, author's emphasis). Obviously, this visible and rigorous approach has been adopted to avoid any suspension of necessary reforms, similar to what the EU experienced in the late stages of Bulgaria's and Romania's accession negotiations. So far, this mechanism concerns only Croatia, for which some screening reports, including the one on 'justice, freedom and security', have led to the stipulation of benchmarks to be attained before negotiations on the respective chapters could begin.

'Advice and twinning'. Twinning is aimed at helping the respective countries bring their administrative and democratic institutions in line with European standards. The twinning programme was invented for the Eastern Enlargement round and has been extended to the Western Balkans in recent years (see Tulmets 2005). It typically involves the secondment of civil servants from EU member states to work as advisers to beneficiary institutions for a period of at least twelve months. During this period, the advisors help work on institution-building programmes. In relation to JHA, the first twinning programme in the region was the project 'Integrated Border Management: Border Police', implemented in Croatia, with Slovenian and

German twinning partners, between 2002 and 2004. By 2003, around a dozen twinning programmes were running or were in preparation in only two of the SAP countries — Croatia and Albania. The 2003 Thessaloniki Agenda stated that this situation was insufficient and that the twinning programme had to be enlarged in order to include all of the states (Council of the European Union 2003a). Additionally, SAP countries became eligible for technical assistance from the Technical Assistance Information Exchange Office (TAIEX). TAIEX was originally set up as part of the pre-accession strategy for the Eastern Enlargement to provide technical assistance to candidate countries in bringing their systems in line with Community legislation. In contrast to the twinning programme, which is based on the longer-term secondment of EU member state experts, the TAIEX programme provides mainly short-term expertise.

Assessing the EU's Pre-accession Strategy

The EU's pre-accession strategy is a major framework for exerting influence on the Western Balkan states. It builds upon the EU's most successful foreign policy tool, namely the incentive of membership. Since the principle of conditionality includes the obligation to implement the EU's *acquis* in JHA in full, it is more a question of when and how, rather than if, these countries will adhere to the *acquis*. The EU has assisted them with substantial financial assistance (in the IPA and CARDS programme), in which JHA has been included in a prominent manner and actually in some countries as the most prominent area of cooperation.

A major difference between the Western Balkans' pre-accession strategy and the Eastern Enlargement is that the EU has raised the hurdles to enter the Union. Due to the failed European constitution and the discussions on the EU's internal absorption capacities, the Western Balkan states have come under a higher degree of scrutiny than any other candidate country before (of course, alongside Turkey). The SAP contains a broader range of political and economic conditions to be met by the aspiring candidates.

Furthermore, the prospect of EU membership for the Western Balkans still has no concrete time frame, and offers a rather remote accession horizon. As a consequence, the EU can offer only a very uncertain time horizon within which compliance with EU rules will be rewarded. This leads to the related problem that the credibility of EU threats and demands is often questionable. In this respect, one has to distinguish between controversial and uncontroversial areas of cooperation. In interviews for this analysis, ministerial officials of the Balkan countries have stated satisfactorily that the CARDS programme has helped to upgrade substantially (or, even to create) domestic JHA systems. This result particularly appeals to policy areas in which adjustment to the EU has not implied difficult reform efforts (such as, for instance, the technical upgrading of border control equipment). The problem for the EU has related to the capacity of inducing changes in areas in which real (and, hence, painful) reform steps were expected or considered necessary. As the membership perspective was remote, the EU's repeated insistence on far-reaching reform of, say, the judiciary sectors in Croatia has trailed off with the promise to do so at a later stage in the *rapprochement* process.[8]

However, the EU has an additional — this time, essentially exclusive — instrument to speed up reform efforts in the Western Balkans' JHA policies: the liberalization of the visa regime.

EC Visa Facilitation and Readmission Agreements: Developing a Policy-related Conditionality

The EU's cooperation in JHA is guided by the principle of safeguarding internal security. A 'safe(r) inside' is contrasted with an 'unsafe(r) outside', 'with the EU's frontiers as the dividing line and law enforcement and border controls as key instruments to maintain and further enhance the distinction' (Monar 2001, 762). EU JHA cooperation has, therefore, created a strong dynamic of inclusion and exclusion between inside and outside countries (see Monar 2000; Lavenex 2005). In the Western Balkans, the EU has used this dynamic to propose partial inclusion in terms of facilitated travel opportunities in exchange for enhanced efforts in reforming domestic JHA.

In the EU's understanding of an effective border control, visa policies take an important role. The visa issuance procedure should allow for separating worthy from unworthy guests, thus preventing unwanted migration flows into the EU. Certain aspects of member states' visa policies were first brought into the Community framework with the Maastricht Treaty, more precisely the determination of those non-EU countries whose nationals must be in possession of visas when crossing the external borders of the member states, and the establishment of a standard model visa. The Amsterdam Treaty (1997) then broke ground for an expansion of the EU's visa policy. Title IV on 'Visas, Asylum, Immigration and other Policies related to free movements of persons' was introduced in the EC Treaty, putting it under the first pillar of the EU's temple structure. In addition, the Schengen *acquis* was integrated into the EU's legal framework. With the Amsterdam Treaty entering into force, the EU used the competences to make up two lists of third countries: the positive visa list, which named the countries whose citizens do not require a visa to enter the EU, and the negative visa list, which specified the countries whose citizens do. In the famous Council Regulation 539/2001, all Western Balkan states, with the notable exception of Croatia, were placed on the negative visa list (Council of the European Union 2001a).

The decision had major implications for the Western Balkans, as it seriously confined their possibilities to travel without restrictions. The costs of the visa fee, travel insurance, translation, notarization of documents, etc. are equivalent to a month's average salary (ICG 2005, 9). Travelling into the EU turned out to be too expensive for many citizens of the Western Balkans. According to some estimates, around seventy per cent of all Serbian students have never left their country (ICG 2005, 8). The visa issue gained political salience when the Central and Eastern European countries joined the EU. As part of the membership conditionality, the new member states were required to impose visa requirements on all countries placed on the EU's negative visa list. The Western Balkans found themselves being surrounded by EU member and Schengen-participating states.

As a consequence, the objective of achieving visa liberalization has ranked high on the political agendas of the Western Balkans. Even though they were lobbying for a quick visa liberalization scheme, the EU recognized a free-visa regime as a long-term objective only. The 2003 Thessaloniki Agenda first introduced the prospect of a liberalized visa regime, once certain conditions have been met:

> The EU is aware of the importance the peoples and governments in the Western Balkans attach to the perspective of liberalisation of the visa regime. Meanwhile, progress is dependent on these countries implementing major reforms in areas such as the strengthening of the rule of law, combating organised crime, corruption and illegal migration, and strengthening their administrative capacity in border control and security in documents (Council of the European Union 2003b).

The promise of a liberalized visa regime was then used to develop a new avenue of external influence based on the implementation of EC visa facilitation and readmission agreements. Any relaxation of the tight visa regime should be achieved only if 'substantial efforts by the countries in question' (Commission of the European Communities 2006c, 9) are observed (e.g. an improved border control) and if a readmission agreement is signed with the European Community. The use of visa liberalization as a major incentive for cooperation was not new, but already applied in the deadlocked negotiations on an EC readmission agreement with the Russian Federation and Ukraine. When proposing facilitated travel opportunities, the two countries finally agreed to sign the EC readmission agreement (Trauner and Kruse 2008, 11).

The EU's approach in the Western Balkans was different, however. Here, visa facilitation and readmission commonly were negotiated right from the start (with the exception of Albania). Moreover, the EU placed stronger emphasis on the fact that the pre-conditions should first be accepted and realized by the partner countries. The reason for this was that the use of visa liberalization as an incentive in the Western Balkans was not uncontroversial among EU member states. A Commission official explained in an interview that some of the EU member states were relatively dissatisfied with their experiences in the wake of the visa liberalization for Bulgaria and Romania. A comparatively high number of people overstayed the permitted three months, and it was rather complicated to 'collect them again and repatriate them'.[9] As a result, EU member states were very reluctant to agree on a quick visa liberalization for any other Balkan state. The International Crisis Group (2005) reported that the Council Working Group (COWEB) was unable to agree on possible first steps for visa facilitation during their discussions on the issue at the beginning of 2005. This would reflect 'a general hardening of the political environment following the negative result of the referendums in

France and the Netherlands on the EU Constitution. Paris argued that the region remains a security threat' (ICG 2005, 7).

Against this background, the governments of the Western Balkans were aware that the EU would not soften the tight visa requirements unless they met the pre-conditions as defined. The EU, in turn, used the political salience of the issue to encourage the Western Balkans not only to sign an EC readmission agreement, but also to align the domestic visa regime with the *acquis*, to reform their external border control system, to fight the spread of fake travel documents, etc. In interviews for this analysis, Commission and Council officials emphasized the strength of this avenue of external influence: 'Visa liberalisation is the issue which is the most relevant for the daily life of the population. ... Now EU member states say that they have to comply with certain standards concerning illegal migration etc. before they qualify for a visa liberalisation. This is a tremendous incentive to speed-up things'.[10]

With the exception of Albania, the negotiations on a visa facilitation and readmission agreements between the EU and the governments of the Western Balkans were initiated at the end of November 2006. Albania's readmission agreement with the EC entered into force on 1 May 2006, and negotiations on a visa facilitation agreement started on 13 December 2006. All agreements were signed officially in September 2007 and entered into force on 1 January 2008. They are now a major means of pushing for further reforms. The former European Commissioner Franco Frattini specified that negotiations for visa-free travel can start only if smooth, functioning visa facilitation and readmission practices are guaranteed. In addition, efforts to fight corruption and improve effective cross-border police cooperation must be evident (Frattini 2006). According to the Commission enlargement strategy for 2008/9, each of the target countries will receive a 'roadmap' defining the exact conditions to be met. These documents will deal with the effective implementation of the readmission agreement and cover other key areas, such as border management, document security and fighting organized crime. 'Such roadmaps will allow the countries concerned to better focus their reform efforts, while also reinforcing the visibility of the EU's commitment to the peoples of the region' (Commission of the European Communities 2007b, 13).

In brief, in the regional setting of the Western Balkans, the EU has developed policy-related conditionality in JHA. EC visa facilitation and readmission agreements were considered to be beneficial to both the EU and the Western Balkans. They gave the EU a strong lever to pressure for reforms and to establish efficient return policies, while they met major grievances of the partner countries by easing the tight visa regime and fostering facilitated travel opportunities for bona fide travellers.

Conclusions

The aim of this paper has been to assess the EU's strategies for encouraging the Western Balkan countries to deepen their reform efforts in the field of justice and home affairs. It has drawn from theoretically informed literature on the Eastern Enlargement and asked whether rational institutionalism

Table 1. State of relations between the Western Balkan states and the EU (as of July 2008)

	Stabilisation and Association Agreement		Application for membership	Candidate country	Accession negotiations
	Date of signature	Entered into force			
Albania	June 2006	—	—	—	—
Bosnia-Herzegovina	June 2008	—	—	—	—
Croatia	October 2001	February 2005	February 2003	June 2004	October 2005
Kosovo	—	—	—	—	—
Macedonia	April 2001	April 2004	March 2004	December 2005	—
Montenegro	October 2007	—	—	—	—
Serbia	April 2008	—	—	—	—

Source: European Commission, DG for Enlargement.

focusing on external incentives underlying EU conditionality is suitable for understanding the Europeanization of the Western Balkans.

The analysis considers the EU's pre-accession strategy as a chief mechanism for stimulating the Western Balkan states to come closer to EU standards in JHA. In exerting influence on the Western Balkan's domestic policy making, the EU has built upon 'mechanisms of Europeanization' similar to those identified for the Eastern Enlargement (see Grabbe 2001) even though the EU's pre-accession strategy contains some new features. The political and economic conditions for entering the EU are more comprehensive, and new instruments were included to pressure for reforms at an early stage of EU integration. Yet, the key challenge has been to render EU membership conditionality credible. As the aspiring candidate countries have only a middle-range membership perspective without a clear time frame for accession, the EU can offer only an uncertain time horizon within which compliance with specific EU rules will be awarded. As a result, possibilities to set concrete deadlines and demand far-reaching reforms in certain issue areas are limited. As the prospect of joining the EU is distant, the credibility of EU threats and demands is often questionable.

To counterbalance these shortcomings, the EU has used its visa regime as a means to developing a new avenue of external leverage: policy-related conditionality. The prospect of a liberalized visa regime was linked with the signing of readmission agreements and other reform steps in domestic JHA. EC visa facilitation and readmission agreements provided the EU with an additional instrument to pressure for reforms in JHA. At the same time, it allowed the EU to meet a major source of discontent for these countries by easing the tight visa regime and fostering facilitated travel opportunities for bona fide travellers. In doing this, the EU also tried to dispel the belief that it was not serious about listening to the problems and priorities of the Western Balkan states.

In conclusion, the key to understanding the Europeanization of the Western Balkans is to take policy-related conditionality into account, in addition to membership conditionality. The experience gained in the Western Balkans concerning how to use policy conditionality in the JHA domain provided the EU with a model to apply in several states participating in the European Neighbourhood Policy (see Trauner and Kruse 2008). According to the former European Commissioner Franco Frattini, the EU seeks to enhance the EU's internal security 'through global visa facilitation and readmission agreements aimed in the longer term at the Union's neighbourhood countries, on the model currently being developed in the Balkans' (Agence Europe 2006). A more relaxed visa regime for certain categories of people in exchange for signing readmission agreements, tightening border controls, aligning the domestic visa policies etc. may prove to become an important tool of the external dimension of JHA.

Acknowledgement

The author gratefully acknowledges the useful comments made by Gregory Mounier, Nicole Wichmann, Sarah Wolff, and the other participants of this special issue, as well as by the anonymous journal referees. The present manuscript is a substantially revised version of a Working Document published by the Centre for European Policy Studies in February 2007 (CEPS Working Document No. 259).

Notes

1. Under the term 'Western Balkans', the EU subsumes Croatia, Albania, Macedonia, Serbia, Montenegro, Bosnia and Herzegovina and Kosovo under UN-Resolution 1244.
2. Regarding numbers, irregular migration from South-Eastern Europe seems to have reached its peak in 2000, when around 50,000 illegal migrants, from Bosnia and Herzegovina alone, passed on their way to the EU (IOM estimation, quoted in Hill 2004, 12). According to the European Commission (2007c, 72), the migratory flows from the Eastern and South-Eastern regions are 'now stabilising if not slightly declining'.
3. Confidential interview, European Commission, 10 February 2006, Brussels.
4. Confidential interview, European Commission, 6 February 2006, Brussels.
5. Ibid.
6. Although initiated by the EU, the Stability Pact for South-Eastern Europe was not another EU institution, but rather a framework agreement to streamline the efforts of the international community in the region. More than forty participating countries and institutions signed the founding document and agreed to develop a shared strategy for stability and growth in South-Eastern Europe.
7. The EU finances only a third of the RCC, equally shared with the participating states of the South-East European Cooperation Process (SEECP) and the rest of the donors of the Stability Pact. The SEECP partly owns the RCC and shares its seat and administrative structure in Sarajevo.
8. Confidential interview, Delegation of the EU to the Republic of Croatia, 11 May 2006, Zagreb.
9. Confidential interview, European Commission, 6 February 2006, Brussels.
10. Ibid. The official referred in particular to the EU–Macedonian relations.

References

Agence Europe. 2006. Brussels, 4 May 2006.
Anastasakis, O., and D. Bechev. 2003. *EU conditionality in South East Europe: Bringing commitment to the process*, South East European Studies Programme Policy Paper. Oxford: University of Oxford.
Commission of the European Communities. 2001a. *CARDS Assistance Programme to the Western Balkans*. Regional Strategy Paper 2002–2006. External Relations Directorate General.
Commission of the European Communities. 2001b. *The Stabilisation and Association Process and CARDS Assistance 2000 to 2006*. European Commission Paper for the Second Regional Conference for South Eastern Europe.
Commission of the European Communities. 2004. Opinion on the application of Croatia for membership of the European Union, April 20 2004, COM (2004) 257.
Commission of the European Communities. 2005a. Communication from the Commission. Commission opinion on the application from the former Yugoslav Republic of Macedonia for membership of the European Union, November 9 2005, COM (2005) 562.
Commission of the European Communities. 2005b. Communication from the Commission: 2005 enlargement strategy paper, November 9 2005, COM (2005) 561.
Commission of the European Communities. 2006a. Communication from the Commission to the Council and the European Parliament of 8 November 2006. Instrument for Pre-Accession Assistance. Multi-Annual indicative financial framework for 2008–2010, March 5 2008, COM (2006) 672 final.
Commission of the European Communities. 2006b. Communication from the Commission to the European Parliament and the Council. Enlargement strategy and main challenges 2006–2007. Including annexed special report on the EU's capacity to integrate new members, November 8 2006, COM (2006) 649.
Commission of the European Communities. 2006c. Communication from the Commission: The Western Balkans on the road to the EU: consolidating stability and raising prosperity, January 27 2006, COM (2006) 27.

Commission of the European Communities. 2007a. Commission decision on a Multi-annual Indicative Planning Document (MIDP) 2007–2009 for Albania, May 31 2007, COM (2007) 2245.
Commission of the European Communities. 2007b. Enlargement strategy and main challenges 2007–2008, November 6 2007, COM (2007) 663 final.
Commission of the European Communities. 2007c. Communication from the Commission. Applying the Global Approach to Migration to the Eastern and South-Eastern Regions Neighbouring the European Union, Brussels, May 16 2007, COM (2007) 247 final.
Council of the European Union. 2000. Council Regulation (EC) No 2666/2000 of 5 December 2000 on assistance for Albania, Bosnia and Herzegovina, Croatia, the Federal Republic of Yugoslavia and the Former Yugoslav Republic of Macedonia, repealing Regulation (EC) No 1628/96 and amending Regulations (EEC) No 3906/89 and (EEC) No 1360/90 and Decision 97/256/EC and 1999/311 EC. *Official Journal of the EU* L306 (December 7).
Council of the European Union. 2001a. Council Regulation (EC) No 539/2001 of 15 March 2001 listing the third countries whose nationals must be in possession of visas when crossing the external borders and those whose nationals are exempt from that requirement. *Official Journal of the EU* L81 (March 21).
Council of the European Union. 2001b. Press release, 2356th Council Meeting, General Affairs, PRES/01/226, June 11-12.
Council of the European Union. 2003a. EU–Western Balkans forum. Joint conclusions, 15578/03, November 28.
Council of the European Union. 2003b. The Thessaloniki agenda for the Western Balkans: Moving towards European integration, Thessaloniki: Western Balkans — General Affairs and External Relations Council (GAERC) Conclusions, June 16.
Council of the European Union. 2005. Stabilisation and Association Agreement between the European Communities and their member states, of the one part, and the Republic of Croatia, of the other part. *Official Journal of the EU* L26/3 (January 28).
Council of the European Union. 2006. Council regulation (EC) No 1085/2006 of 17 July 2006 establishing an Instrument for Pre-Accession Assistance (IPA). *Official Journal of the EU* L210 (July 31).
Di Puppo, L. 2009. The externalisation of JHA policies in Georgia: Partner or hotbed of threats? *Journal of European Integration* 31, no. 1: 103–18.
Emerson, M., S. Aydin, J. De Clerck-Sachsse, and G. Noutcheva. 2006. Just what is this 'absorption capacity' of the European Union?. CEPS Policy Brief No. 113, Centre for European Policy Studies, September.
European Council. 2000. Presidency conclusions, Santa Maria da Feira, June 19 and 20.
European Council. 2003. Presidency conclusions, Thessaloniki, June 19 and 20.
Frattini, F. 2006. The role of internal security in relations between the EU and its neighbours. Speech held at the Ministerial Conference Vienna, May 4, http://www.libertysecurity.org/article907.html.
Grabbe, H. 2001. How does Europeanization affect CEE governance? Conditionality, diffusion and diversity. *Journal of European Public Policy*, 8, no.6: 1013–31.
Grabbe, H. 2002. Stabilising the East while keeping out the Easterners: internal and external security logics in conflict. In *Migration and the externalities of European integration*, eds. S. Lavenex and E.M. Ucarer, 91–104. Lanham, MD: Lexington Books.
Grabbe, H. 2003. Europeanization goes East: Power and uncertainty in the EU accession process. In *The politics of Europeanization*, eds. K. Featherstone and C.M. Radaelli, 303–31. Oxford: Oxford Univ. Press.
Hill, A. 2004. Assumptions, principles and strategy. *Adelphi Papers* 44, no. 371: 11–40.
ICG. 2005. *EU visas and the Western Balkans*, Europe Report Nr 168, November 29. Brussels: International Crisis Group.
Kelley, J.G. 2004. *Ethnic politics in Europe: The power of norms and incentives*. Princeton, NJ: Princeton Univ. Press.
Lavenex, S. 2005. The politics of exclusion and inclusion in 'wider Europe'. In *Soft or hard borders? Managing the divide in an enlarged Europe*, ed. J. DeBardeleben, 123–45. Cornwall: MPG Books Ltd.
Lavenex, S., and E.M. Uçarer. 2004. The external dimension of Europeanization: The case of immigration policies. *Cooperation and Conflict: Journal of the Nordic International Studies Association* 39, no. 4: 417–43.

March, J.G., and J.P. Olsen. 1998. The institutional dynamics of international political orders. *International Organisation* 52, no. 4: 943–69.

Monar, J. 2000. *Justice and home affairs in a wider Europe: The dynamics of inclusion and exclusion.* ESRC 'One Europe or Several?' Programme Working Paper 07/00, Leicester, http://www.one-europe.ac.uk/pdf/monarW7.PDF.

Monar, J. 2001. The dynamics of justice and home affairs: Laboratories, driving factors and costs. *Journal of Common Market Studies* 39, no. 4: 747–64.

Pippan, C. 2004. The rocky road to Europe: the EU's Stabilisation and Association Process for the Western Balkans and the principle of conditionality. *European Foreign Affairs Review* 9: 219–45.

Pridham, G. 2005. *Designing democracy: EU enlargement and regime change in post-communist Europe.* New York: Palgrave Macmillan.

Radaelli, C. 2000. Whither Europeanization? Concept stretching and substantive change. *European Integration On-Line Papers* 4, no. 8, http://eiop.or.at/eiop/texte/2000-008.htm.

Schelter, K. 2003. Challenges for non (and not-yet) Schengen countries. Paper presented at the Workshop 'Managing International and Inter-Agency Cooperation at the Border', Geneva Centre for the Democratic Control of Armed Forces (DCAF).

Schimmelfennig, F., S. Engert, and H. Knobel. 2003. Costs, commitment and compliance: the impact of EU democratic conditionality on Latvia, Slovakia and Turkey. *Journal of Common Market Studies* 41, no. 3: 495–518.

Schimmelfennig, F., and U. Sedelmeier. 2005a. *The Europeanisation of Central and Eastern Europe.* Ithaca, NY: Cornell Univ. Press.

Schimmelfennig, F., and U. Sedelmeier. 2005b. Introduction: Conceptualizing the Europeanization of Central and Eastern Europe. In Schimmelfennig and Sedelmeier 2005a, 1–29.

Sedelmeier, U. 2006. Europeanisation in new member and candidate states. *Living Reviews in European Governance* 1, no. 3, http://europeangovernance.livingreviews.org/Articles/lreg-2006-3/.

Trauner, F. 2007. From membership conditionality to policy conditionality: EU external governance in South-Eastern Europe. Paper presented to the EU Consent conference 'Deepening in an enlarged Europe: Integrative balancing in the new member states', Budapest, November 16–17 2007.

Trauner, F., and I. Kruse. 2008. *EC visa facilitation and readmission agreements: implementing a new EU security approach in the neighbourhood.* CEPS Working Paper No 290, Centre for European Policy Studies, April.

Tulmets, E. 2005. The management of new forms of governance by former accession countries of the European Union: Institutional twinning in Estonia and Hungary. *European Law Journal* 11, no. 5: 657–74.

UNHCR. 2003. *The EU enlargement process and the external dimension of the EU JHA policy.* Geneva: United Nations High Commissioner for Refugees.

Vachudova, M.A. 2005. *Europe undivided: Democracy, leverage and integration after communism.* Oxford: Oxford Univ. Press.

Wolff, S., N. Wichmann, and G. Mounier. 2009. The external dimension of Justice and Home Affairs: A different security agenda for the EU? *Journal of European Integration* 31, no. 1: 9–23.

The External Governance of EU Internal Security

SANDRA LAVENEX & NICOLE WICHMANN

Department of Political Science, University of Lucerne, Lucerne, Switzerland

ABSTRACT This article analyses the modes of governance through which the EU seeks to ensure the European Neighbourhood Policy (ENP) countries' participation in the realization of its internal security project. Although the EU, given the strong interdependence in these 'soft security' issues, has strong incentives to govern by conditionality in order to ensure the ENP countries' compliance, efforts to transfer policies by such hierarchical means encounter serious limitations as a result of lack of supranational competence and insufficient incentives that the EU can offer third countries to compensate for adaptation costs. By comparing Justice and Home Affairs (JHA) issues with different degrees of communitarization and representing different constellations of interests in relations with ENP countries, we find that the EU increasingly focuses on the extension of internal transgovernmental networks as an alternative form of external governance. Although theoretically allowing for horizontal patterns of co-owned cooperation, the integrative potential of these networks is hampered by the lack of mutual trust and institutional incompatibilities in ENP countries. As a result, extended network governance becomes an attempt at unilateral policy-transfer by 'softer' means.

Introduction

The emergence of an external dimension to EU internal security cooperation is part of two broader trends in contemporary Europe: first, the blurring of the distinction between internal and external security and, secondly, the gradual extension of EU policies to associated non-member states, recently coined as 'external governance'. Whereas the first trend is a distinctive feature of the security landscape in Western Europe of the post-Cold War era (Bigo 2001; Pastore 2002; Lutterbeck 2005), the attempt to bind neighbouring countries into common policy frameworks has been interpreted as an answer to this changed geopolitical landscape (Lavenex 2004).

Motivated and inspired by the experience of Eastern enlargement, the European Neighbourhood Policy (ENP) basically consists of promoting the EU's Eastern and Southern neighbours'[1] approximation to the EU's *acquis*, without, however, offering a membership perspective. In the words of Andreas Herdina (2005), one of the crafters of the ENP in the Commission, 'the majority of agreed measures consists of projecting first pillar Community policies beyond our external borders'.

The external projection of internal policies constitutes a new kind of foreign policy, which is usually referred to as the 'external dimension' of a policy field. This development has been particularly prominent in the area of Justice and Home Affairs (JHA) where cooperation within the EU has, from the outset, also involved third countries (Lavenex 2006). A major motivation is the transnational character of associated threats. According to the Commission, 'the projection of the values underpinning the area of freedom, security and justice is essential in order to safeguard the internal security of the EU. Menaces such as terrorism, organized crime and drug trafficking also originate outside the EU. It is thus crucial that the EU develop a strategy to engage with third countries worldwide' (European Commission 2005a, 3). Whereas these endeavours to involve third countries in the realization of Europe's internal security project has by now raised increased scholarly attention (Lavenex and Uçarer 2002; Geddes 2006; Trauner 2007; Wichmann 2007a; Wolff 2007), the ways how the EU seeks to ensure third countries' participation and the question whether it succeeds in doing so are not always well understood. To address these research objectives the article proposes to compare the attempts at governing the ENP countries, which is one of the outputs of the JHA external dimension, across different countries and issue areas (Wolff, Wichmann, and Mounier 2009, this issue, 9–23).[2]

Inspired by the analyses of Eastern enlargement that highlighted the predominance of conditionality and unilateral policy transfer in involving third countries into EU policies, scholars have tended to emphasize similar patterns in the ENP (Cremona and Hillion 2006; Kelley 2006; Magen 2006; Maier and Schimmelfennig 2007). This tendency seems particularly salient in JHA, given the security interests involved for the EU and its member states. However, this policy field poses a number of challenges to the traditional external governance approach. First, in contrast to most 'first pillar Community policies' mentioned by Herdina, it is not fully communitarized: incomplete communitarization coexists with non-legislative and more operational modes of governance that put into question the EU's capacity to exert policy transfer. Relating to the introduction to this volume, this means that characteristic features of the input impinge upon the resulting policy output (Wolff, Wichmann, and Mounier 2009, this issue, 9–23). Secondly, and linked to that, it is unclear how the leverage mechanism of policy transfer — conditionality — shall work in the absence of both communitarization and strong incentives for adaptation. And, finally, interdependence in relation with the ENP countries is strongly asymmetric, with the EU having much stronger interests in cooperation with most aspects of JHA than its neighbours.

Comparing communitarized ('1st pillar') with intergovernmental ('3rd pillar') JHA policies and such with stronger and weaker asymmetry of interests, our analysis shows that three factors seriously limit the EU's ability to engage in unilateral policy transfer. Rather than replicating the conditionality approach to external governance, the EU has developed a variety of institutional settings with ENP countries that mirror, to a certain extent, the internal modes of governance in this field, while bringing in some important modifications. After briefly introducing the internal patterns of JHA cooperation, we will show that external governance by transgovernmental networks plays a crucial role in replacing more hierarchical attempts at policy transfer. While theoretically allowing for more horizontal patterns of co-owned cooperation, however, extended network governance also presupposes some important institutional and ideational features that are not necessarily given in the external realm. The last part of our article identifies the challenges facing these hitherto under-studied forms of EU external governance and closes with a general conclusion on the chances and limits of associating third countries to internal policy goals.

Governance in External Relations

Originally focused on the politics of Eastern enlargement studies, the emerging literature on EU external governance has a tendency to emphasize EU endeavours to ensure third countries' cooperation through what has been detected as its 'most successful foreign policy instrument' (European Commission 2003, 5): governance by conditionality. This is basically a hierarchical approach in which the EU capitalizes on its superior bargaining power in order to induce third country compliance. It is hierarchical in the sense that it works through a vertical process of command — where the EU transfers predetermined, non-negotiable rules — and control, where the EU ensures compliance through regular monitoring mechanisms (Schimmelfennig and Sedelmeier 2004, 674 ff.).[3]

External governance by conditionality presupposes the existence of a clear supranational *acquis* to be exported as well as strong leverage on the part of the Union. Whereas the ENP lacks the leverage of membership incentives, in JHA large parts of the *acquis* consist less in transferable legal instruments than in operational cooperation. A particular feature of cooperation in JHA is its network character and the predominance of transgovernmentalism as a mode of governance (see below).

Drawing on Slaughter's (2004, 52ff.) work on transgovernmental networks, we distinguish conceptually between three different types of networks depending on their main functions.[4] Most EU agencies and programmes operate according to one of these models of network governance, as they are based on the coordination of responsible sections of national bureaucracies. JHA agencies are Europol (network of national police offices), Eurojust (network of national prosecutors) or Frontex (network of national border control services). Policy networks can, however, also be fully horizontal without supranational European coordination and less formalized.

- *Information networks* — they do not produce regulatory instruments but are set up to diffuse policy-relevant knowledge and ideas among the members. Usually, this goes hand in hand with the objective of distilling this information and identifying best practices. Expertise and professional reputation play an important role in these networks.
- *Implementation networks* — they focus primarily on enhancing cooperation among national regulators to implement/enforce existing laws and rules — be they national, international or European. In EU law these networks are complementary to the hierarchical modes of governance in that they add a more cooperative implementation structure to the essentially unilateral decision-making process. Often, implementation networks also promote capacity building through technical assistance and training.
- *Regulatory networks* — they are the most powerful ones in terms of governance since they have an implicit or explicit legislative mandate and are geared at the formulation of common rules and standards in a given policy area. According to Slaughter (2004, 59), 'behind the facade of technical adjustments for improved coordination … and uniformity of standards lie subtle adjustments' of national laws. In so far as they are inclusionary and voluntary, these networks represent the most advanced form of flexible sectoral integration in terms of shared governance.

Table 1 summarizes two idea-typical models of external governance. It excludes modes of interaction that — because of their lesser degree of institutionalization and commitment — do not qualify as governance, such as traditional intergovernmental cooperation.

In the following sections, we first specify the internal modes of governance in JHA before analysing their reflection in JHA external relations. Drawing on the characteristics of internal modes of policy making and hypotheses derived from theories of institutional design, we will identify the conditions under which different modes of external governance prevail.

The Governance of Internal Security in the EU

The internal governance of JHA is marked by the co-existence of weak hierarchical legal integration through the Community method and intergovernmental procedures, as well as the dominance of network governance through intensive transgovernmentalism. Integration occurs not only or primarily through legislation but first and foremost through operational cooperation in transgovernmental networks.

Legislative Level

At the legislative level the interaction in JHA is structured according to two different procedures: either through the 'communitarized' ('1st pillar') or

Table 1. Modes of external governance

Modes of interaction		Instruments	Output	Actors
Hierarchy		EC and EU law, precise requirements	Policy transfer	Supranational EU institutions and Council vis-à-vis third country governments
Networks	Information networks	Voluntary instruments, process-orientated: Data, information, best practices	Coordination	Multilevel: transgovernmental and transnational (including supra- and subnational actors) Non-State actors: bodies, agencies Private actors
	Implementation networks	Voluntary instruments, process-orientated: Data, information, ooperational cooperation, capacity building		
	Regulation networks	Voluntary instruments, process-orientated: Benchmarks, common standards		

through intergovernmental decision making ('3rd pillar'). The communitarized aspects of JHA policy making prevail in the areas of visa, asylum and some aspects of irregular migration control. The Community method assigns a central role to the Commission as the policy initiator, the formal rule of decision taking in the Council is Qualified Majority Voting, and the output of cooperation is legally binding EC norms.

The second modus of legislative interaction is the intergovernmental mode of decision making. The Commission is associated with the work in this area, but it does not have the same prerogatives as in the Community area. Both the European Parliament and the European Court of Justice (ECJ) are excluded from decision making. Decisions are adopted by unanimity in the Council, and the legislative outcome frequently reflects lowest common denominator solutions. The legislative output produced in this setting consists of framework decisions and conventions. The legal instruments pursue the double objective of approximating the substantive elements of criminal law and of simplifying the procedural aspects of cooperation in criminal and judicial matters (by, for example, introducing mutual recognition). In practice, a common feature of the legal instruments adopted in both first and third pillar JHA matters is the weakness of obligations implied. This means that the member states retain a high margin of discretion, when they transpose the adopted legal instruments in to their domestic legal system (Weyembergh 2006).

Operational Level

A particularity of internal security governance is the important role played by operational cooperation. The operational level is characterized by 'intensive transgovernmentalism' (Slaughter 1997; Wallace 2000; Lavenex and Wallace 2005), i.e. by the existence of a number of networks of law enforcement officials, which are established on the basis of similar functions, tasks and levels of seniority. Transgovernmentalism is one form of 'network governance'; it can occur both on the meso-level of law enforcement officials (e.g. magistrates) and, on the micro-level, where police officers and judicial authorities work together to enforce the law in a cross-border setting (Benyon 1996). On the meso-level, networks of law enforcement officials are created for exchanging information, for conducting joint investigations to enforce the law and for setting standards of cooperation in the form of memoranda of understanding. Network governance in horizontal networks fulfils one or several of the following objectives: information exchange, law enforcement or standard setting for future cooperation (=regulation).[5] While regulation networks may come close to legislative functions when they produce mutually agreed standards, these outputs retain a different legal quality as 'soft law', which is the reason why they are not included in the analysis of legislative decision making.

These 'bottom-up' or horizontal-level activities of law enforcement do not stand alone in European internal security governance; they are complemented by vertical or top-down support structures, which have been created at the European level to facilitate cooperation between national law enforcement officials. The most prominent examples of vertical coordinating structures are Europol, Eurojust and Frontex. These bodies provide a platform for the exchange of information between the member states, and they facilitate the conduct of joint operations (Schalken and Pronk 2002). The coordinating bodies help the law enforcement officials involved in international cooperation to identify the competent authorities in the other states, so that they know who to contact for formal assistance requests (Bigo 2000b). The major weakness of these vertical networks is the absence of executive policing powers, which makes them reliant upon the information provided by the member states. By and large, the top-down networks are limited to exchanging information and providing support for joint implementation.

The existence of these top-down networks is linked closely to the emergence of an EU competence in the field of criminal law. They are frequently created by European instruments (decisions, conventions) and established for the purpose of implementing European criminal law instruments. The importance of the vertical networks should not be underestimated, as their remit of activities of the coordinating bodies is expanded constantly. In sum, we find a complex maze of law enforcement institutions in the EU that cooperate with each other in a system of 'multilevel governance'. Theoretically, this system of multilevel governance is more open to flexible forms of participation, including that of third countries, than legislative integration under supranational procedures. In the following section, we investigate the role of these networks in the external dimension of JHA in relation with ENP countries.

The External Dimension of JHA

Our analysis of external governance of JHA starts from the general assumption that the external modes of interaction will, to a large degree, reflect the internal modes of policy making in the respective fields (Longo 2003). The way EU policies are promoted or extended abroad depends on how these policies are produced internally. On the one hand, hierarchical policy transfer presupposes the existence of a clear *acquis* and strong EU competence to both act externally and monitor compliance. Therefore, we expect this mode of governance to prevail in the more communitarized areas (such as asylum and visa policy). In contrast, we expect network governance or intergovernmental cooperation in those areas where the EU does not have strong competence, but is dominated by transgovernmentalism.

Apart from these institutional configurations or 'input' factors, interest constellations between the EU and the third countries in question are likely to impact on the modes of governance prevailing. In areas in which the EU has strong interests in third country 'compliance', the EU will try to resort to more hegemonic or hierarchical modes of interaction. Yet, the degree to which the EU is able to exercise hegemony depends on competence, that is the existence of a clear *acquis*, supranational powers and monitoring mechanisms — and, in so far as conditionality presupposes positive incentives, also the capacity to offer attractive rewards in return for costly compliance. In areas characterized by a strong asymmetry of interests, where compliance with EU demands would impose high costs and few benefits on the third country, attempts at hierarchical policy transfer are likely to involve interest-based bargaining in the definition of conditionality in terms of positive rewards. This corresponds to the case of irregular migration/readmission. The European Commission acknowledged the problem of 'lack of incentives', when it stated that, 'in the field of JHA, there is little that can be offered in return ...' (European Commission 2002).

Given the attraction of hierarchy or governance by conditionality in asymmetric interest constellations, network governance is likely to predominate under two conditions: first in more technocratic or at least less politicized areas, where both sides share an interest in cooperation, such as the fight against corruption. Secondly, in those areas where the EU lacks the resources necessary for hierarchical governance by conditionality. In this case, network governance may emerge as a default option as a means to promote cooperation despite the inability to agree on binding obligations. Our empirical analysis will show that this constellation is frequent in JHA, and that extended network governance can — contrary to its proclaimed inclusiveness and voluntariness — be hegemonic.

In order to examine the impact of these variables on the choice of external governance modes, we chose cases reflecting different degrees of communitarization and constellations of interests. Our more communitarized cases are irregular migration and asylum (mainly 1st pillar), the still predominantly intergovernmental ones are drugs and corruption (mainly 3rd pillar). These cases also differ with regard to the urgency the EU attributes to them in relations with the third countries and the latter's situation with regard to the underlying problems. We refer to this dimension as symmetry or asymmetry of interests. Asymmetry is stronger when an issue is politicized or even securitized in the EU, leading it to put strong emphasis on third country compliance. This is the case for irregular migration and drugs, which also figure in the EU's security strategy and for which ENP countries are both countries of origin and transit. By contrast, asylum as a humanitarian concept and the fight against corruption as element of good governance do not feature as prominently in the EU external policies under the ENP and enjoy — at least rhetorically — more support also from ENP country governments. The case selection is summarized in Table 2.

Table 2. Case selection

Interests constellation	Degree of communitarization	
	Communitarized	Less communitarized
Strong asymmetry of interests	Irregular migration	Drugs
Stronger symmetry of interests	Asylum	Corruption

Asylum and Immigration Cooperation

External action in the field of asylum focuses primarily on legislative aspects and, in the second instance, on operational and technical cooperation, whereas with regard to legal and irregular migration various forms of operational cooperation and networking prevail. This is partly a function of the higher level of legalization in asylum matters, with the existence of an international regime and — at least in a few respects — stronger *acquis*.

The overarching goal of asylum cooperation as stated in all ENP Action Plans is the spread of the international refugee regime through the implementation of the Geneva Convention and its 1967 Protocol. Action Plans towards Ukraine and Moldova furthermore require the approximation of legislation and of the system of state authorities responsible with EU norms and standards (European Commission 2004c; EU–Ukraine Co-operation Council 2007), whereas towards Morocco and Tunisia, the EU merely agrees to put at disposition 'the European experience and expertise with the transposition of the 1951 Convention' (authors' translation), including, with Morocco, support for competent authorities and professional training for persons dealing with the asylum procedure and reception (European Commission 2004a, 2004b). With this focus on rule-transfer, asylum cooperation is dominated by a hegemonic mode of governance, where the EU tries to expand the geographical scope of European asylum traditions in an attempt to increase the number of countries sharing the 'burden' of refugee protection.

However, policy transfer is not really pursued in a consistent manner. The review of JHA-subcommittee meetings with Ukraine and Moldova and Social Affairs Committees established with Morocco and Tunisia shows a greater focus on irregular migration than on the implementation of asylum systems. External asylum governance has received new impetus with the decision to establish Regional Protection Programmes (RPP) in third countries in cooperation with UNHCR and involving capacity building in the area of asylum (European Commission 2005c). In parallel, regional networks have been created to promote cooperation in asylum and immigration matters, both to the East and South. Launched in 2001 on an informal basis by Sweden to address the challenges of EU eastward enlargement, the so-called Söderköping Process focuses since 2004 on transferring the experience of the newly acceded EU member states to the Western New Independent States (NIS) 'in aligning their migration and asylum related legislation, policies and practices with the EU acquis standards' (Söderköping Process 2005). The stated aim is to develop the Western NIS 'into safe countries of asylum through alignment with EU standards'. In terms of our network typology, the Söderköping process can be seen as an information and implementation network that also aims to foster capacity building. However, as the quotation shows, the transfer of EU policies and practices is at the core. This turns an organizationally horizontal mode of governance into an instrument of hegemonic policy-export. The weaker status of asylum cooperation with the Southern Mediterranean neighbours, and the total lack of relevant clauses in agreements with

Tunisia is interesting, given the countries' geographical location as both sending and transit countries of asylum seekers. In line with earlier Association Agreements, these countries clearly give priority to cooperation on legal migration and the rights of their nationals living in the EU, while both Action Plans and subcommittee documents reflect the lack of responsiveness on the part of the EU. With the Valencia Action Plan adopted in 2002, attention has clearly shifted to the issue of irregular migration (Presidency 2002), notwithstanding the more recent rhetorical embracement of a 'global approach' invoking also other forms of migration (Lavenex and Kunz 2008).

The priority attributed to irregular migration is also reflected in the European Security Strategy, which lists 'illegal migrants' among the 'key threats' facing the Union (Council of the European Union 2003, 4). Although the EU by now has a considerable *acquis* relating to border security, visa policy and the fight against irregular migration, the Action Plans mainly focus on three issues: improvement of information exchange on migration flows; practical operational support and capacity building to third country authorities dealing with border control and migration; and the conclusion of readmission agreements.

The modes of interaction applied are the linkage of conditionality with intergovernmental bargaining and an increasing number of operational network-activities. Conditionality and intergovernmental bargaining concentrate on the negotiation of readmission agreements with the EU. These agreements specify the obligations to take back their own and third country nationals having travelled through one of the contracting parties and who are illegally staying in the other party and, in exchange, offering visa facilitations for certain categories of persons, such as students, journalists, government officials etc. Whereas with Ukraine and Moldova, agreements could be negotiated in exchange for visa facilitations, the Mediterranean ENP countries have proved less responsive to this policy export by conditional rewards. Probably because they do not share the Eastern neighbours' ambitions to join the Union — despite the absence of an official membership perspective — Southern Mediterranean countries have hitherto rejected any binding commitments, thereby forcing the EU to recourse to alternative modes of interaction (Lavenex 2006, 341ff.). In particular, EU member states have engaged in an 'informalization' strategy that focuses on a broader framework of cooperation based on administrative arrangements, bilateral deals and exchanges of letters and memoranda of understanding, including operational cooperation (e.g. police cooperation, joint border operations) (Carrera 2007; Cassarino 2007).

This mode of external governance through transgovernmental networking also predominates in other aspects of migration and asylum policy, both bilaterally and multilaterally. It usually takes the form of information and implementation networks involving consultative, financial and expert assistance to responsible government services, including twinnings with EU countries.[6] Operational network governance often occurs through 'projects' financed by the EU budget (e.g. the AENEAS and AGIS programmes in JHA), where member states, third countries or international organizations compete for tender. Such project-based networks often involve — apart from member and non-member states — NGOs and international organizations. They may also be set up to support the implementation of international and European standards. That such projects are not void of more hegemonic forms of policy transfer is revealed when we take a closer look at their description. For instance, with regard to trafficking in Eastern Europe, Project JAI/2004/AGIS/031 (15) foresees next to the identification and exchange of best practices, the aim of 'uniform application of international/EU law and practices' (European Commission 2005d). Such hegemonic elements have started to figure more prominently in operational border politics recently. In 2005, the EU launched a border control mission at the Ukrainian–Moldovan border, EUBAM, giving fifty EU experts a free hand to monitor the comings and goings across the border. In July and August 2006, the first joint operations started under the coordination of the new European Frontex agency, composed of patrol boats, planes and helicopters from several member states to patrol sea borders in the Atlantic Ocean and the Mediterranean. In its 2005 Communication on priority actions for responding to the challenges of migration, the Commission also announced it would extend the newly created Mediterranean Coastal Patrols Network to the Mediterranean third countries 'as soon as technically feasible' (European Commission 2005b). In the meantime, joint operations are also carried out in the framework of 'training' activities.

Beyond official EU activities, networking on migration control cooperation has developed at a purely transgovernmental level between law and order officials both to the east and the south. Whereas eastern networks, such as the Budapest process, have focused exclusively on repressive measures, the informal 5+5 Ministerial Western Mediterranean Dialogue to the south has taken on a broader mandate, also covering legal migration. Recognizing the socialization potential of such bottom-up, horizontal transgovernmental networks, recent Commission documents declare the aim to link them more closely to ENP activities and, in particular, discussions in technical subcommittees (European Commission 2005b).

In sum, the evidence gathered so far indicates that attempts at hierarchical governance or policy transfer face strong difficulties due to the weakness of the *acquis*, the lack of incentives the EC can offer to compensate significant interest asymmetries, and the weak level of legalization in relations with third countries. The negotiations on readmission agreements show despite all difficulties that countries with membership aspirations (Moldova and Ukraine) are more prone to accept external governance by conditionality, in return for limited visa facilitations, whereas the southern Mediterranean countries have hitherto declined the (weak) incentives offered. In contrast, the resort to networks is much more frequent than the conditionality model of interaction. Yet, differences in the perception of the underlying problems and preferred solutions, as well as lack of trust between the partners, tend to replicate the asymmetry of overarching relationships, thus giving clear preference to EU concepts and priorities over those of the third countries. Enhanced dialogue within relevant subcommittees and networks also opens the possibility for voicing third countries' concerns. For instance, the EU's 'global approach' to immigration launched in 2005 and aiming at a pan-African strategy of immigration management, was influenced strongly by exchanges with Moroccan officials. Pressure by Mediterranean countries has also provoked more thought on the role of mobility within the ENP and the desire to promote the 'migration–development nexus' in foreign policies (Lavenex and Kunz 2008).[7] Beyond the production of policy documents, however, this awareness has given rise to few concrete actions. A precursory look at the Aeneas projects and the Country Strategy Documents reveals a bias in favour of the more traditional instruments of migration control.

Drug Trafficking and Corruption

External action in the field of police and judicial matters focuses on technical cooperation, operational cooperation and the transfer of legislative standards. Two issue areas were chosen for closer investigation: cooperation to fight drugs and anti-corruption. The external dimension of drugs policy is characterized by hierarchical policy transfer, which manifests itself through the insertion of cooperation clauses on drugs in international agreements, combined with technical and operational cooperation, whereas in the anti-corruption policy a 'softer' mode of governance is identified, which lays the emphasis on peer review, dialogue and the elaboration of national Action Plans.

The overarching goal of the EU's external anti-drugs policy is to assist third countries, including ENP countries, and key drug-producing and transit countries 'to be more effective in both drugs supply and demand reduction' (Council of the European Union 2004). The actions with which the EU intends to achieve this objective are the implementation of the UN Drugs Conventions (1961, 1971, 1988), and the UN Convention on Transnational Organised Crime, the elaboration of national drugs action plans, assistance for demand reduction measures and institution building in the law enforcement sector. The minutes of the Sub-Committee meetings with Moldova and Ukraine reveal that discussions have been limited to the presentation of the EU's activities. With Morocco, the EU refuses to talk about drugs before the country delivers on its promise to elaborate a National Drugs Strategy.[8] The overall external drugs policy puts a strong emphasis on supply reduction measures, as documents on the funding and the thematic distribution of EU Drug Projects confirm (Council of the European Union 2006). External drugs policy has received a further boost through the adoption of the European Security Strategy and the Strategy for the External Dimension of the Area of Freedom, Security and Justice, as both of these documents list drugs as one of the main threats to EU security (Council of the European Union 2003, 2005a).

In terms of the main mode of interaction in the drugs field, policy transfer based on the insertion of drugs cooperation clauses in international agreements prevails. All Association (AA) and Partnership and Cooperation

Agreements (PCA) contain a clause on the need to cooperate on drugs issues, and a recent EC regulation declares that preferential access to the internal market is dependent upon cooperation on drugs matters (Council of the European Union 2005b). The partner countries have committed themselves to implementing UN Conventions and to complying with the recommendations of the International Narcotics Board (INCB), the quasi-judicial monitoring body established by the UN. In other words, the EU is contributing to exporting the founding pillars of the global drugs prohibition regime to neighbouring countries hegemonically, i.e. by inserting mandatory drugs cooperation clauses and monitoring through international bodies. The promotion of the demand reduction and harm reduction, on the other hand, was delegated to development cooperation agencies. In this domain there are no binding international policy prescriptions.

In the external domain, networks are set up for training and capacity-building purposes. Training and capacity-building measures in the drugs field consist of financial, infrastructure support and the organization of training sessions. In the Eastern European ENP countries, the EU has launched a specific anti-drugs project, BUMAD (Belarus, Ukraine, Moldova Anti-Drugs programme). The latter is a joint EU/UNDP initiative that covers many activities, both in the field of capacity building for law enforcement officers and in the area of demand reduction (e.g. working with NGOs or the support of rehabilitation centres etc.). In some cases, the EU provides the country with support to conduct operations against drug trafficking, through Frontex operations in the south or the EU Border Assistance Mission (EUBAM) on the Moldovan–Ukrainian border.

The EU also hopes to attain a higher level of information exchange with the ENP countries by improving their methods of data collection, and by concluding association agreements between the ENP countries and Europol, and the European Judicial Network. Further important sources for data collection are the meetings of the Drugs Liaison Officers and the Dublin Group meetings in the neighbouring countries. These meetings bring together either the officials of member states (Liaison Officer Networks) or the authorities of member states and those of other drugs donor countries (USA, Norway, Japan and Australia). These networks are generally not accessible for representatives of the ENP countries, but, at times, the authorities of the host country are invited to meetings to provide supplementary information.[9]

The main objective of the EU's external anti-corruption policy is to promote a ring of well-governed countries in the neighbourhood. The actions listed to achieve the objective of 'better governance' are accession of the neighbouring countries to international conventions on fighting corruption, political dialogue, the elaboration of national action plans, technical cooperation with law enforcement agencies, involvement of civil society and the adoption of codes of conduct for civil servants. The Sub-Committee minutes show that the focus so far has been laid on the elaboration of National Anti-Corruption Action Plans. The relevance of the fight against corruption for security is stated in a number of documents (Council of the European Union

2003, 2005a), but, in practice, the EU has not forcefully promoted its policy outside of the enlargement context (Tivig and Maurer 2006).

The EU's interaction with third states in the field of anti-corruption is characterized by political dialogue in the south and by intensive socialization based on 'naming and shaming' through implementation networks in relations with Moldova and Ukraine. The EU bases its anti-corruption dialogue with third countries on international anti-corruption agreements, such as the 2003 United Nations Convention against Corruption and the Council of Europe's conventions. The EU has to resort to these international instruments, because it does not have an anti-corruption *acquis* that is exported readily to third countries.

In the area of anti-corruption the EU relies on cooperation with an implementation network, the Council of Europe's GRECO (*Groupe d'Etats contre la Corruption*) in relations with eastern neighbours. GRECO has been set up to implement and monitor implementation of the Council of Europe's anti-corruption instruments.[10] It is open to accession by all Council of Europe member states and other countries that participated in the elaboration of the agreement, such as, for example, the USA. The GRECO plenary brings together high-level officials from Ministries of Justice, Ministries of the Interior and specialized anti-corruption bodies. In a first step, the GRECO Plenary specifies the provisions of the Council of Europe's anti-corruption *acquis* on which the country evaluations will be based (e.g. financing of political parties). The evaluations are carried out by teams composed of experts designated by the member state and appointed by GRECO.[11] Replies to questionnaires, the intensive study of legislation and implementation practices, and on-site visits feed into the evaluation reports. The reports are drawn up at the end of the on-site visit, and the results are discussed with the authorities of the evaluated country. Finally, the reports and recommendations are submitted to a GRECO plenary meeting for adoption. The compliance with GRECO's recommendations is subject to monitoring under the compliance procedure. After adoption by the GRECO plenary, the reports and recommendations are made available on the internet.

The last instrument through which the EU promotes the principles of anti-corruption in neighbouring countries is technical assistance. Many of the assistance activities are carried out jointly with the Council of Europe under the Joint Programmes formula, according to which the EC finances or co-finances projects in Moldova and Ukraine.[12] Technical assistance activities cover study visits to the EU, training sessions on fighting corruption in various sectors, legal advice on drafting laws to protect whistle-blowers, information on how to further integrity in the public administration and the role of the press in anti-corruption. The anti-corruption activities, which are carried out in Eastern Europe have a broad focus extending to the involvement of civil society in the fight against corruption. By and large, these programmes fulfil the purpose of transferring Western rule of law standards to these countries. In the Mediterranean countries, technical assistance activities in the anti-corruption field are more limited. The EU has put in place a few MEDA technical assistance projects aimed at the modernization of the justice system, but those projects are focused strongly on enhancing the efficiency of the judiciary and less on eradicating corruption and improving the political environment of justice reform (Wichmann 2007b).

The Limits of External Governance

The case studies above give a mixed picture of JHA external governance. Our initial assumption was confirmed that, due to the internal structure of JHA cooperation and limited capacities to offer attractive incentives in the ENP, network governance is more frequent than hierarchical policy transfer through the conditionality method. However, these transgovernmental networks are not void of hegemonic traits and frequently reflect the dominance of EU interests and actors. On the one hand, this asymmetry in networks is due to the constellations of interdependence, where the EU's interest in cooperation is not matched by the third country. On the other hand, however, our case studies also reveal more endogenous limits to extended network governance that may apply also to other fields of external relations (Lavenex, Lehmkuhl, and Wichmann 2007; Lavenex 2008). To expand transgovernmental networks successfully the EU has to be able to rely on compatible administrative structures and expertise in the partner countries. Such networks require the existence of strong administrative actors, police officials or border guards with a certain degree of independence from central government, pertinent expertise and resources. In contrast to political actors, who must maintain national interests, technocrats and experts are apt to succumb to the functional, problem-orientated dynamics of mutual learning and adaptation that the EU seeks to unleash. Governance capacity also requires that the partner countries have an appropriate level of expertise in national administrations and that these bodies have the necessary financial resources at their disposal to ensure adequate implementation. Governance capacity does not merely refer to the resources of a third country, but it also has a 'qualitative' connotation. In other words, government capacity also alludes to the manner in which a third country exerts its repressive functions. Abidance to rule of law standards, compliance with international human rights standards and the absence of corruption in the state administration are crucial prerequisites for successful JHA cooperation. That these issues remain major challenges for the ENP countries is revealed, for example, in the GRECO evaluation reports on Ukraine and Moldova (*Groupe d'Etats contre la Corruption* 2006, 2007).

The two last crucial preconditions for external governance, both hierarchical and horizontal, concern the relation between the parties involved and, in particular, the high degree of legalization or institutionalization of overarching external relations and the degree to which both sides share fundamental values and trust each other. The overarching legal framework, Association Agreements and Partnership and Cooperation Agreements, need to foresee mechanisms for joint decision making, implementation and monitoring. In the absence of such provisions, the EU has to resort to softer mechanisms of interaction, such as political dialogue, which, due the voluntarism implied, no longer qualifies as governance. Whereas legalization is particularly important for hierarchical modes of interaction, socialization, mutual trust and the existence of a shared professional 'ethos' are co-substantial to network governance and transgovernmentalism (Benyon 1996; Den Boer 2005; Sheptycki 2000). The absolute centrality of these two factors became apparent during Eastern enlargement, when it proved difficult to intensify JHA cooperation with the acceding countries owing to the widespread distrust prevailing in the EU member states with respect to the policing practices of the Central and Eastern European Countries (Gregory 1994; Bigo 2000a). Adherence to common values, similar legal cultures and shared problem perceptions facilitate successful law enforcement cooperation. The absence of these background conditions in relations with ENP states constitutes a structural barrier to the extension of bottom-up, inclusive and voluntary modes of interaction.

Faced with these obstacles, the EU has started devising a number of tools to tackle the deficiencies in the areas of governance capacity. These shall also contribute to fostering a shared professional ethos, similar problem perceptions and, above all, an increase in the level of trust that the EU law enforcement agencies have in the ENP countries' authorities. The main instruments put in place to achieve this objective are the provision of technical assistance, as well as inter-administrative exchanges through twinnings and TAIEX activities (Tulmets 2007).[13] Another tool to foster governance capacity is the extension of vertical coordination networks in relations with ENP countries. Coordinating bodies or agencies, such as Europol, Eurojust, CEPOL, are becoming involved in information exchange through the conclusion of cooperation agreements, for example (Europol 2004). They thereby operate as information networks providing partner countries with technical assistance and expertise.[14]

The way in which the EU seeks to tackle the deficiencies reveals many new interesting research questions; in particular, it draws attention to the question of how network governance interacts with more hierarchical forms of steering. Indeed, one could argue that technical assistance networks are being used as a tool for 'socializing' third countries in to common European standards of law enforcement.[15] Hence, in the context of JHA cooperation, networks have come to serve the purpose of domination rather than engaging the partner countries in participatory governance.

Conclusion

The 'external dimension' has become an integral part of EU JHA cooperation. New notions of security not only entail a blurring of the distinction between internal and external threats, they also lead to new forms of political cooperation that transgress the traditional division between foreign and domestic policy. It has been argued that new and hybrid forms of political interaction are emerging, which result from an incapacity to exert policy transfer through conditionality.

Given asymmetries of interests between the EU and its neighbours, we expected a tendency towards more hierarchical, hegemonic modes of interaction, which would, however, be influenced by the consolidation of an internal *acquis* as well as supranational competence to act externally. The comparison between more and less communitarized policy fields yields a number of interesting findings. In cases where EC/EU legislation exists, we do observe a tendency for policy transfer, but the asymmetry of interests, the weakness of monitoring mechanisms and the absence of compensatory rewards limit the portent of this model of interaction.

In order to cope with these obstacles, two hitherto under-investigated strategies of interaction have developed. First, in the more intergovernmental areas of JHA, the lack of an own *acquis* does not preclude attempts at legislative approximation. In this case, the EU compensates the lack of internal templates with the mobilization of international conventions and their monitoring mechanisms. Similar to traditional policy transfer, however, and although this strategy may increase the legitimacy of EU requirements, it lacks strong leverage in cases when it does not meet the interest of the third countries.

The second strategy identified, which corresponds to the internal predominance of transgovernmentalism in JHA, is the extension of network governance. Yet, at least in the short run, without a common legal background and mutual trust, these networks lack their social fabric. Differences in problem perceptions and lack of trust undermine their effectiveness and integrative dynamics in terms of participatory structures and joint decision making. Either the third states send high-ranking officials who, rejecting the idea of functional cooperation, politicize the networks and move them closer to classic intergovernmentalism, or the third state representatives lack the necessary resources to participate on equal footing in the deliberations. Under these circumstances, transgovernmental networks are a hitherto under-investigated vehicle for policy transfer through 'softer' means, adding to the EU's toolbox in extending external security governance in spite of a lack of leverage through conditionality.

Acknowledgement

This paper was written in the framework of a broader cooperative research project entitled 'Inside-Out. New Modes of Governance in relations with non-Member States' within the NEWGOV consortium funded under EU-contract no. CIT1-CT-2004-506392. Other areas of external governance covered in the project are environmental, transport and research policy. For an overview of the first overall project results, see Lavenex, Lehmkuhl, and Wichmann (2007). Funding by the European Commission and Swiss State Secretariat State Secretariat for Education and Research (SER) is gratefully acknowledged.

Notes

1. Algeria, Armenia, Azerbaijan, Belarus, Egypt, Georgia, Israel, Jordan, Lebanon, Libya, Moldova, Morocco, the Palestinian Authority, Syria, Tunisia and Ukraine.

2. Under the term 'internal security', we understand the entirety of activities covered by the EU under the title cooperation on Justice and Home Affairs. This means that we include cooperation on asylum and irregular migration. In police and judicial cooperation, we have decided to focus on two issue areas linked to the fight against organized crime (cf. section on case selection).
3. This emphasis on quasi-hierarchical instruments in external action departs from some important elements of the original governance literature, which takes its point of departure in the broader transformation from the interventionist to the cooperative state (Mayntz 2005).
4. In order to avoid conceptual confusion with EU jargon, we modify Slaughter's terminology slightly and speak of implementation instead of enforcement networks and regulatory instead of harmonization networks.
5. Here, we draw on Slaughter's differentiation of networks.
6. The first ENP country to carry out a twinning 'light' project with the EU in the area of migration and border management is Morocco.
7. Morocco's input on this strategy can be retraced in the documents of the subcommittee meetings on 'social affairs and migration' as well as the recent 'JHA subcommittee' and was confirmed in interviews with Commission officials, such as with DG JLS representatives on 17 April 2007 and 3 May 2007.
8. Interview DG JLS, May 2006.
9. Interview DG JLS, May 2005.
10. Council of Europe's Civil and Criminal Law Conventions and the Council of Europe's Twenty Guiding Principles on Fighting Corruption.
11. Each country presents a list of three to five available experts on a given question. For each evaluation, GRECO appoints experts for carrying out the assessment. They make sure that the teams are representative and that there is at least one country expert. Interview GRECO Secretariat, June 2007.
12. http://www.jp.coe.int/CEAD/JP/Default.asp (accessed 6 May 2007) provides an overview of the joint projects with the Council.
13. Twinning is a cooperation tool aimed at developing the capacity of the public administration in enlargement and ENP countries. It involves the longer-term secondment of an EU expert to the administration of a partner country. TAIEX assistance covers a number of short-term activities, such as seminars, study visits and workshops in the partner country on JHA issues, for example.
14. See, for example, CEPOL's involvement in the regional Eurmed programme. At times, the agencies are also asked to provide TAIEX seminars or similar activities for third countries. Interview Europeaid, May 2007.
15. This 'instrumental' reasoning was apparent in a series of interviews conducted in April–May 2007 in Brussels.

References

Benyon, J. 1996. Policing the European Union: The changing basis of cooperation on law enforcement. *International Affairs* 70, no. 3: 497–517.

Bigo, D. 2000a. *Border regimes and security in an enlarged European Community police co-operation with CEECs: Between trust and obligation.* Working Paper 2000/65. Florence: EUI.

Bigo, D. 2000b. Liaison officers in Europe, new actors in the European security field. In *Issues in transnational policing*, ed. J. Sheptycki, 67–100. London: Routledge.

Bigo, D. 2001. The Möbius Ribbon of internal and external security(ies). In *Identities, borders, orders — Rethinking IR theory, borderlines, vol. 18*, eds. M. Albert, D. Jacobson and Y. Lapid, 91–116. Minneapolis: Univ. Minnesota Press.

Carrera, S. 2007. *The EU border management strategy — FRONTEX and the challenges of irregular immigration in the Canary Islands.* Working Document 261/March 2007. Brussels: CEPS.

Cassarino, J.-P. 2007. Informalising readmission agreements in the EU neighbourhood. *International Spectator* 42, no. 2: 179–96.

Council of the European Union. 2003. *A secure Europe in a better world — European Security Strategy.*

Council of the European Union. 2004. *15074/04, EU Drugs Strategy 2005–2012.*

Council of the European Union. 2005a. *14366/05, A strategy for the external dimension of JHA: Global freedom, security and justice — Contribution of the Council Secretariat.*

Council of the European Union. 2005b. Council Regulation No. 980/2005 of 27 June 2005 applying a scheme of generalised tariff preferences. *Official Journal of the EU* L169 (June 30).

Council of the European Union. 2006. 9376/06, *The level of funding and the geographic and thematic distribution of EU drug projects*.

Cremona, M., and C. Hillion. 2006. L'Union fait la force? Potential and limitations of the European Neighbourhood Policy as an integrated EU Foreign and Security Policy. Working Paper LAW No. 2006/39. Florence: EUI.

Den Boer, M. 2005. Copweb Europe — venues, virtues and vexations of transnational policing. In *Transnational Europe — Towards a common political space*, eds. W. Kaiser and P. Starie, 191–209. London: Routledge.

EU–Ukraine Co-operation Council. 2007. *Revised EU–Ukraine action plan freedom, security and justice: Challenges and strategic aims*.

European Commission. 2002. Communication from the Commission to the Council and the European Parliament — Integrating migration issues in the European Union's relations with third states. COM (2002) 703 final.

European Commission. 2003. Wider Europe — Neighbourhood: A new framework for relations with our eastern and southern neighbours. COM (2003) 104 final.

European Commission. 2004a. *Plan propose d'action UE/Maroc*.

European Commission. 2004b. *Plan propose d'action UE/Tunisie*.

European Commission. 2004c. *Proposed EU/Moldova Action Plan*.

European Commission. 2005a. Communication on a strategy on the external dimension of the Area of Freedom, Security and Justice, COM (2005) 491 final.

European Commission. 2005b. Communication on priority actions for responding to the challenges of migration: First follow-up to Hampton Court, COM (2005) 621 final.

European Commission. 2005c. Communication on regional protection programmes, COM (2005) 388 final.

European Commission. 2005d. Second annual report to the European Parliament and the Council on the implementation of the AGIS programme, YEAR 2004, SEC (2005) 1764.

Europol. 2004. 9670/04, *Europol's External Relations*.

Geddes, A. 2006. Europeanisation goes south: The external dimension of EU migration and asylum policy. *Zeitschrift für Staats- und Europawissenschaften/Journal for Comparative Government and European Policy* 3, no. 2: 275–93.

Gregory, F. 1994. Unprecedented partnerships in crime control: law enforcement issues and linkages between Eastern and Western Europe since 1989. In *Policing across national boundaries*, eds. M. Anderson and M. Den Boer, 85–105. London: Pinter Publishers.

Groupe d'Etats contre la Corruption. 2006. Second evaluation report — Evaluation report on Moldova.

Groupe d'Etats contre la Corruption. 2007. Joint first and second evaluation rounds — Evaluation report on Ukraine.

Herdina, A. 2005. The European Neighbourhood Policy (ENP) — A partnership for reform. Paper presented at the Institute of European Affairs, Dublin.

Kelley, J. 2006. New wine in old wine skins: Policy adaptation in the European Neighbourhood Policy. *Journal of Common Market Studies* 44, no. 1: 29–55.

Lavenex, S. 2004. EU external governance in 'wider Europe'. *Journal of European Public Policy* 11, no. 4: 688–708.

Lavenex, S. 2006. Shifting up and out: the foreign policy of European immigration control. *West European Politics* 29, no. 2: 329–50.

Lavenex, S. 2008. A governance perspective on the European Neighbourhood Policy: integration beyond conditionality? *Journal of European Public Policy* 15: 938–55.

Lavenex, S., and R. Kunz. 2008. The migration–development nexus in EU external relations. *Journal of European Integration* 30, no. 3: 439–57.

Lavenex, S., D. Lehmkuhl, and N. Wichmann. 2007. Die Nachbarschaftspolitiken der Europäischen Union: zwischen Hegemonie und erweiterter Governance. In *Politische Vierteljahresschrift Sonderheft 40/2007*, ed. I. Tömmel, 367–88. Wiesbaden: VS Verlag für Sozialwissenschaften.

Lavenex, S., and E. Uçarer. 2002. *Migration and the externalities of European integration*. Lanham, MD: Lexington Books.

Lavenex, S., and W. Wallace. 2005. Justice and Home Affairs: 'Towards a European public order?'. In *Policy-making in the European Union,* eds. H. Wallace, W. Wallace and M. Pollack, 457–80. Oxford: Oxford Univ. Press.

Longo, F. 2003. The export of the fight against organized crime policy model and the EU's international actorness. In *Understanding the European Union's external relations,* eds. M. Knodt and S. Princen, 158–72. London: Routledge.

Lutterbeck, D. 2005. Blurring the dividing line: The convergence of internal and external security in Western Europe. *European Security* 14, no. 2: 231–53.

Magen, A. 2006. The shadow of enlargement: Can the European Neighbourhood Policy achieve compliance?. *Columbia Journal of European Law* 12: 383–427.

Maier, S., and F. Schimmelfennig. 2007. Shared values: Democracy and human rights. In *Governing Europe's neighbourhood,* eds. M. Baun, M.E. Smith and K. Weber, 39–57. Manchester: Manchester Univ. Press.

Mayntz, R. 2005. Governance theory als fortenwickelte Steuerungstheorie?. In *Governance-Forschung, Vergewisserung über Stand und Entwicklungslinien,* ed. G.F. Schuppert, 11–20. Baden-Baden: Nomos.

Pastore, F. 2002. The asymmetrical fortress: The problem of relations between internal and external security policies in the European Union. In *Police and justice cooperation and the new European borders,* eds. M. Anderson and J. Apap, 81–102. The Hague: Kluwer Law International.

Presidency. 2002. Conclusions of Euro-Mediterranean conference of foreign ministers, Valencia 22–23 April 2002.

Schalken, T., and M. Pronk. 2002. On joint investigation teams, Europol and supervision of their joint actions. *European Journal of Crime, Criminal Law and Criminal Justice* 10, no. 1: 7–82.

Schimmelfennig, F., and U. Sedelmeier. 2004. Governance by conditionality: EU rule transfer to the candidate countries of Central and Eastern Europe. *Journal of European Public Policy* 11, no. 4: 661–79.

Sheptycki, J. 2000. *Issues in transnational policing.* London: Routledge.

Slaughter, A.-M. 1997. The real new world order. *Foreign Affairs* 76, no. 5: 183–97.

Slaughter, A.-M. 2004. *A new world order.* Princeton: Princeton Univ. Press.

Söderköping Process. 2005. Roadmap of the Söderköping Process, http://soderkoping.org.ua/files/en/pub/ROADMAP_eng2.pdf (accessed July 7, 2006).

Tivig, A., and A. Maurer. 2006. *Die EU-Antikorruptionspolitik — Erfolgsbedingungen einer Korruptionsbekämpfung auf mehreren Ebenen.* Diskussionspapier der FG 1, 2006/03. Berlin: SWP Berlin.

Trauner, F. 2007. *EU Justice and Home Affairs strategy in the Western Balkans — Conflicting objectives in the pre-accession strategy.* Working Document 259/February 2007. Brussels: CEPS.

Tulmets, E. 2007. Policy adaptation from the enlargement to the Neighbourhood Policy: A way to improve the EU's external capabilities?. *Politique Européenne* 20, no. 2: 55–80.

Wallace, H. 2000. The policy process. A moving pendulum. In *Policy-making in the European Union,* eds. H. Wallace and W. Wallace, 39–64. Oxford: Oxford Univ. Press.

Weyembergh, A. 2006. Approximation of criminal laws, the Constitutional Treaty and the Hague Programme. *Common Market Law Review* 42: 1567–97.

Wichmann, N. 2007a. *The intersection between Justice and Home Affairs and the European Neighbourhood Policy: Stocktaking logics, objectives and practices.* CEPS Working Document 275/October 2007. Brussels: CEPS.

Wichmann, N. 2007b. Promoting the rule of law in the ENP — Strategic or normative power EU. *Politique Européenne* 20, no. 2: 81–104.

Wolff, S. 2007. La dimension méditerranéenne de la politique Justice et Affaires intérieures. *Cultures et Conflits* 66: 77–99.

Wolff, S., N. Wichmann, and G. Mounier. 2009. The external dimension of Justice and Home Affairs: A different security agenda for the EU?. *Journal of European Integration* 31, no. 1: 9–23.

The Externalization of JHA Policies in Georgia: Partner or Hotbed of Threats?

LILI DI PUPPO

PhD candidate, European Viadrina University, Frankfurt/Oder, Germany

ABSTRACT This paper argues that the European Union's attempts to externalize JHA policies and turn neighbouring countries into partners contributing to its internal security are hampered by numerous factors, including its obvious ambivalence towards these countries. The limitations of pursuing internal security objectives through a 'soft' partnership approach are particularly visible in the South Caucasus. The paper examines the EU's policies in Georgia and finds that they lack strategic vision and coherence. EU activity in Georgia illustrates three major challenges to the export of JHA policies in the neighbourhood: (1) the form of relations between the EU and its supposed partners ('modes of governance'); (2) the EU's policies vs. local expectations; and (3) the contradictions in the EU's objectives (democracy vs. efficiency).

Introduction

In its neighbourhood, the European Union is attempting to promote long-term democratic and market-based reforms with the aim of sustainably changing its environment. At the same time, it is addressing short-term 'soft' security threats through cooperation with neighbouring countries. A number of these threats (e.g. organized crime, terrorism, trafficking) fall under the domain of Justice and Home Affairs (JHA). JHA-related issues have gained a prominent place in the cooperation agreements signed under the European Neighbourhood Policy (ENP) framework. The South Caucasus is an area that represents some of the new types of security threats identified by the EU in its 2003 security strategy.

Using Georgia as an example, I want to illustrate the difficulty of externalizing JHA policies in the EU's neighbourhood. It is argued that both the form and content of the EU's JHA policies in Georgia are incoherent and thus fail to produce a strategic vision. The incoherence stems from the EU's attempt to deploy a partnership approach within the context of a securitization strategy. EU–Georgia relations, in turn, reflect a more fundamental dilemma between security and integration in the neighbourhood policies.[1] I will analyse three different aspects of the EU's JHA policies in my discussion of the dilemmas faced by the EU: (1) ambiguity in the form of relations; (2) diverging views regarding the contents of the EU's policies; and (3) contradictory EU objectives. The first challenge is concerned with the form of relations the EU wants to establish with neighbouring countries. The EU's position with respect to the South Caucasus countries is clearly ambivalent. On the one hand, these nations are viewed as failing states that potentially represent a source of threats. At the same time, they are being wooed as partners in the EU's endeavour to address 'common threats'. Secondly, the EU tends to define threats in its neighbourhood from its own perspective, and the EU's vision of security does not necessarily correspond to local security needs. Georgia is preoccupied with state building and regaining its territorial integrity. In the absence of a consensus on what constitutes threats, the EU might find it difficult to convince neighbouring countries of the benefits of contributing to its security. The EU wants to intervene in Georgia's domestic affairs, while nevertheless 'keeping it at arm's length' (Lynch 2006, 69). Finally, the EU's JHA policies in Georgia try to reconcile normative and strategic goals, with ambiguous results. To show this, various examples of JHA policies in Georgia, such as the EU's 2004 'rule-of-law mission' (EUJUST Themis), as well as the attempts to reform the criminal justice and penitentiary system in post-revolutionary Georgia, will be analysed in detail.

Rational choice institutionalism assumes that an actor's behaviour is constrained by its institutional environment. The institutional setting determines the incentive structure and the cost–benefit calculus of the rational actor. The EU's JHA activities in Georgia are driven by the pursuit of internal security objectives within an ENP framework. The EU has not defined clear foreign policy goals in the South Caucasus.

The evolution of the JHA or Area of Justice, Freedom and Liberty (AJFL) domains has been influenced by the increasing fuzziness in the boundary between internal and external security in the EU's strategic thinking. JHA issues have become a major aspect of the EU's relations with third countries, as reflected in their prominence in cooperation agreements, in particular the recent ENP Action Plans. Literature on external governance provides a conceptual framework to analyse how JHA, a policy designed to address internal policy goals, is increasingly being externalized. Lavenex (2004, 682) defined external governance as the extension of the regulatory scope of parts of the *acquis communautaire* to the EU's neighbourhood through the inclusion of third countries in the pursuit of EU's internal policy goals. In this process, internal and foreign policy goals come together. Lavenex referred to M. Smith's (1996) distinction between different EU boundaries: geopolitical, institutional/legal, transactional and cultural. External governance shifts the EU's 'legal boundary' to include neighbouring countries, but the opening of the 'institutional boundary' is limited. Prodi has characterized the ENP as 'everything but institutions'; it does not offer membership, yet does not entirely preclude it, either. Lavenex (2004, 681) distinguished two goals in the EU's neighbourhood policies: increasing the efficiency and the problem-solving capacity of internal policies (functional needs) and stabilizing the neighbourhood (foreign policy goals).

Increasingly, internal JHA policy objectives are being pursued with foreign policy instruments, such as European Security and Defence Policy (ESDP) missions. JHA is not only a first (asylum and immigration) or third (police and judicial cooperation in criminal matters) pillar issue, but has been integrated into the second pillar as an element of the Common Foreign and Security Policy (CFSP). New ESDP missions targeting the reform of the police and justice systems in third countries, such as a police mission in Bosnia-Herzegovina and rule of law missions in Georgia and Iraq, illustrate this trend. ESDP missions are civilian crisis management operations aimed at security sector reform in failed states. The security sector encompasses various institutions, including the armed forces, police, border guards and the judiciary, whose function is to guarantee public safety and order. Institution building and the strengthening of the rule of law are viewed by the EU as tools to create a safe environment, which it feels the military alone cannot provide. This combination of JHA objectives with foreign policy instruments results in the merging of different agendas, i.e. a development agenda with a security agenda. However, this combination can easily lead to incoherence in the EU's external policies and raise confusion about the EU's role as an external actor. As Berenskoetter (2006, 13) remarked, 'Turning instruments and strategies of domestic law enforcement ... into instruments of foreign policy involves significant adjustments'. In the following, I aim to demonstrate how this lack of coherence reveals itself in different dimensions of EU–Georgia relations.

Threat Perceptions in the South Caucasus: Partners or Sources of Threats?

In its attempts to project JHA policies into its neighbourhood, the EU is confronted with the challenge of how to shape its relations with bordering countries. The clash between the two different logics the EU deploys in its relations with neighbouring countries, i.e. 'the politics of inclusion' and the 'politics of exclusion' (Smith 1996), is particularly evident in the South Caucasus. The South Caucasus countries are identified as 'outsiders', 'others' and 'threats' in the form of failing states, but they are also viewed as partners in the pursuit of the EU's policy goals, countries that could potentially benefit from the construction of an area of stability.

Security considerations inform the EU's relations with neighbouring countries. As Lavenex (2004, 685) remarked, the externalization of the EU's internal policies in its neighbourhood is driven by the EU's perceptions of interdependence and vulnerability. The EU tends to look at the South Caucasus through a security lens. As a major transit region between Central Asia and Europe, the South Caucasus is an area replete with the new security threats that are identified in the EU's security strategy: state failure, organized crime, terrorism, money laundering and illegal migration. According to Lynch (2006, 8), Georgia embodies the main challenges that the EU faces as a security actor at the start of the twenty-first century. The South Caucasus first entered the EU's 'radar' as a security threat in a footnote in the 2003 Communication on a Wider Europe, illustrating how the EU is constantly redrawing its boundaries as a result of its security perceptions.[2]

The concept of security interdependence forms the core of the EU's security strategy and implies that the EU's security begins beyond its borders. As the EU's security strategy states, 'The first line of defense will often be abroad' (European Security Strategy 2003). Internal security is linked to the exercise of national sovereignty on a defined territory. Its main instruments are policing, prosecution, the administration of justice and border control (Monar 2006, 497). Policing and the administration of justice are traditionally the prerogatives of a domestic authority, however, and do not belong to the domain of foreign policy. In its 2003 security strategy, the EU formulated a new concept of internal security, which is defined neither territorially nor militarily. The strategy cites new security threats, such as energy security, migration flows, demography, failing states and organized crime. Although these threats originate in territories outside the EU's borders, particularly in weak or failed states in the EU's neighbourhood, they have an impact on the EU's internal security. As a consequence, the problems these states have with policing and ensuring domestic order are seen as directly affecting the EU's security. The reform of the neighbouring countries' security apparatus is thus an EU concern. The EU tries to consolidate cooperation with neighbouring countries in combating these threats through agreements. To this end, it has developed a range of instruments in recent years to intervene in issues of domestic order in third countries, with the ultimate objective of transforming neighbouring countries into partners in security.

However, the EU faces certain challenges when trying to incorporate neighbouring countries into its security planning in that it also considers these nations to be potential exporters of instability. While the blurring between 'inside' and 'outside' is a central tenet of the EU's security thinking, these two categories still appear to determine relations with neighbouring countries. The EU tends to project a threat image onto its neighbourhood (Berenskoetter 2006, 14). The EU's security strategy states that 'Neighbours who are engaged in violent conflict, weak states where organised crime flourishes, dysfunctional societies or exploding population growth on its borders all pose problems for Europe' (European Security Strategy 2003, 7). The image of weak or failing states as territories nurturing organized crime, terrorism and other threats guides the EU's security thinking. Its citizens, meanwhile, are also viewed as security threats, as potential illegal migrants or victims of trafficking. While in EU declarations neighbouring countries are also referred to as 'borderlands' that can help to contain the threats emerging from unstable areas, the Southern Caucasus has been mentioned as a zone of instability in the EU's security strategy.

Diez (2005, 613) argued that the discursive construction of a European identity as a normative power has an 'othering' quality, as it has the effect of turning third parties into 'others'.[3] The EU constructs its identity against an image of others in the 'outside world' (Diez 2005, 614). The ENP's discourse tends to present the EU as a 'civilized island' surrounded by a disorderly and dangerous neighbourhood. Smith (1996, 14) referred to this particular representation of the EU as an 'island of stability' as the construction of a 'geopolitical boundary'. In the neighbourhood, the EU applies two different forms of 'othering': the representation of the 'other' as an existential threat ('securitization') and the representation of the 'other' as 'violating universal principles' (Diez 2005, 628, 629). While the second form of othering was applied during the enlargement process, in which the Copenhagen criteria set the standards for EU membership, the securitization strategy is applied to the neighbourhood within the discourse on values. At the same time, the EU is constantly redrawing boundaries in the post-Cold War context, oscillating between 'the politics of inclusion' and 'the politics of exclusion'. A fixed set of boundaries can no longer contain disturbances in the EU's environment, however, and the EU must thus develop new methods to contain new threats (Smith 1996, 23). Neighbouring countries are not clear 'outsiders' in that the EU wants to transform them into partners who can help further the EU's objectives abroad. The ENP aims at creating a 'ring of well-governed countries' and 'friends'; there is eagerness to avoid the emergence of 'new dividing lines in Europe', and it is implied that neighbouring countries can also benefit from the construction of an area of stability. Referring to boundaries, Smith (1996, 23) said, 'In relation to the changing European order, they uncover the tension between the notion of the EU as an island and an example, and the impression that the EU's benefits can be multilateralized and disseminated'.

The EU's ambivalence towards its neighbouring countries, such as Georgia, has consequences on the form of relations that it tries to establish with them. The EU oscillates between two different approaches, soft partnership and a securitization strategy, both of which are problematic. In the 'partnership approach', the EU defines the threats to its security as 'common threats', with the promise of including neighbouring countries in an 'area of stability and prosperity'. Viewing Europe as a 'civilian power', Duchêne (1973, quoted in Lavenex 2004, 684) described how the 'domestication' of inter-state relations brings to international problems a sense of common responsibility and introduces structures of contractual politics, mechanisms that had previously been reserved for domestic affairs. However, exporting the civilian approach outside the EU is questionable in the absence of membership prospects for the ENP countries, and the use of conditionality departs from the voluntarism implicit in the concept of civilian power (Lavenex 2004, 684). Furthermore, in order for a soft approach to be effective, the EU needs to offer substantial incentives to convince neighbouring countries of the benefits of cooperating in tackling threats to the EU's security. The use of conditionality — both positive and negative — evidently has a limited impact within the ENP framework. While the concept of a single 'area of freedom, security and justice' (AFSJ) is an attempt at transcending the territoriality principle inherent in the concept of internal security, the neighbourhood is also presented as a future coherent 'area of stability and prosperity'. Nevertheless, the creation of a single area with the EU remains a vague prospect in the absence of clear membership commitments. Moreover, this inclusion of partner countries in an 'area of stability and prosperity' is not benevolent, but motivated by strategic interests. As noted by Lavenex (2004, 695), there is a strategic aspect in the EU's projection of values, '[e]specially when applied towards third countries which lack the prospect of membership, the attempt to extend the EU's legal boundary is not only a benevolent projection of acquired civilian virtues but also a more strategic attempt to gain control over policy developments through external governance'. The EU's relations with its neighbourhood tend to be rather asymmetrical, as it is the EU that sets the terms and conditions of the relations and defines to what extent neighbouring countries have made progress or not towards 'common values'. The EU defines what these 'common values' are, as well as the nature of 'common security threats'. The two forms of logic that shape the EU's relations with its neighbours are visible in the Council's declaration on a strategy for the external dimension of JHA. As stated in the declaration, 'The development of the area of freedom, security and justice can only be successful if it is underpinned by a partnership with third countries on these issues' and 'EU action is most effective where it is based on a partnership with third countries to tackle common problems and meet shared policy objectives' (European Council 2005, 2, 5). However, the declaration states in the next sentence,

> The EU should use its significant relationship with third countries as an incentive for them to adopt and implement relevant international standards and obligations on JHA issues. Countries should be aware that the nature of their relationship with the EU will be positively affected by their level of co-operation, given the central importance of these issues for the EU and its Member States (European Council 2005, 5).

The declaration thus tries to have it both ways: after defining JHA issues as 'common problems' and 'shared policy objectives' for EU member states and ENP countries alike, it goes on to suggest that the neighbouring countries will be rewarded for their cooperation. The 'borderlands' are hence cast as both equals and subordinates or 'others'. This mixed message shows the ambiguity in the EU's relations with third countries in the pursuit of JHA objectives.

The major problem that the EU encounters in shaping relations with neighbouring countries, such as Georgia, is that the countries in question do not share the EU's conception of what constitutes a threat. The rather weak incentives to enlist as partners contributing to the EU's security are compounded by the presence of differing priorities. Ambiguities in the form of the transfer of norms and standards are thus coupled with scepticism towards the content of the EU's policies.

EU and Georgia: Diverging Expectations?

In its attempts to mould domestic areas linked to public order and security through ESDP missions in the neighbourhood, the EU provides technical assistance and cooperation based on its own notions of security and order. These notions, of course, derive from its own experiences and needs, and do not necessarily reflect the concerns of the recipients of its aid. The EU thus projects European standards of internal security and imposes its own solutions to the problems it identifies. Law enforcement institutions must not only be made more effective, but these institutions must also be 'Europeanized' and their reform guided by EU standards. The Commission communication on a strategy on the external dimension of AJFL states, 'The projection of the values underpinning the area of freedom, security and justice is essential in order to safeguard the internal security of the EU' (European Commission 2005, 3). The question is whether the EU is successful in exporting its vision of the problems affecting the neighbourhood. Its perceptions might not necessarily be in line with local demands and expectations. Following a short overview of the EU's engagement in Georgia, I will explain how the EU's threat perception diverges from Georgia's own security needs.

The EU's policies towards the South Caucasus have been the object of a continuous debate between different EU member states over the last fifteen years. The EU views the resolution of conflicts as a precondition for increased EU involvement in the region. The EU's perception of its own role in the settlement of conflicts is rather uncertain; it has limited itself to supporting the Organisation for Security and Cooperation in Europe's (OSCE) conflict resolution efforts. The EU has traditionally had a cautious attitude with a weak presence in conflict negotiating mechanisms and no involvement in mediation, but it has upgraded its profile in recent years. The EU is engaged in 'conflict management' rather than in 'conflict resolution' in the South Caucasus (Tchanturia 2007). It has supported the rehabilitation of the conflict zones and confidence-building measures and has become the largest donor in the secessionist territories of Abkhazia and South Ossetia. The first phase of the EU's assistance to Georgia consisted of technical assistance in specific areas. The Partnership and Cooperation Agreement (PCA) signed in 1999 between the EU and Georgia provides the legal framework for EU–Georgia relations. The Commission has focused traditionally on four main areas: governance and rule of law with support for institution building, support for market reforms, addressing the social consequences of transition, and conflict resolution. Until recently, the TACIS programme was the instrument for financing projects in these areas. Starting in 2007, financial assistance took the form of budgetary support with the introduction of the European Neighbourhood Partnership Instrument (ENPI). No emphasis was put on the political dimension of the EU–Georgia relations within the PCA framework; the focus was on technical and economic assistance. The EU's assistance to Georgia amounted to 420 million between 1992 and 2004. Despite substantial EU assistance, Georgia did not achieve any visible results during former president Eduard Shevardnadze's terms in office (1995–2003). Along with the kidnapping of an EU expert in Tbilisi in 2002, this lack of results led to the revision of the Country Strategy Paper. New priorities were thus defined for 2003–2006, with a stronger emphasis on rule of law, support for civil society, poverty reduction and conflict resolution. The Council has become more involved in the region since the appointment of an EU Special Representative (EUSR) for the South Caucasus in 2003, whose task is to develop recommendations for the peaceful resolution of conflicts. The 2004 Rose Revolution was a determining factor behind the decision to include the Southern Caucasus in the ENP, whereby a rule of law mission to Georgia was launched in 2004 and the EUSR's mandate was extended in 2005. In the 2003 Communication on Wider Europe, the South Caucasus initially was excluded from the ENP due to its geographical location (European Commission 2003, 4). The South Caucasus was mentioned in the EU's security strategy published the same year, however: 'We should take a stronger interest in the problems of the Southern Caucasus, which in due course will also be a neighbouring region' (European Security Strategy 2003, 8). Since 2004, the Commission has provided advice to the Georgian Ministry of Justice, which focuses on penitentiary reform (e.g. the establishment of a probation service, the strengthening of the penitentiary administration and the rehabilitation of the penitentiary infrastructure). It has also provided assistance to the Prosecutor's office and to the Ministry of Internal Affairs; the aim is to reform the Ministry into a civilian institution (Helly 2006, 89).

The EU's tendency to define threats and solutions in its neighbourhood from its own perspective is visible in Georgian reactions to the deployment of an EU rule of law mission in 2004. This mission to Georgia, also known as EUJUST Themis, operated from June 2004 to July 2005. The first of its kind, it built to a certain extent on the previous Commission work in the justice sector, but this time under an ESDP framework. The mission was viewed as a contribution to political stability in Georgia in its post-transition phase. It was also considered to be a solution to potential security problems in Georgia, as well as a way to defuse the risk of regional instability (European Council 2004). The mission's stated objectives were to provide guidance to the Georgian government in implementing the new criminal justice reform strategy; to support the overall coordinating role of the relevant Georgian authorities in the field of judicial reform and anti-corruption; to aid in the planning of new legislation as necessary; and, as an additional point, to assist in the development of international as well as regional cooperation in the area of criminal justice (European Council 2004). The mission was also an attempt to conciliate short-term security measures with long-term assistance for institutional reform (Helly 2006, 92).

The rule of law mission was not exactly the type of support that the Georgian government had envisioned from the EU after the Rose Revolution.[4]

The Georgian government, instead, wished for more direct EU assistance with short-term national security issues, including help in resolving conflicts and training for border guards. In fact, it wanted conflict resolution to be the first priority in the ENP Action Plan (Popescu 2007, 9). As it turns out, Georgia appears more interested in promoting a traditional concept of domestic security, i.e. one based on the classical categories of territorial sovereignty and the state monopoly on violence, than in embracing the protection of the EU's internal security against transnational threats. The Georgian government would like to see the EU use traditional diplomatic overtures rather than soft instruments and become more engaged in conflict resolution. Until now, however, the EU has been rather reluctant to engage directly in conflict resolution, preferring to defer to the OSCE's efforts. Compared to other players in the region, the EU favours the use of soft instruments and rejects zero-sum approaches. As Lynch (2006, 72) observed, '[t]he EU does not act in the same geopolitical game with the US and Russia'. After Russia vetoed the continuation of the OSCE border monitoring mission at the Russo-Georgian border in 2004, Georgia invited the EU to take over the border mission from the OSCE. The EU refused to assume control of the mission under the EU flag, offering instead the more modest option of deploying a small team of experts under the EUSR. This decision showed that the EU's policy in the South Caucasus is constrained by the reluctance of certain EU member states to irritate Russia. The EU preferred to engage in low profile missions. The Georgian–Russian conflict of August 2008 has forced the EU to upgrade its involvement in Georgia. EU member states agreed in September 2008 on the deployment an EU observer mission.

The Georgian government's post-Rose Revolution priorities are obvious: the defence budget reached almost 1.5 billion Georgian laris in 2007 and 1.1 billion Georgian laris in 2008 (about $US850 million for 2007 and $US623 million for 2008) (Civil Georgia 2008). The fight against corruption and organized crime is one of its top priorities. These objectives are integrated into a more ambitious state-building and modernization project that also aims at the restoration of the state's legitimacy and normative influence. The Georgian government is also trying to combat organized crime networks, as well as the traditional tolerance towards criminal groups in Georgian society; in other words, the state is determined to eradicate parallel monopolies of violence. As a result of this repressive logic, the prison's population has increased dramatically (nearly doubling since the Rose Revolution) and new prison facilities are being built. The Georgian government's objective is more to inspire respect for the state than for the rule of law. It follows a 'law and order' logic relying on 'efficient' and loyal law enforcement agencies. Major government efforts have targeted the reform of security structures, and have apparently succeeded in improving the police's image among the population and inspiring confidence in it.[5] At the same time, human rights associations and opposition parties are increasingly critical of the government's repressive approach. The government defends its heavy-handed style as necessary for restoring respect for the state, which has long been associated with foreign rule. Fear of punishment by the state is seen as a means of ensuring that laws are respected, even if the government itself is increasingly perceived as violating them. In a country where parallel justice systems and sources of violence previously were allowed to flourish, the state must now be seen as the sole player. The EU and the Georgian government thus have very different understandings of the rule of law. The former places emphasis on predictability and legal certainty for business and investments, as well as a judiciary that is both modelled on the EU's standards and capable of implementing them. The latter's vision of 'law and order' is based on the restoration of state control via the destruction of parallel sources of legitimacy and violence.[6]

Another example of how the EU tries to define threats and solutions in the South Caucasus in the JHA domain is the Integrated Border Management project. The EU hopes to develop a single border management system for the whole South Caucasus region (Armenia, Azerbaijan and Georgia), entailing cooperation between the three countries' law-enforcement agencies. The project's objectives are to increase efficiency in the fight against drugs and human trafficking as well as to prevent conflicts.[7] Similar EU projects include the Border Management Programme for Central Asia (BOMCA), plus a border management project between Ukraine and Moldova. However, seen from a South Caucasus perspective, the project appears to be difficult to implement, especially given Azerbaijan's reluctance to engage in regional projects with Armenia.[8] Georgia, for its part, has expressed its interest in being included in a Black Sea dimension with Ukraine, rather than as part of the South Caucasus region. In the document 'Priorities of the Georgian government for the ENP Action Plan', the Georgian government claims to want 'to promote regional cooperation with respect to Integrated Border Management within the framework of the Black Sea region as well as the South Caucasus'.[9] Furthermore, the Georgian government's desire to secure borders has more to do with addressing the 'frozen conflicts' with Abkhazia and South Ossetia than with hindering the flow of drugs and human trafficking from Central Asia to Europe. The UNDP project Southern Caucasus Anti-Drug Programme (SCAD), funded by the EU, was refocused on narcotics prevention after an internal evaluation revealed that the equipping and training of Georgian law enforcement agencies in combating drugs from 2001 to 2006 had not been particularly effective. Given the weak incentives contained in the ENP Action Plan, however, the Georgian government's readiness to cooperate with the EU on JHA issues, such as border management, migration and money laundering, is far from certain.[10]

Georgia is interested in the 'positive' aspects inherent in the concept of the AFSJ, namely the freedom of movement and preferential trade agreements. However, the freedom of movement and visa provision presuppose Georgia's readiness to cooperate with the EU on readmission agreements. As noted by Monar (2006, 498), among the public goods associated with the concept of AFSJ, security is placed above freedom, as the 'effective exercise of freedom is made dependent upon the guarantee of security'. Freedom is not primarily associated with the freedom of movement, but with freedom from insecurity and crime and the right to live in a safe and law-abiding environment (Monar 2006, 498). When it comes to public security, the EU aims primarily at designing instruments that protect its own citizens. The Council's 2005 declaration on a strategy for the external dimension of JHA stated that 'it is no longer useful to distinguish between the security of citizens inside the European Union and those outside' (European Council 2005, 2). However, the protection of EU citizens appears to be what matters when trafficking, organized crime and migration problems are addressed through readmission agreements. Citizens in neighbouring countries are themselves included in the threat construction as trafficked victims or labour migrants. The Council's declaration on a strategy for the externalization of JHA also states its agenda in unequivocal terms: 'The EU's objective in engaging with third countries on JHA issues is to respond to the needs of its citizens' (European Council 2005, 5). In the case of Georgia, the building of institutions modelled on European standards appears more geared towards exporting the EU's vision of how a local judiciary can contribute to the EU's security than responding to the needs of Georgian society. This logic has consequences for the EU's ambition of exporting democratic values to neighbouring countries, especially if we consider that democratizing law enforcement institutions depends primarily on reinforcing their accountability towards nationals.

JHA Policies in Georgia: Normative and Strategic Goals

Not only do the EU's policies not necessarily correspond with the Georgian government's expectations and its own concept of security, but the EU's various goals are often contradictory. The concept of 'civilian power' in Europe refers to the EU's use of soft instruments (economic incentives and values) in its external relations that differ from traditional foreign policy instruments (military and diplomatic) and power politics. These two modes of influence and logics were described by Smith (2003) as possession and milieu goals.[11] Milieu goals refer to the processes by which the EU shapes its environment through the combination of socialization instruments (e.g. the export of democracy and rule of law standards) and positive conditionality (economic incentives). Possession goals correspond to a more traditional concept of foreign policy aimed at promoting and protecting national interests abroad. According to Youngs (2004), the normative and strategic aspects of the EU's external policies complement rather than oppose each other. They coexist in one policy, or strategic objectives can be integrated into a broader normative framework. As Diez (2005, 625) argued, the spread of particular norms and values to third countries necessarily implies strategic interests and the two cannot be distinguished easily. With the externalization of JHA policies, the EU is trying to combine internal goals with foreign policy objectives. However, these two sets of goals are not necessarily compatible. The traditional dilemma between the promotion of rule of law and 'efficiency', or between 'democracy' and 'security', is visible in the EU's JHA policies in Georgia. The transformation of institutions of domestic order in neighbouring countries is aimed primarily at ensuring the security of EU citizens. Hence, the EU contradicts its own objective of promoting democratic and rule of law standards abroad. Indeed, domestic law enforcement institutions derive their legitimacy from their role as providers of security and order for nationals.

Criminal justice reform is one of the EU's top priorities in Georgia, as reflected in the ENP Action Plan and the launch of a rule of law mission in 2004, with the objective of advising the Georgian government on a criminal justice strategy. The EU's engagement in criminal justice reform in Georgia revolves around normative and strategic goals. In the export of rule of law standards, the EU uses two means: approximation of legislation and administrative capacity building. The former mechanism is aimed at aligning national legislation with EU standards and filling some gaps, for example in introducing the prosecution of certain crimes. Criminals can easily exploit loopholes and differences in national criminal legislation; national criminal codes vary from one country to another and depend on national legal traditions (Monar 2006, 505). As the Council's declaration on a strategy for an external dimension of JHA states, 'The EU must tackle the underlying factors that enable organised criminality to exploit and operate across the EU's external borders, including by removing obstacles to judicial cooperation in criminal and, as appropriate, civil matters' (European Council 2005, 3). Administrative capacity building aims at making institutions more efficient and better equipped for grappling with illegal migration and other menaces. Capacity building is often not limited to equipping certain ministries, but also takes the form of training, with an emphasis on human rights and democracy standards. The reform of the criminal justice system in post-Soviet countries is linked intimately to the challenge of exporting democracy standards. Criminal justice reform and penitentiary reforms have been areas of interest for the EU in Georgia for many years, as areas in which human rights standards are particularly lagging.[12] The Georgian criminal justice system still has some characteristics of the Soviet system and changes initiated during the Shevardnadze era tended to be rather cosmetic. The criminal justice system is still characterized by an imbalance between different bodies. The prosecutorial branch is strong in the investigation and trial phases and subject to political interference, while the judiciary and the defence are weak (Helly 2006, 90). These conditions have reinforced public distrust in the justice system.

The rule of law mission in Georgia was hampered by the presence of two different approaches to fighting corruption. During the phase of justice system reform, the mission staff encountered obstacles in fulfilling their objectives when Georgian authorities attempted to take over the judiciary under the banner of stamping out corruption. While these clean-up efforts might have some genuine motivation, it is clear that the executive is trying to exert control over the courts and reinforce the prosecution office's powers. As in other ministries, the Georgian government launched a radical purge in the judiciary. A large number of judges were labelled as incompetent and corrupt and were fired. Under these conditions, the mission found it increasingly difficult to carry out its objectives. Two different ministers were in charge of the reform in the space of one year (Helly 2006, 96). The head of the mission, Sylvie Pantz, pointed to the problems of political interference in the work of the judiciary (Lobjakas 2005). Further difficulties were caused by the hybrid nature of ESDP missions, which have the effect of creating overlapping competencies between the Council and the Commission. In the case of the rule of law mission to Georgia, cooperation between the mission and the Commission was not smooth (Helly 2006, 94). In contrast to the traditional low profile adopted by officials in the EC delegation, Pantz favoured a hands-on approach when dealing with Georgian authorities. In an interview with Radio Liberty, Pantz explained how she achieved results by seeking more direct involvement in the daily affairs of the Georgian judicial system: 'We were very anxious when we heard that three, four judges of the Supreme Court had been asked to resign', Pantz says.

> So, what I initiated outside [my official] mission [was that] I put round the table the OSCE, the Council of Europe, the [European Commission] delegation, Americans — USAID and the [US] Department of Justice — and all together we went to see the president of the Supreme Court of Georgia in order, in order to [say] collectively that it was not the right way to proceed. Since then, no more judges have been asked to resign at the level of the Supreme Court (Lobjakas 2005).

The EU faces a similar dilemma in law enforcement reform, as it must answer to efficiency demands while simultaneously ensuring that these institutions comply with human rights standards. In post-Soviet countries, the challenge is to democratize policing and transform a state organ with a repressive mentality into a body accountable to citizens and aimed at guaranteeing their safety. In order to gain the society's trust, law enforcement institutions need to respect human rights and rule of law standards. Furthermore, these organs need to be perceived as protecting citizens rather than serving state interests. The Georgian government's crackdown on organized crime has resulted in overcrowded prisons, police abuses, cases of torture in prisons and harsh penalties against juvenile delinquency; all of these developments violate the EU's human rights standards. The Commission is cautious in its assistance *vis-à-vis* the reform of the Ministry of Internal Affairs, as it is wary of losing its credibility. With respect to infrastructure, the EU has supported the rehabilitation of the Rustavi prison, but has refused to provide financial support for the building of new prison facilities.[13] As for training, the EU is engaged only in the training of the border police, a project being conducted by Finnish border guards. The dilemma between efficiency and the protection of fundamental rights can also be seen in the example of Georgia's efforts to reform the civil registry. In the absence of sufficient legal guarantees on data protection, the EU was reluctant to support the reform in its initial stages after the Rose Revolution.[14]

Conclusion

The EU faces a number of limits in the implementation of its foreign and internal policy goals in the South Caucasus. An important obstacle is the limited leverage the EU has on ENP countries in the absence of membership prospects for these nations. The EU's policy in the region is also constrained by its eagerness to avoid a confrontation with Russia. It remains to be seen how the recent Georgian–Russian conflict will affect the EU's relations with Russia as well as the EU's engagement in its eastern neighbourhood.

This paper has argued, however, that another major stumbling block to the effective implementation of EU policies in Georgia is the EU's ambivalent perception of Georgia. The EU tries to address threats in its neighbourhood through a partnership approach, but at the same time applies a securitization and 'othering' strategy to neighbouring countries that has the effect of including them in its threat perception. As a result of this ambiguity, there is a lack of strategic vision in the region. The EU's attempt to export JHA policies to Georgia showcases several of the complex issues it faces in its endeavours to externalize its policies: it is concerned with the issues of security and integration on the one hand and with efficiency and the promotion of human rights and democracy standards on the other. Beyond this conundrum, the EU faces two additional major problems in the South Caucasus: first, it is difficult to transplant its own security vision in an environment where classical notions of security as territorial defence prevail. The Georgian–Russian conflict has illustrated the gap between the EU's soft security policies and Georgia's security needs. It has shown that military power is still a relevant category in the post-Cold War context. Secondly, the EU is having difficulty addressing pressing security issues on the ground with soft instruments and assistance for long-term reforms. The EU's efforts to externalize JHA policies as well as enlist third countries to help it realize its internal goals are impeded further by its unilateral imposition of priorities and solutions. If there is no consensus among the EU and Georgia on the threat analysis and the instruments needed, the implementation of JHA policies in Georgia will prove difficult.[15] Regarding JHA issues, the emphasis put on drug trafficking and illegal migration appears to be out of synch with Georgia's needs and what it expects from an increased EU presence. Furthermore, the externalization of JHA policies is driven by the EU's perceptions of interdependence and vulnerability, along with its desire to protect its own citizens. Citizens in neighbouring countries are not necessarily seen as the victims, but to some extent as threats in themselves. It is not clear how the EU can turn domestic law enforcement institutions, whose primary function is to ensure domestic security, into instruments aimed at protecting the EU's internal security and countering transnational threats. This objective is especially challenging if these institutions are supposed to comply with human rights and democracy standards.

The EU's vision of the South Caucasus region as a coherent entity is self-serving and does not reflect local perceptions. As the head of the EC delegation to Georgia and Armenia, Per Eklund, declared in an interview, '[f]rom the EU's perspective, the need to find alternative energy providers is one key issue that can bind Georgia, Armenia and Azerbaijan together in the future, in their role as transit countries' (Di Puppo 2007). These three countries do not perceive themselves as a regional unit, however. Finally, by insisting on long-term institutional reform and the export of EU standards, the EU is perhaps misjudging the environment that it is trying to shape. The countries of the region are still closer to a state building than a transition phase. The ENP's approach, which shares similarities with the enlargement policy and utilizes the same instruments, is perhaps better tailored to states that are slated to join the EU than to countries like Georgia. Georgia is still in a state-building phase and coping with its own security challenges. Popescu (2007, 22) remarked, '[i]n a constantly degenerating security environment around Abkhazia and South Ossetia and increasing tensions between Russia and Georgia, the long-term focus of the ENP has been increasingly out of touch with the pressing realities on the ground'. The Georgian–Russian conflict has confirmed that long-term reforms cannot answer appropriately Georgia's immediate security needs. Lynch (2006, 74) viewed the strengthening of the state as Georgia's top priority, thinking that

> [t]he first objective (of the EU) should be to strengthen the Georgian state in terms of its ability to enjoy full sovereignty. Here, the EU should support first-order reforms now being undertaken by the Georgian government. Georgia must become a fully-fledged state before it can undertake the integration reforms that will draw it closer to the EU as a political, economic and social model.

Notes

1. See Tassinari (2005, 6) on the integration/security dilemma.
2. The EU's security strategy states, 'We should now take a stronger and more active interest in the problems of the Southern Caucasus, which will in due course also be a neighbouring region' (European Security Strategy 2003, 8).
3. See Manners (2002) on the concept of 'normative power Europe'.
4. Interview with the Georgian–European Policy and Legal Advice Centre (GEPLAC), Tbilisi, 13 July 2007.
5. Public confidence in the police has increased after the Rose Revolution. See International Republican Institute et al. (2007, 95–6).
6. Kleinfeld Belton (2005) distinguished between five different ends-based definitions of the rule of law, including 'law and order' and 'predictable, efficient justice'.
7. Interview with the EC delegation to Georgia and Armenia, Tbilisi, 24 August 2007.
8. *Ibid.*
9. Georgian government: Priorities of the Georgian government for the ENP Action Plan, http://www.parliament.ge/files/292_901_909756_priority_en.pdf.
10. Interview with the EC delegation to Georgia and Armenia, Tbilisi, 24 August 2007.
11. Smith (2005), drawing from A. Wolfers (1962, 73–6).
12. Interview with the EC delegation to Georgia and Armenia, Tbilisi, 20 July 2007.
13. *Ibid.*
14. *Ibid.*
15. See Berenskoetter (2006) on the problem of the agreement on the threat image in the case of the EU police mission in Bosnia Herzegovina (EUPM).

References

Berenskoetter, F. 2006. *Under construction: ESDP and the 'fight against organised crime'.* CHALLENGE Working Paper, July 5.

Civil Georgia. 2008. 2008 State budget approved, 28 December 2007, http://www.civil.ge/eng/article.php?id=16708 (accessed May 2008).

Diez, T. 2005. Constructing the self and changing others: reconsidering 'normative power Europe'. *Millennium: Journal of International Studies* 33, no. 3: 613–36.

Di Puppo, L. 2007. The present situation concerning the South Caucasus conflicts cannot go on forever, there must be some movement. Caucaz.com, July 10 2007, http://www.caucaz.com/home_eng/breve_contenu.php?id=319 (accessed May 2008).

Duchêne, E. 1973. The European Community and the uncertainties of interdependence. In *A nation writ large? Foreign-policy problems before the European Community*, eds. M. Kohnstamm and W. Hager, 1–21. London: Macmillan.

European Commission. 2003. Communication on wider europe — Neighbourhood: A new framework for relations with our eastern and southern neighbours, March 11 2003, COM (2003) 104 final.

European Commission. 2005. Communication from the Commission 'A strategy on the external dimension of the Area of Freedom, Security and Justice', October 12 2005, COM (2005) 491 final, Brussels.

European Council. 2004. Council Joint Action 2004/523/CFSP of 28 June 2004 on the European Union Rule of Law Mission in Georgia, EUJUST THEMIS.

European Council. 2005. A strategy for the external dimension of JHA: Global freedom, security and justice.

European Security Strategy. 2003. A secure Europe in a better world — European Security Strategy, Brussels, December 12, http://ue.eu.int/uedocs/cmsUpload/78367.pdf.

Helly, D. 2006. EUJUST Themis in Georgia: An ambitious bet on rule of law. In *Civilian crisis management: The EU way*, ed. A. Nowak, 87–102. Chaillot Paper 90, EU Institute for Security Studies, June.

International Republican Institute (IRI), Baltic Surveys Ltd/The Gallup Organisation, The Institute of Polling and Marketing (IPM). 2007. Georgian National Voter Study, February.

Kleinfeld Belton, R. 2005. *Competing definitions of the rule of law: implications for practitioners.* Carnegie Paper 55.

Lavenex, S. 2004. EU external governance in 'wider Europe'. *Journal of European Public Policy* 11, no. 4: 688–708.

Lobjakas, A. 2005. Chief of EU judicial mission leaves with mixed feelings, RFE/RL, July 20 2005, http://www.rferl.org/featuresarticle/2005/07/21fd4483-0ba0-46fd-9442-e245d767acb9.html (accessed May 2008).

Lynch, D. 2006. *Why Georgia matters?* Chaillot Paper 86.

Manners, I. 2002. Normative power Europe: a contradiction in terms. *Journal of Common Market Studies* 40, no. 2: 235–58.

Monar, J. 2006. Cooperation in the Justice and Home Affairs domain: Characteristics, constraints and progress. *Journal of European Integration* 28, no. 5: 495–509.

Popescu, N. 2007. *Europe's unrecognised neighbours: The EU in Abkhazia and South Ossetia.* CEPS Working Document 260. Brussels: CEPS.

Smith, M. 1996. The European Union and a changing order: establishing the boundaries of order. *Journal of Common Market Studies* 31, no. 1.

Smith, K. 2005. 'Still "Civilian Power EU?"', European Foreign Policy Unit Working Paper 2005/1. London: London School of Economics.

Tassinari, F. 2005. *Security and integration in the EU neighbourhood: the case for regionalism.* CEPS Working Document 226. Brussels: CEPS.

Tchanturia, K. 2007. It is more apt to speak of 'management' than of 'resolution' of the conflicts in the South Caucasus. Caucaz.com, July 26 2007, http://www.caucaz.com/home_eng/breve_contenu.php?id=324 (accessed May 2008).

Wolfers, A. 1962. *Discord and Collaboration: Essays on International Politics.* Baltimore: Johns Hopkins University Press.

Youngs, R. 2004. Normative dynamics and strategic interests in the EU's external identity. *Journal of Common Market Studies* 42, no. 2: 415–35.

When the EU is the 'Norm-taker': The Passenger Name Records Agreement and the EU's Internalization of US Border Security Norms

JAVIER ARGOMANIZ

School of Politics & International Relations, University of Nottingham, Nottingham, UK

ABSTRACT European Union efforts to diffuse its internal security policies to neighbouring countries have attracted increased interest by EU scholars. Yet, significantly less attention has been placed on the fact that the Union also undergoes socialization practices of security norms promoted by other international actors. The article aims to address this gap by focusing on the transatlantic relationship in border security and, more specifically, the Passenger Name Records (PNR) agreement. By applying a new institutionalist approach to the analysis of this case study, the article argues that the EU's internalization of US-produced border security norms is developed following three interrelated stages: unilateral and forceful norm advocacy by the USA, a process of negotiation and bargaining and, eventually, norm mirroring and imitation from EU authorities.

Introduction

Since the Treaty of Amsterdam and the 1999 Tampere Summit, the transformation of the European Union into an international actor in the domain of Justice and Home Affairs (JHA) has been followed closely by an emerging body of JHA literature. Thus, authors have placed increasing attention on the blurring of 'internal' and 'external' security dimensions and the growing perception amongst EU policy makers of the need to address transnational threats at their origin (Anderson 1995; Bigo 2000; Mitsilegas, Monar, and Rees 2003; Monar 2004). In this context, key debates have emerged on whether the EU has behaved as a strategic or normative power when encouraging and pressurizing 'near-abroad' countries to adopt certain norms and values, the tension between normative visions of inclusiveness and the obligation to protect European citizens, and the EU's real potential to influence third countries' internal security arrangements.

Yet, there has been hitherto little notice of the fact that the EU does not only export its own security norms but is also a receptor of policies. This is not only from international organizations, such as the G-8 or the United Nations, or global standards-setters bodies, such as the International Civil Aviation Organisation (ICAO) or the International Maritime Organisation (IMO), but, more importantly, from its transatlantic 'partner', the USA.

This process has been particularly remarkable in the field of border security, especially following the 9/11 events, which led the US government to commit a comprehensive overhaul of its border management architecture. Measures affecting US authorities' institutional infrastructure and competencies have included the creation of a Department of Homeland Security (DHS), stricter immigration rules, more stringent screening methods and wider dissemination of intelligence between security agencies. Predictably, as America and Europe experience a huge amount of cross-border traffic in people and goods, these measures have had an important effect on European interests in parallel with becoming a key element of the transatlantic counter-terror cooperation.

Formally, collaborative efforts in this area have been portrayed in glowing terms on both sides of the Atlantic. The EU ex-counter-terror coordinator, Gijs de Vries (2005) has described this relationship as 'wide-ranging', whilst US officials have claimed that the Europeans are among the 'closest and most reliable partners' and 'truly it may be said that it is one of our best relationships' (US Congress 2004, 11, 49).[1] This article will argue, by contrast, that the official discourse has obscured the fact that border security cooperation is far from being a 'partnership', resembling instead an asymmetrical relationship. Structural imbalances based on the nature of these two actors have led the EU to adopt, sometimes reluctantly, Washington's security policies, some of which did not fit easily with the European threat perceptions and strategy of response. In essence, a pattern of norm promotion and acceptance has come to characterize transatlantic cooperation in border management.

In developing this general argument, the article will focus on the Passenger Name Records (PNR) agreement. The PNR agreement has emerged as one of the most controversial issues in the transatlantic security relationship. Crucially, it also explicitly exhibits the conditions that have often come to characterize the EU–US border security relationship, namely, a European internalization of US-advocated security norms. This process of 'norm internalization' is understood here as the fulsome assimilation of international norms, where 'norms' are authoritative rules or standards regulating patterns of behaviour in an area of international relations. Moving away from Manners' (2002, 239) broad definition as 'conceptions of normal', this article uses the term 'norm' less in an ideological sense but, more narrowly, as a framework of legal and political agreements acting as a model of action for international actors. Internalization of norms in the context of this paper would then reflect a consensus established between the advocating and the complying actor on the adequacy of a particular set of legal instruments and/or policies to address a problem; in this case, the protection of a state from terrorist infiltration at the point of entrance.

It will be argued here that norm internalization practices in the transatlantic border relationship have generally developed following a three-stage process: norm advocacy and/or imposition by US authorities; norm acceptance as a result of an interactive bargaining process; and, in some instances, voluntary imitation and borrowing by EU actors. Importantly, as shown by the PNR case, these practices of internalization of US security norms have the potential to affect European travellers' privacy rights significantly.

Given the PNR agreement's suitability as a case study of norms internalization practices, this paper will approach the issue mainly following a sociological institutionalist angle, a strand of new institutionalism that has offered an important contribution to the study of the transmission of norms in the international system. Hence, the first part of the paper introduces the paper's theoretical framework based on a number of conceptualizations emerged in institutionalist studies of EU's norm diffusion. This will be followed by an overview of the background of the PNR agreement's protracted negotiation process. The discussion will then move to scrutinize, from a sociological institutionalist perspective, the three-stage course of action through which the exportation of US border security has led to the EU's internalization of security norms and the significant parallels with the EU's own practices of norm diffusion to neighbouring countries. The paper will then conclude by underlining the wider contribution of this case study to the analysis of the transatlantic border relationship and to the broader process of international norm promotion and adoption.

Theoretical Setting

EU scholars arguing that the Union is a producer and exporter of norms to third states have generally approached the problem by following the rational choice and sociological strands of new institutionalism. As shown in Wolff, Wichmann, and Mounier's (2009) opening paper, these two schools are separated by clear ontological gaps in the character and influence of institutions in the shaping of agents' interests and political action. As a consequence, these differences are directly reflected in their perspectives on the practices of norm compliance by international actors.

In this regard, rationalist approaches have tended to focus on 'coercion, cost–benefit calculations and material incentives' (Checkel 2001, 553). Utility-maximizing agents' adoption of norms is based on strategic choices shaped by existing punitive and/or incentive structures. Hence rationalist scholars have been generally sceptical of the transformative capacities of international norms and compliance is described as 'most often a game of altering strategies and behaviour only' (Checkel 2001, 556). Norm compliance is considered as an interactive, deliberative and iterative process of bargaining between strategically calculating national governments where choices are made on the basis of cost–benefit estimations. In other words, actors in the international system will comply with a particular norm according to the benefits or costs implied in the rule-following action.

In this vein, a particular rationalist notion that is highly relevant to the policy bargaining process in the PNR case is that of 'first mover' strategies. Drawing upon Scharpf's (1997) ideas, Aus (2006) has shown in his study of the Council's negotiation of biometric passports regulation how 'first move' strategies is an effective option when utility-maximizing 'players' are engaged in what rationalists define as 'Battle-of-the-sexes' game. This game-theory model engages actors that disagree over the contents of a proposal but are forced to reach a negotiated solution as failure to agree on the policy represents the worst-case scenario for all bargaining actors involved.

In this situation, a successful strategic calculation from a player is to 'move first', to restrict the other player's alternatives by unilaterally establishing a particular policy. By exploiting the first mover advantage, later players must adjust their moves to the initial mover's preferred solution. They may also find it necessary to converge towards the first player's solution even if it does not represent their preferred answer, as the necessity to reach an agreement offers no rational alternative. As will be shown later, rational choice institutionalism will offer valuable insights in the analysis of the bargaining stage of the process of internalization of the PNR norm.

On the other hand, according to a sociological institutionalist perspective, norm adoption by international actors is not a clear-cut or automatic development, instead being seen as an interactive and incremental process of persuasion through various means. Thus, emphasis is put on processes of social learning and socialization, highlighting how actors' interaction and social learning shape interests and how mutual learning and the selection of new preferences may lead to normative compliance. In this account, 'state compliance results from social learning and deliberation that lead to preference change' (Aus 2006, 560). Under this perspective, the impact of argumentative persuasion as a mechanism of norm adoption is emphasized and the consensual and iterative methods in which the EU diffuses its norms in international relations is highlighted (Manners 2002).

Drawing upon these constructivist analyses of norm compliance, Björkdahl (2005) has transferred Checkel's (2001) notions of 'norm-maker' and 'norm-taker' into the analysis of EU's external relations in the Western Balkans. Björkdahl's (2005) argument, from which the theoretical framework of this paper draws, points out that the EU, as the 'norm-maker' is in a strong position to exert a normative influence on 'near-abroad' countries, or 'norm-takers'. Norm adoption, however, is by no means a forgone conclusion, as EU efforts to export specific norms may be met, not only with their adoption or the localization of the norms to the local pre-existing context, but also with resistance or rejection. Whereas some norms are more likely to be accepted due to a goodness-of-fit that allows an uncomplicated localization of the norm to match the recipient's normative context, others demand reinterpretation or re-framing efforts to match. Furthermore, external normative compliance is more likely if the norms are perceived as not being imposed by overtly or covertly coercive means by the norm-maker: 'forceful norm export may result in resistance' (Björkdahl 2005, 274). On the other hand, adoption is more probable if the normative change is perceived as domestically driven and voluntary.

Ultimately, however, the EU's capacity for norm diffusion is boosted by way of its capability of combining attractive positive incentives with harsh negative sanctions to ensure norm acceptance in its asymmetrical relationship with third states. The former is represented by external trade dialogue, economic cooperation and contractual relations in the form of association agreements that have been used increasingly to promote normative standards. Most importantly, it is also highlighted how a relationship of trust conducive to norm acceptance can be established between the EU and a third state's domestic actors through interaction, technical assistance, argumentation and exchange of views.

It is argued here that, although a rational choice perspective offers a valid contribution to the analysis of some elements of the process, it is this sociological institutionalist approach that is most productive when studying the dynamics of norms advocacy and acceptance that characterize the transatlantic relationship in border security. This argument will be constructed in the analysis of the different stages of the internalization process that follows the account of the PNR negotiation process presented below.

Background to the EU–US Passenger Name Records Agreement

The origins of the PNR agreement can be traced back to the 19 November 2001 US Aviation and Transportation Security Act. This US domestic legislation requested that airlines flying from, to or through the US share, before every departure, their passenger name records[2] data with authorities in the Customs and Border Protection Bureau (CBP) and the Transportation Security Administration (TSA).

A crucial obstacle to this US request, however, was that transfer of PNR information contravened Article 25 of the EU's Data Protection Directive 95/46/EC, which impedes the transfer of EU citizens' data to another country when an adequate level of protection cannot be ensured. The high penalties facing European companies, stemming from the US unilateral decision, put significant pressure on the Commission to resolve this legal limbo by negotiating a temporary settlement with the US in a high-level meeting on 17–18 February 2003. Despite strong opposition from European Data Protection authorities, privacy rights' advocates and the European Parliament's (EP) LIBE Committee (Civil Liberties, Justice and Home Affairs Committee),[3] the European Commission and the US Department of Homeland Security signed a permanent PNR agreement on 17 May 2004.

As a response, EP President Pat Cox announced on 25 June 2004 that the Parliament would bring the case before the European Court of Justice (ECJ) to have the accord overturned. Although there was a reference to the legal weakness of the agreement, the EP's opposition was based mostly on the insufficiency of US undertakings to guarantee the protection of European citizens' data. On 30 May 2006, the ECJ announced that the 2004 PNR agreement lacked an 'appropriate legal basis'. The ruling contended that handing over PNR information falls under member states' criminal law legislation, within the third pillar, and not under the social and economic first pillar law.

Ironically, the ECJ ruling would prove counterproductive to the EP's efforts to ensure a greater protection of Europeans' privacy rights since the Parliament holds no consultation powers on the negotiations of third pillar agreements. This factor contributed to the swift conclusion of a final permanent agreement between the Presidency, on behalf this time of the EU instead of the Community, and US authorities on June 29 2007.

The resulting PNR agreement disposes that passenger data would be kept for fifteen years, seven as 'active' and eight as 'dormant' data with stricter access rules. There would be nineteen accessible data fields, including passengers' names, address, credit card information and travel history. Whereas a 'pull' system had been used since 2003 to transfer the data, meaning that the US enjoyed immediate access to the airline databases, the US 'committed' to change this to a 'push' system by January 2008, where US authorities would have to ask for filtered-out data on a case-by-case basis. Importantly, the DHS would also be allowed to pass the data to other US security agencies. Finally, the agreement would be valid for seven years, a substantial period of legal certainty.

The Internalization of US Passenger Name Records Rules: A Three-stage Process

It is argued here that the developments leading to the 2007 PNR agreement represent a salient instance of the EU acting as a 'norm-taker' in relation to another international actor. Adopting an institutionalist perspective, norm socialization can be conceptualized in this case as a three-stage process: an initial forceful norm advocacy by the US, ensuing bargaining leading to norm acceptance and, finally, norm incorporation is accompanied by mirroring and imitation. Formally, these stages could be described as in an incrementalist pattern, where developments in one stage restrict choices in subsequent periods. In reality, practices of norm adoption and borrowing take place in parallel, lending credence to the hypothesis of socialization and social learning as key mechanisms for norm diffusion.

Unilateral Policy Promotion

Whereas the EU has acted traditionally as initiator and transmitter ('norm-maker') of JHA initiatives in its relationship with third countries, the PNR agreement underscores, on the other hand, a key element in the transatlantic security relationship, which is US pro-activeness as a producer and catalyst of initiatives in contrast to the more reactive role that the EU has adopted.

As Rees (2006, 99) noted, ideas were 'incubated inside the US bureaucracy without a clear understanding of the implications that they would have for Western Europe' and this has generally left the EU reacting to a US-inspired agenda. Unsurprisingly, this has led EU officials to the impression that they were being rushed into provisions because of Washington's unilateral steps. The point of US forceful diffusion of its own internal security policies has been argued by some leading counter-terror experts who claimed that there is a 'strong sense that the latest anti-terrorist strategies are directed by the USA and merely co-produced by the EU' (Den Boer and Monar 2002, 25). A prominent MEP from the Civil Liberties Committee has gone as far as to claim that 'we see today that policies are not made in national capitals, nor are they made in Brussels, they are made in Washington' (EurActiv 2006).[4] Under this highly critical perspective, the EU's main, almost sole, function has been to provide a legal basis for the US' security policies.

This is typically a product of the differing perceptions and strategic analysis of the threat existing at both sides of the Atlantic. A major US priority since 9/11 has been to encourage European states to strengthen transport and travel document security, as this is seen as crucial for America's own internal security. This comes down to the fact that, in contrast with the US' relative success in assimilating its own Muslim immigrants, the phenomenon of radicalization of Muslim youth across Western Europe is seen with grave concern by US authorities, particularly after the July 2005 bombings in London and subsequent foiled terrorist plots planned by European nationals. Infiltration by passport-carrying, visa-exempt Western European *jihadist* is perceived as a significant security risk by US authorities, who remind Europeans that the members of the Hamburg cell, Moussaoui and Richard Reid came by air without a visa. Thus, EU states are not only seen as allies in the US 'war on terror' but also as a potential platform for terrorism (BBC 2008).[5]

This explains US irritation with the delays in the implementation of border security policies by member states and US willingness to pressurize European authorities to produce similar sorts of measures. In this context, it is revealing that the transmission of air passenger data to the US had never been part of the EU antiterrorist agenda until the unilateral US authorities' decision to oblige European carriers to provide these data. PNR exchange had been neither part of the EU antiterrorist action plan nor previously discussed in JHA meetings. In fact, the EU's reaction can be perceived more as an attempt to minimize the damage of the American requests on passengers' privacy rights than as a conscious decision to develop stronger EU–US intelligence exchange in this area.

The fact that the US authorities did not contemplate negotiating an agreement with European authorities before announcing the measure, or even consult sufficiently in advance with their counterparts considering the significant costs that the scheme would represent for European airlines, signalled a general reluctance from US authorities to engage with their

European allies in this area and a preference for unconstrained and extraterritorial action.

Furthermore, the US has not refrained from using its political and economic clout in order to pressurize the EU to accept its demands for tighter border control. Indeed, the US government has used coercive means to force norm compliance from their European (and non-European) allies in the process. This approach follows closely from the July 2002 National Strategy for Homeland Security that made it clear, as Rees (2006, 97) noted, 'that the US would be unwilling to let countries enjoy privileged access to their territory unless they implement the same sorts of security measures as the US'. Incidentally, the US government threatened European carriers with strong economic sanctions, such as the removal of landing rights, which would have kept companies off the American market. Resembling a 'Battle-of-the-sexes' game, a negotiating solution became indispensable as the *status quo* would have resulted in a legal limbo and the severe disruption of transatlantic travel. Moreover, by unilaterally forcing the transmission of PNR data upon foreign carriers, US authorities acted as a 'first mover', setting the terms of the negotiation and ensuring a position of strength in the bargaining process.

Ironically, in a number of ways this development is an inverse mirror image of the EU's own promotion of internal security policies to neighbouring countries and third states. As remarked by Björkdahl (2005), under the EU's External JHA domain, institutional affiliation or financial support towards particular third countries was made conditional on security apparatus reforms through the adoption of policies produced in Brussels. Rather than a basic procedure of policy transfer, this has involved, in places, protracted negotiations concerning issues such as visa facilitation or readmission agreements, which very often involve a 'quid pro quo' bartering, where Brussels' demands on internal reforms, intelligence sharing and operational collaboration are met with requests for socio-economic assistance. As addressed below, this description holds important similarities with the second stage in the EU's internalization of PNR rules.

Negotiation and Bargaining

Not unlike the EU's security dialogue with neighbourhood countries, the EU's adoption of US security norms was channelled through two related mechanisms: a US-dominated hierarchical relationship where the US applies political and economic coercion to ensure European compliance, and an ensuing process of interaction and bargaining between US and EU authorities. As part of the latter, during the PNR negotiation process, EU negotiators have attempted — once forced to deal with US attempts to exercise a normative influence — to address the *reciprocity deficit* that emerged as a logical by-product of an asymmetrical relationship.

EU–US asymmetrical relationship. Similar to the EU's relationship with European Neighbourhood Policy (ENP) countries, the transatlantic relationship is far from being a 'partnership' in border security and can be better defined as an asymmetric framework of cooperation. This statement should come as counter-intuitive to some students of the transatlantic relationship. Both actors' economies are roughly equal in size, they are each other's main commercial partner and their primary trade and investment targets each other. Considering the strong economic interdependence between the two blocs, it would be possible to assume in theory that power relations work in both directions and both actors would possess similar bargaining powers on this matter. In fact, that is not so.

An asymmetry in this area has been facilitated by a number of factors. First, there has been a rapid development of US counter-terrorism architecture in the aftermath of 9/11, leading to fundamental institutional reorganization, the creation of the DHS behemoth, the rapid formulation of policies aiming to enhance international cooperation with US partners and the beefing up of US border security. Hampered by its non-state nature, no equivalent of this comprehensive approach has been forthcoming from the EU. Whereas the US is a hegemonic nation-state, the EU is a multilateral organization that lacks the supranational power to produce and harmonize radical and swift changes in the member states' counter-terror structures. Faced with US superior capabilities and the immediacy and salience of the threat, member states have tended to adopt the more developed US solutions to the problem. In fact, it has been argued that the rapid progress made by the Union in the aftermath of 9/11 in passing counter-terror instruments, such as the European arrest warrant and a common definition of terrorism, have been motivated, in part, by an intention to prove to the US that the EU could be a credible partner in this area.[6]

A second factor is the US' own unilateral and extraterritorial approach. The present US administration's disregard for European allies' views on some aspects of the US 'war on terror' has been documented widely. The reorganization of the US' internal security structure similarly has been conducted with little reflection on the potential impact of these policies on third countries. Even assuming the profound disparities in the institutionalization procedures, US unilateral strengthening of the security rules to enter its territory would have caused less friction with the EU's own arrangements had US authorities considered close dialogue with European partners as a prerequisite for security rules acceptance.

Thirdly, in the period following the 9/11 attacks, the US started to exert sustained influence on the EU's JHA policies based on the privileged access by US officials to Council working groups. Such access guaranteed that US requests for US-compatible reform concerning border management and intelligence exchange found a sympathetic forum. This influence is further sustained through periodic high-level meetings of US and EU JHA officials, where, as highlighted by Guild and Brower (2006), US authorities are aiming to obtain personal data from EU citizens and residents in Europe in more ways than with the PNR system.[7]

Hence, the opening of the EU's internal decision-making structures to US influence, combined with the US' immense hard power capabilities and a persistent long history of broader strategic cooperation between both sides, has been a major contributing factor in cementing US dominance of the relationship.

Such US dominance has been apparent in the negotiations as well as in the final contents of the 2007 PNR agreement. In this respect, the EU negotiators have been forced to accept changes on the original undertakings after claiming initially that they were 'untouchable'. As a result, the US undertakings accepted by the Commission give the US plenty of leeway to modify the agreement unilaterally. As a UK House of Lords (2007) report on PNR argued, 'an undertaking which includes a provision allowing the party giving it to amend it virtually at will is of very limited value and scarcely deserves the name'.

The structural inequality of the relationship has been reflected further in the humiliating conditions put by US authorities on high-ranking EU officials during the joint 2005 review: the first, and so far last, assessment on the US use of European PNR data.[8] The US also pressurized the EU side into leaving the most important information out from their watered-down report. Eventually, DHS negotiators succeeded in removing data protection authorities from the July 2007 agreement.

Finally, the asymmetry is particularly salient when the EU–US agreement is compared with a similar PNR accord signed in October 2005 with Canada. Canadian authorities receive only filtered-out data on a case-by-case basis and their 'commitments' to data protection are legally stronger than the US 'undertakings'. Moreover, none of these commitments permits the Canadian authorities to unilaterally change aspects of the agreement. The Canada PNR agreement proves that the US' superior bargaining power, and its privileged access to EU JHA decision-making structures, has given it a potential for norm advocacy and promotion unmatched by any other international actor in relations with the EU.

Bargaining and reciprocity deficit. The reciprocity deficit emerging from this asymmetrical relationship has been addressed only partially by the Commission and the Presidency. This has been done, first, by incorporating to the Presidency negotiating mandate the expansion of the Visa Waiver Programme (VWP) to the citizens from those twelve member states[9] who are still not part of the scheme. US authorities have been very receptive to the idea of US–EU visa reciprocity as a bargaining chip for PNR data. In fact, the US has long established a connection between the extension of the VWP and the member states' cooperation with US border security policies. Even if European representatives officially insist that these are separate issues, Justice Liberty and Security (JLS) Commissioner Frattini himself remarked that 'it is our aim to have all EU member states in the Visa Waiver Program' and 'the Commission raises this issue at every relevant meeting with US representatives'.[10] The success of this strategy is open to question, however, as the expansion of the VWP to these countries has finally been dependent on bilateral negotiations in which these states had to accept additional demands from US authorities, far beyond what had been granted under the PNR agreement.[11] These US negotiations with individual member states contribute to undermining Community competences in what is, in principle, a communitarized policy area and have been seen with concern and irritation by EU officials.

EU authorities have also been exploring other avenues of reciprocity during the negotiations. EU negotiators have sought and obtained the US promise of the transfer of terrorist intelligence obtained on the analysis of European citizens' data to Europol, Eurojust and member states' police and judicial authorities. This has been a key issue in the European negotiating mandate: Jonathan Faull, JLS Director-General at the Commission, has emphasized how 'the intelligence work, the analysis made of PNR data, particularly in relation to transatlantic travel, should be of benefit to our security as well as to theirs', while remarking on the importance of PNR to trace back terrorists or criminals' travelling patterns (House of Lords 2007, 41). As with the Central Intelligence Agency (CIA) extraordinary renditions, where European agents interrogated unlawfully arrested terrorist suspects in Guantanamo and third countries' prisons (Geyer 2007), while their governments officially opposed the practice, the Europeans are willing to outsource to the US a task that they cannot presently perform due to lack of resources and limitations imposed by their own legal systems. The flow of analytical information back from US agencies inevitably raises questions concerning its transmission outside the framework of the existing transatlantic agreements on mutual legal assistance and extradition and its potential intra-European exchange through the 'principle of availability', further undermining citizens' privacy rights.

In sum, the process becomes one where strategically calculating actors interact and one of these offers external incentives (extension of VWP to other EU countries, terrorist intelligence exchange) to the other to comply with the passengers' data request. As a rationalist approach would contend, by enhancing the cost–benefit balance the US expects to improve the possibilities for a rule transfer. Similar to the EU's promotion of JHA norms, external positive (and negative) incentives and compensatory measures do affect domestic rule acceptance.

Norm Mirroring

The Commission has acknowledged that full reciprocity is ultimately unattainable unless the EU develops its own PNR system. An opening in EU proposals for the use of passenger data had already occurred when, following calls from the 25 March 2004 European Council Declaration, the Council adopted on 29 April 2004 a Directive obliging carriers to communicate Advanced Passenger Information (API). API data are strictly biographical and travel information data principally used to run names against suspects lists. In principle, the directive forces the authorities to delete the data 24 hours after the transmission. PNR, in contrast, adds a wealth of information that is non-existent within API and allows *post-ante* intelligence analysis on travel patterns and other trends and associations between known and unknown criminals.

With these distinctions in mind, Commissioner Frattini announced a Commission draft framework decision for a European PNR scheme in the aftermath of the June 2007 failed car bomb attacks in London and Glasgow Airport. The proposal would oblige airlines flying to and from EU territory to share private data on their passengers with European governments' security services. Data would be transferred to a national competent authority, or 'Passenger Information Unit' (PIU), which would then proceed to analyse the data and reach a 'risk assessment' for each passenger; in other words, profile all passengers according to the corresponding national watch list. National PIUs would then be able to transfer their national data amongst themselves and to non-EU states, such as the US.

Significantly, the proposal is in a number of areas almost the exact mirror of the transatlantic PNR system. To begin with, both schemes would access nineteen very similar data categories. Data would then be used for both terrorist *and* organized crime investigations. Except when being used for an ongoing investigation, the data are to be preserved 'active' for five years and 'dormant' for a further eight years: for seven and eight in the US scheme. As in the 2007 agreement, a 'push' system will be implemented. Similarly, sensitive personal data (i.e. ethnic origin, religious beliefs) that can be inferred from fields, such as birth place or dietary choices, are to be deleted.

Considering these similarities, it is difficult not to argue that the US PNR scheme has been a precursor of the Commission's own policy. As one Commission official noted, it would have been difficult to explain to European passengers that US authorities would receive more information than their own national services.[12] The fact that the US scheme served as a model for the European PNR proposal further signifies the ideational adoption by the Commission of US norms in passenger control. Indeed, the Commission's borrowing and mirroring of the US initiative constitutes the last piece in the puzzle of the internalization process.

In this regard, it was during the negotiations with their US counterparts that Commission officials became increasingly aware of the importance of air travel as a tool for radicalization and for the preparation of terrorist attacks. There was also a growing realization that European countries were far more vulnerable in this area and that there was a need for 'self-defence'.[13] A quote from the 2007 Commission proposal is highly revealing in this respect:

> On the basis of an exchange of information with these third countries [USA and Canada], the EU has been able to *assess the value* of PNR data and to *realise its potential* for law enforcement purposes. The EU has further been able *to learn from the experiences* of such third countries in the use of PNR data, as well as from the experience of the UK from its pilot project (European Commission 2007, author's emphasis).

As expected by sociological institutionalist authors, the Commission approach to the transmission of passenger's data for security purposes has been fundamentally shaped by its interaction with other international actors; leading to learning practices, compliance and full normative socialization.

These processes actually began at a relatively early stage with the 2003 Communication 'Transfer of air passenger name record (PNR) data: A global EU approach'. This Commission document outlined the core elements of an EU policy in this area and, revealingly, the Communication stated that 'the EU's approach cannot be limited to responding to the authorities of others'. It also claimed that by 2007 'the EU will have developed its own policy on the use of PNR' (European Commission 2003, 4). Furthermore, it was also postulated that the principle of reciprocity should be the base of 'any possible information exchange with US authorities' (European Commission 2003, 9). The Commission aimed with this document to consolidate its central position as the main EU negotiator in this area by insisting upon a global approach to this problem through international standards agreed at the ICAO (Mitsilegas 2005).

Thus, the Commission had consistently worked on a European PNR policy for four years *in parallel* to the negotiation process. In fact, the Commission organized several meetings and consultations under the PNR negotiations, which were further expanded with a questionnaire sent out in December 2006 to relevant stakeholders and a February 2007 meeting in Brussels with state representatives. This time, member states were clearly more receptive. By 2007 only UK, France and Denmark had enacted national PNR legislation but, according to a European Commission official, the US–EU negotiations had contributed to a 'massive' change of opinion and greater national interest and involvement on a European PNR scheme.[14] Supported by national representatives and long convinced of the value of the US programme, the Commission was aiming to create a similar scheme to the one which it was formally negotiating with DHS officials.

The Commission's position during the negotiations, and the decision in 2003 to work on a parallel European PNR scheme, was influenced undoubtedly by the positive view expressed by member states regarding this instrument. Thus, the Commission's (2007, 3) proposal stated clearly that member states' support for the use of passengers' data for law enforcement purposes had been consistent since the European Council of 25–26 March 2004 and reiterated twice in The Hague Programme and the extraordinary Council meeting of 13 July 2005. Considering this evidence and member states' approving reception accorded to the 2007 proposal (Council of the European Union 2007a, 2007b), it is difficult to picture national governments pressurizing the Commission to adopt a tougher stance during the negotiating process. One could argue, in fact, that this process of norm adoption also occurred in parallel at the national level after witnessing the adoption of similar schemes by some member states.

In sum, either seeking reciprocal arrangements in an unequal relationship or simply persuaded by the benefits of the scheme, the EU's import of this norm has involved acquiescence with US demands and then voluntary imitation and borrowing of policies. This means that, first, the sociological institutionalist perspective is fundamental in order to understand the process and, secondly, that the PNR agreement is a process of norm assimilation as well as of policy transfer. This is highly significant insofar as this leads to the transformation of US norms into global standards since both the US and European governments are the most dynamic actors in counter-terrorism. Moreover, EU-adopted rules can be transmitted subsequently through EU dialogue with third countries and international organizations, a process facilitated by the EU's higher international legitimacy *vis-à-vis* the Bush administration and the EU's, relatively successful, self-constructed image of a moral 'leader for good' (Chaban, Elgstrom, and Holland 2006). Critics, however, have referred to the corrosive effect of this transfer on citizens' civil liberties, dubbing it 'policy laundering' as international forums are used as an indirect means to push policies that could prove very unpopular in the domestic political process (Hosein 2005).

More significantly, contestation has also emerged *from within* the EU's institutional structure. This has reflected the fact that the position of the EU negotiating agents (i.e. the Commission and the Presidency) has been markedly different from that of those EU actors (i.e. European Parliament, Article 29 Working Party, the European Data Protection Supervisor), who had been kept excluded from the negotiations. Whilst the former have been willing to compromise and cooperate with the US, the latter have worked closely together to challenge some of the US demands. Under their perspective, the EU's acquiescing and mirroring of US policies has the potential to erode European citizens' civil liberties and privacy rights.[15] The fact that these measures are seen as being imposed from outside has strengthened such contestation. Thus, the EU's fragmented governance has lent itself to power struggles between EU institutions that have impeded the EU from acting with institutional coherence to US demands. Inter-institutional conflict and internal division have reflected the fact that the Union has not acted as a unitary actor in regards to the internalization of US border security policies.

Conclusion

This paper has argued that the process of internalization of border security norms present in the PNR agreement is constituted by three subsequent stages: first, an initial stage of US unilateral norm imposition, followed by rule compliance articulated as US–EU negotiations characterized by bargaining and cost–benefit calculations from both actors, and, finally, a parallel process of policy socialization by EU executive bodies, in particular the European Commission, contested by other European actors. Resistance to norm internalization within the Union has originated mainly from data protection officers and MEPs concerned about data protection and democratic accountability shortcomings.

This case study is important insofar as it provides lessons applicable to other aspects of the transatlantic border security relationship where the EU has acted as a norm-taker to the US norm-maker. Thus, the impact of American pressures has been manifest in the Container Security Initiative (CSI), the inclusion of Biometric identifiers in European passports or the Sky Marshals proposal.

To begin with, and as part of the CSI scheme, the US government demanded major European ports establish dedicated shipping terminals and allow the deployment of US custom officers to screen containers identified as posing a potential risk for terrorism.[16] A December 2004 Council Regulation on the inclusion of digital facial images and fingerprints on passports also came as a result of American legislation requiring states participating in the US VWP to use passports with biometric features (Council of the European Union 2004b).[17] In parallel to these measures, the US demanded European airlines in December 2003 to accept the deployment of Sky Marshals on particular transatlantic flights under the threat of revoking their licences.[18] Finally, an August 2007 US law forced foreign travellers to give US authorities at least 48 hours' notice of their plans to visit the country.[19]

These and other initiatives reinforce the impression that some of the most significant EU measures in recent years in the field of border management have come as a result of direct US pressure or unilateral decisions. In other words, US forceful norm promotion, although creating friction in transatlantic relations, has ultimately been met by European compliance. This merits attention.

On the other hand, PNR as a case study also provides a contribution to the study of the mutually reinforcing practices of promotion and internalization of international norms. It is argued in this paper that sociological institutionalism can deliver unmatched insights on the different dimensions that act in the assimilation of norms, a final stage in a process initiated by external rule abidance.

Assuming rational choice contribution in explaining norm incorporation, sociological institutionalism, however, allows moving the analysis beyond this initial stage to engage with the further and related processes of voluntary imitation and borrowing. It would be limiting, on balance, to explain the EU's internalization of US demands by making exclusive reference to US pressure and coercion or both actors' bargaining strategies. On the other hand, mutually shared values, interests and common principles are crucial to facilitate cooperation in the high-politics area of security. This finds a reflection here as both sides are affected and place a similarly high value on combating international terrorism. There is certainly a 'logic of appropriateness' in the EU's compliance since member states acknowledge that international cooperation is key in counter-terrorism. In this context, passenger information exchange is considered an appropriate and legitimate course of action to improve counter-terror cooperation. These common principles act as a counterbalance to the existing differences in their counter-terror strategic culture, where the US sees itself involved in a 'war on terror', whereas Europe places less importance on the military aspects and more on diplomatic tools, multilateral institutions and addressing the 'root causes'. Notwithstanding these divergences, which in any case have been progressively reduced in recent years, the PNR case proves the importance of a strong consensus on common values, such as the strengthening of counter-terror cooperation, and social learning and interaction as factors facilitating the diffusion and adoption of norms in the international domain.

Notes

1. Quoted by William T. Pope (US Department of State's Office of the Coordinator for Counterterrorism).
2. A Passenger Name Record is the generic name given to the files created by airlines for each journey any passenger books. They are stored in the airlines' reservation and departure control databases.
3. A 24 October 2002 opinion from the Article 29 Data Protection Working Party criticized the legality and proportionality of the US requests and raised concerns over the adequacy of data protection in the US. Similar criticisms were voiced by the European Parliament in March 2003 when overwhelmingly voting in favour of a very critical resolution drafted by the Civil Liberties (LIBE) Committee. Moreover, a coalition of privacy and civil liberties organizations in Europe launched a campaign in May 2003 against the transfer of data.
4. Quoted by MEP and Rapporteur, Sophie in't Veld.
5. Quoted by Michael Chertoff (DHS Secretary).
6. Argued by Den Boer, Dubois or Monar, amongst other experts.
7. At the 2–3 March 2006 EU–US summit, for instance, US officials remarked that they would approach member states to ensure access to retained communication data while warning against the adoption of the data protection framework in the third pillar.
8. EU officials were forced to sign confidentiality agreements exposing them to criminal sanctions for any breach and their access to some records was limited by US authorities.
9. Currently: Greece, Malta, Cyprus, Bulgaria, Romania, Slovakia, Czech Republic, Poland, Hungary, Latvia, Lithuania and Estonia.
10. Statewatch (2007), http://www.statewatch.org/news/2007/may/eu-dp-swift-frattini-letter.pdf.
11. Including in-flight Sky Marshals, electronic authorization system and information on travel documents. See EUobserver (2008).
12. Interview with a Commission official, Brussels, April 2008.
13. Ibid.
14. Ibid.
15. As an example a European Parliament 12 July 2007 Resolution criticized the deal for being 'substantively flawed' by 'open and vague definitions and multiple possibilities for exception'. A 17 August 2007 opinion from the Article 29 Data Protection Working Party also claimed that 'the new agreement leaves open serious questions and shortcomings' and that 'safeguards provided for under the previous agreement have been markedly weakened'.
16. Concerned about being cut off from the lucrative US market, major ports member states, such as France (Le Havre), the Netherlands (Rotterdam) or Belgium (Antwerp), conducted secret bilateral negotiations with US authorities. Thus, the Commission was forced to intervene to protect its competences under the Community pillar leading to the April 2004 Custom cooperation accord, which subsumed all previous bilateral accords and expanded the programme to almost twenty ports in ten member states. See *Official Journal of the EU* L304 (30 September 2004) (Council of the European Union 2004c).
17. In spite of European compliance, and in a politically sensitive decision, the US VISIT programme was extended since September 2004 to those fifteen member states which were under the VWP; allowing US authorities to collect biometric identifiers (two digital fingerprints and a photograph) from European visitors upon arrival to the US for their storage in a database.
18. US demands clashed with some member states' strict regulations against armed personnel in-flight. Member states also found particularly irksome the US authorities' lack of interest in contacting their allies to communicate their unilateral demands (some governments learnt about the measure from the media) and the vagueness of their requirements. Even so, EU transport ministers agreed on 12 October 2006 on European legislation allowing armed officers on board (Council of the European Union 2006).
19. As a response to the US government's disregard of repeated appeals to reconsider these measures, the Commission has prepared plans to mirror this system with an electronic traveller authorization scheme similarly requiring foreigners, including US citizens, to give notice of their plans (*Financial Times* 2007).

References

Anderson, M. 1995. The merging of internal and external security. In *Policing the European Union*, eds. M. Anderson, M. den Boer, P. Cullen, W. Gilmore, C. Raab and N. Walker, 156–80. Oxford: Clarendon Press.

Article 29 Data Protection Working Party. 2007. Opinion 5/2007 on the follow-up agreement between the European Union and the United States of America on the processing and transfer of passenger name record (PNR) data by air carriers to the United States Department of Homeland Security concluded in July 2007, August 17.

Aus, J.P. 2006. *Decision-making under pressure: The negotiation of the Biometric Passports Regulation in the Council*. Oslo: ARENA Working Paper 11.

BBC. 2008. US fears Europe-based terrorism, January 15.

Bigo, D. 2000. When two become one: internal and external securitisations. In *International relations theory and the politics of European integration*, eds. M. Kelstrup and M. Williams, 171–204. London: Routledge.

Björkdahl, A. 2005. Norm-maker and norm-taker: Exploring the normative influence of the EU in Macedonia. *European Foreign Affairs Review*, 10, no. 2: 257–78.

Chaban, N., O. Elgstrom, and M. Holland. 2006. The European Union as others see it. *European Foreign Affairs Review* 11, no. 2: 245–62.

Checkel, J.T. 2001. Why comply? Social learning and European identity change. *International Organization* 55, no. 3: 553–88.

Council of the European Union. 2004a. Council Directive 2004/82/EC of 29 April 2004 on the obligation of carriers to communicate passenger data. *Official Journal of the EU* L261 (August 6).

Council of the European Union. 2004b. Council Regulation on standards for security features and biometrics in passports and travel documents issued by Member States, 15152/04, December 10.

Council of the European Union. 2004c. Council Decision 2004/634/EC of 30 March 2004 concerning the conclusion of the Agreement between the European Community and the United States of America on intensifying and broadening the Agreement on customs cooperation and mutual assistance in customs matters to include cooperation on container security and related matters. *Official Journal of the EU* L304 (September 30).

Council of the European Union. 2006. COREPER proposal for a regulation of the European Parliament and of the Council on common rules in the field of civil aviation security Political agreement, 13599/06, October 6.

Council of the European Union. 2007a. Extraordinary Meeting of the Permanent Representatives Committee (Part 2) held in Luxembourg on June 12 2007, 10994/07, June 19.

Council of the European Union. 2007b. Processing and transfer of passenger name record data by air carriers to the United States Department of Homeland Security- 'PNR', 11304/07, June 28.

De Vries, G. 2005. *Working together in the fight against terrorism, 16 September*. Brussels: EPC.

Den Boer, M., and J. Monar. 2002. Keynote article: September and the challenge of global terrorism to the EU as a security actor. *Journal of Common Market Studies* 40, no. 1.

EUobserver. 2008. US flight security demands ruffle EU feathers, February 11.

EurActiv. 2006. We can't trust Americans blindfolded, October 25.

European Commission. 2003. Communication from the Commission to the Council and the Parliament. Transfer of Air Passenger Name Record (PNR) data: A global EU approach, December 16 2003, COM (2003) 826.

European Commission. 2007. Proposal for a Council framework decision on the use of Passenger Name Record (PNR) for law enforcement purposes, October 22 2007, COM (2007) 654.

European Court of Justice. 2004. Action brought on 27 July 2004 by the European Parliament against the Commission of the European Communities. Case C-318/04. *Official Journal of the EU* C228/32 (September 11).

European Court of Justice. 2006. The Court Annuls the Council Decision concerning the conclusion of an agreement between the European Community and the United States of America on the processing and transfer of personal data and the Commission decision on the adequate protection of those data. Press release, CJE/06/46, May 30.

European Parliament. 2007. European Parliament resolution of 12 July 2007 on the PNR agreement with the United States of America, P6_TA-PROV(2007)0347, July 12.

Financial Times. 2007. Travellers from US face EU crackdown, August 7.

Geyer, F. 2007. *Fruit of the poisonous tree. Member states' indirect use of extraordinary rendition and the EU counter-terrorism strategy.* Brussels: CEPS Working Document 263.

Guild, E., and E. Brower. 2006. *The political life of data. The ECJ decision on the PNR agreement between the EU and the US.* July. Brussels: CEPS.

Hosein, G. 2005. On international policy dynamics: challenges for civil society. *Privacy International* (April 8).

Manners, I. 2002. The normative power Europe: a contradiction in terms. *Journal of Common Market Studies* 40, no. 2.

Mitsilegas, V. 2005. Contrôle des étrangers, des passagers, des citoyens: surveillance et anti-terrorisme. *Cultures & Conflits* 58: 151–81.

Mitsilegas, V., J. Monar, and W. Rees. 2003. *The European Union and internal security. Guardian of the people?.* Basingstoke: Palgrave Macmillan.

Monar, J. 2004. The EU as an international actor in the domain of justice and home affairs. *European Foreign Affairs Review* 9, no. 4: 395–415.

Rees, W. 2006. *Transatlantic counter–terrorism cooperation. The new imperative.* Abingdon: Routledge.

Scharpf, F.W. 1997. *Games real actors play. Actor-centered institutionalism in policy research.* Boulder: Westview Press.

UK House of Lords. 2007. *The EU/US Passenger Name Record (PNR) Agreement.* London: Stationary Office.

US Congress. 2004. Committee on international relations joint hearing. US–European cooperation on counterterrorism: achievements and challenges, Washington, September 14.

Wolff, S., N. Wichmann, and G. Mounier. 2009. The external dimension of Justice and Home Affairs: A different security agenda for the EU?. *Journal of European Integration* 31, no. 1: 9–23.

The Mediterranean Dimension of EU Counter-terrorism

SARAH WOLFF

Department of International Relations, London School of Economics and Political Science, London, UK

ABSTRACT Key to the Mediterranean dimension of the European Union's internal security is the fight against terrorism, which has captivated most of European policy making in recent years. Counter-terrorism initiatives aimed at the Mediterranean region have multiplied, taking the form of technical assistance, funding and training. One striking feature of this recent evolution is the use of first pillar and second pillar instruments to achieve objectives of the EU's internal security. The development of a foreign policy dimension to the EU's counter-terrorism policy towards neighbouring countries, in particular, is one of the aspects through which the external dimension of Justice and Home Affairs (JHA) has materialized. This article proposes to investigate the input and output dimensions of the EU's counter-terrorism policy in the Mediterranean. For that purpose, an institutionalist approach casts some light on the weight of history, critical junctures, the role of cultural frame and of the persisting differences between the member states, to build up a common counter-terrorism policy. Then, turning to the second level of analysis, which investigates the 'external' actors that are the Mediterranean partners, an overview of counter-terrorism cooperation reveals that, whereas multilateral actions have blossomed, the thrust of the cooperation occurs at a bilateral level, mainly between some EU member states and some of their ex-colonial powers.

Introduction

Key to the Mediterranean dimension of the EU's internal security is the fight against terrorism, which in recent years has captivated policy making activity in Europe. Counter-terrorism initiatives aimed at the Mediterranean region have multiplied, taking the form of technical assistance, funding and training. One striking feature of this evolution is the use of first pillar and second pillar instruments to achieve the objective of EU's internal security. The development of a foreign policy dimension to the EU's counter-terrorism policy towards neighbouring countries is one of the aspects through which the external dimension of Justice and Home Affairs (JHA) has materialized.

In accordance with the research framework proposed in the introduction to this special issue, this article espouses an institutionalist approach, combined with a two-level analysis of the input and output dimensions. From an *input perspective*, the ambition is to understand why and how the foreign policy dimension of EU counter-terrorism policy has developed. A historical institutionalist approach is used to argue that the development of a foreign policy dimension to EU counter-terrorism policy has been caused by a series of 'critical junctures'. Furthermore, despite the persistence of differences between national law enforcement practices, a new 'permissive consensus' has enabled the aggregation of the various national interests under a single political objective: the achievement of an Area of Freedom, Security and Justice (AFSJ). This is explained using the sociological concept of 'cultural frame'.

The second level of analysis investigates the 'external' actors; the Mediterranean partners (the *output dimension*). Cooperation has also been made possible by the spill-over of a 'permissive consensus', prevalent amongst European and North African elites. Here it is not possible to talk about a 'cultural frame', though, since the *rapprochement* of security discourses serves different interests. In addition, the weight of past counter-terrorism cooperation with ex-colonial powers still plays an important role. Indeed, while multilateral actions have blossomed, the thrust of the cooperation occurs at a bilateral level, notably between France, Spain and North African countries.

The Development of a Foreign Policy Dimension of Counter-terrorism: the Input Dimension

In understanding why and how the EU and its member states have developed a foreign policy dimension to their counter-terrorism policies, a historical institutionalist perspective appears relevant. The current policy towards the Mediterranean cannot, indeed, be understood without taking into consideration past decisions in the field of counter-terrorism and their influence on the current context. These path-dependent patterns, which reproduce routinization practices, have nonetheless been challenged by some 'critical junctures', which provided some opportunities for policy change and to rupture with incremental policy patterns. 'Critical junctures', such as the 1972 Munich Olympic Games, the 1999 Tampere summit or 9/11, have been identified as formative events that have influenced the current outlook of EU counter-terrorism policy. These critical junctures have occurred within the context of a new cultural frame, a new 'permissive consensus' regarding security issues. A detailed analysis of the institutional and policy innovations since 2001 reveals that the thrust of legislative activity has focused on the mainstreaming of counter-terrorism into external relations.

Critical Junctures and Cultural Frames

From a historical institutionalist perspective, institutions are sticky; in the sense that there is a certain resistance to change from institutional actors, and that reproduction of similar patterns and past decisions are characteristics of policy evolution. Policy change is still possible, and can happen through the occurrence of a 'critical juncture', an event that can provoke reform and have 'lasting consequences' for institutions (Pierson 2000, 263). Critical junctures are interpreted as key moments; these can be generated by big events, exogenous shocks, but also by small decisions. What is important is temporality and to analyse when political change might occur. The case of counter-terrorism in the Mediterranean reveals that despite the existence of 'critical junctures', or events combining a series of factors leading to policy change, EU counter-terrorism policy presents some path-dependent features such as lack of cooperation, lack of sufficient resources and shortcomings in implementation of common agreements. Although it is shown in this article that historical institutionalism is an appropriate approach to understand counter-terrorism policy developments, one must also acknowledge that it is necessary to look at new policy orientation in 'normal times', when there is not necessarily a crisis or a critical juncture. It is, therefore, important for researchers to combine a historical institutionalist perspective with the analysis of JHA incremental change through daily politics.

In the field of terrorism cooperation with Mediterranean countries, several critical junctures can be identified. The 1972 Munich Olympic Games marked the first irruption of the Middle East conflict in the European arena, which had until then been considered a remote security problem. The massacre of eleven Israeli athletes and one German officer marked a turning point in police cooperation amongst EU member states to fight terrorism. Thus, 1972 was a critical moment during which terrorist attacks were securitized and internalized by European leaders. Bicchi (2007, 73) explained that, due to the uncertainty generated by the new phenomenon irrupting on the European scene, leaders were ready to cooperate and look for common solutions to the issue, for instance through the European Policy Cooperation framework. It is the argument of this article, though, that this uncertainty did not really lead to the quest for common solutions, but for national solutions under a transgovernmental framework. Moreover, it is important to stress that, at the time, *ad hoc* groups, such as the TREVI group, remained secretive and worked behind closed doors (Bigo 1996; Pastore, Friedrichs, and Politi 2005, 5).

While the 1970s constituted an opportunistic moment to set up *ad hoc* working groups, such as TREVI or the Police Working Group on Terrorism (PWGT), the 1990s were none the less a period during which terrorism was not anymore perceived as a European problem, but rather as a domestic problem. Basque nationalism was a problem circumscribed to the Spanish territory, while Islamic terrorism was mainly the deed of the Algerian GIA, active only on French territory (Fijnaut, Wouters, and Naert 2004, 17).

The summit of Tampere in 1999, organized under the Finnish presidency, also presents the features of a critical juncture in the sense that it introduced for the first time a political objective: the achievement of the Area of Freedom, Security and Justice (AFSJ). This evolution has been described as a 'normative shift away from a full preservation of national sovereignty towards to partial pooling of national sovereignty with limited mandates and weak institutional instruments and structures' (Kaunert 2005, 469). It was also the first time ever that the 'external dimension' of JHA was mentioned in Council conclusions (Wolff, Wichmann, and Mounier 2009, this issue, 9–23).

Another critical juncture was 9/11, which acted as a window of opportunity to adopt long-standing proposals that were lying on the desk of EU officials. It helped to accelerate the taking of decisions that had already been discussed in the past, and reflected the different visions of the EU member states in conceiving an EU counter-terrorism policy; such as the debate over the joint investigation teams, which started in 1999 at the Tampere summit (European Council 1999). Nonetheless, it is important to underline that the prospect of enlargement acted as important leverage to foster integration in the field of JHA and police cooperation well before 9/11. The prospect of expansion of EU borders to new neighbours, such as Ukraine, Belarus, or even Turkey, acted as a formidable incentive to move from the constraints introduced by Maastricht to a much more integrated JHA policy within the Amsterdam treaty. As a consequence, the foreign policy dimension of JHA, and 'the need for the Union to integrate JHA matters fully in the Union's external policy so that a comprehensive, integrated, cross-pillar action is carried out by the Union as a whole' (Coreper 2000, 2) in the field of the fight against terrorism, were considered seriously well before 9/11.

This historical analysis puts the emphasis on the necessity to take into account past decisions, and the importance of different cultural practices amongst the member states, when it comes to counter-terrorism. The existence of critical junctures helped the EU to accelerate decision taking in that field, and to decide upon some common measures at the most critical moments. Indeed, under certain conditions, short-term interests can lose some ground in favour of collective action. The evolution of the perceptions and nature of terrorism, as well as the position of European public opinion on the issue, convinced EU member states that collective action was necessary, and that the EU was probably the most innate arena of action for that purpose. In that sense, a helpful way to reconcile both the rationalist and the historical analyses is to adopt a 'cultural frame' institutionalist approach. Such an approach draws from sociology and argues that the presence of certain 'cultural frames' might 'convince actors about the general contours of new arrangements' (Fligstein and Mara-Drita 1996, 3).

The cultural frame approach reconciles rational choice with more sociological and historical branches of institutionalism by 'emphasizing the need to take path dependency created by existing institutions, the social context of interaction between the relevant actors as well as the role of institutional entrepreneurs into consideration' (Stetter 2000, 97). In the field of counter-terrorism, this combination of the three institutionalisms is particularly useful, since one cannot take for granted that this policy is merely the result of inter-institutional competition between actors driven by rational calculations. Internal and external, but also sociological and historical factors, explain the evolution of counter-terrorism policies towards the Mediterranean and other neighbouring countries. Internally, the lack of coordination is explained by the permanence of different national practices and the culture of intelligence sharing. The weight of decisions taken within the context of *ad hoc* groups, such as TREVI or the Berne Group, has conditioned current institutional developments. Externally, past commitments within the Euro–Mediterranean relationship conditioned current developments of the partnership, as well as the security context in which the dialogue on counter-terrorism takes place.

As at the time of the 1992 Single Programme, the objective of achieving an AFSJ has gathered under one banner the interests of the different member states who are willing to cooperate to protect the EU as well as their own internal security. The difficulties encountered with the pillarized system introduced by Maastricht, as well as the prospect of the enlargement, gave some impetus to the consensus around the concept of AFSJ well before the context created by 9/11. The political objective of AFSJ is, in fact, the result of the spreading of a new post-Cold War cultural frame; according to which, in order 'to protect the EU's internal security regime from external threats, the EU must project its norms and standards of security' (Mounier 2007, 8). Similarly, in the context of the Euro–Mediterranean Partnership, it has long been demonstrated that the deadlock of the 2000 Charter on Peace and Stability pushed the discussion away from hard security issues towards soft security issues (Bicchi 2002, 8).

Mainstreaming into External Relations and Institutional Reorganization

If counter-terrorism cooperation dates back to the time of the Brigades Rouges with the TREVI group, it is true that 9/11 has considerably intensified the fight against terrorism. Only a few days after the attacks on American soil, an extraordinary European Council summit on 21 September 2001 adopted the first ever EU action plan for the fight against terrorism, which was the first document in a series that would follow (European Council 2001).

The 2001 action plan was thought through in a multi-dimensional manner (Monar 2006, 152). First, it combines both legislative and operational measures, which was quite innovative at EU level. Secondly, it is multidimensional

> in the sense that it integrates both internal and external (international) measures, providing the so far most prominent example of putting the whole range of external EU instruments — including those of the Common Foreign and Security Policy and of European Community (EC) external economic relations instruments — at the service of an

internal security objective, namely the protection of European citizens against terrorism (Monar 2006, 152).

Finally, the action plan presents characteristics of cross-pillarization, involving all three pillars at the service of the fight against terrorism.

Despite important reforms on an internal level,[1] it is on an external level that most of the policy innovations took place, with EU counter-terrorism policy acquiring a foreign policy dimension. Although first conceived at an internal level, in recent years it has spilled over into the EU's external relations, to the extent that some have described a 'mainstreaming' of the fight against terrorism into external relations (Monar 2007, 276). Accordingly, this mainstreaming has been accompanied by cross-pillarization and, therefore, by the use of first and second pillar policy tools in EU counter-terrorism policy. In particular, Common Foreign and Security Policy (CFSP) political dialogues with third countries (in the form of partnership and association agreements), and the active role of the EU within United Nations' working groups dealing with terrorism, have been used to profile the foreign policy dimension of EU counter-terrorism policy (Monar 2007, 276).

This mainstreaming of counter-terrorism into external relations resulted in the elaboration of an external strategy for the fight against terrorism, as expressed by the European Council in June 2004 in the document 'Integrating the fight against terrorism into EU external relations policy' (Council of the European Union 2004), and the 'Declaration on Combating Terrorism' adopted by the European Council in March 2004 (European Council 2004a). This external strategy is based on the general objective of 'deepen[ing] the international consensus and enhanc[ing] international efforts to combat terrorism' (Objective 1) and 'target[ing] actions under EU external relations towards priority Third Countries where counter-terrorist capacity or commitment to combating terrorism needs to be enhanced' (Objective 7) (Council of the European Union 2004, 2). As a result, commentators have pointed to the increasing blurring of internal and external security, and to 'the internationalisation of what were traditionally national internal security policies' (Cottey 2007, 177).

In parallel to the development of a foreign policy dimension to EU counter-terrorism policy, the EU's internal structure was reorganized, with the intention of promoting coordination and cross-pillarization, with mixed results. In particular, a reform of the working groups in the Council took place. Two groups are now devoted to the fight against terrorism: the Terrorism Working Group (TWG), a working group on terrorism in charge of the internal aspects and gathering interior ministers; and the Counter-Terrorism Working Group (COTER) under the CFSP pillar, which is in charge of the external aspects and meets at least once a month. Although the creation of these groups can be seen as a positive development, they duplicate structures for interior ministers and diplomats instead of creating only one counter-terrorism working group. Coordination efforts are, therefore, needed and, since 2003, the TWG and the COTER have held joint meetings and work on a common assessment of the threat (Lugna 2006, 109). A new *ad hoc* group, enabling security and intelligence services to cooperate, was also created in 2005. The Situation Centre (SitCen) is based in the Council Secretariat, and 'provides the Council with strategic analysis of the terrorist threat based on intelligence from the Member States' security [internal security services] and intelligence services [external services] and, where appropriate, on information provided by Europol' (Lugna 2006, 110). Similarly, the Police Chiefs Task Force,[2] set up in October 1999 after the Tampere Summit, was mandated to improve cooperation with third countries, notably at an operational level but also to guarantee a high level of air safety (Anderson and Apap 2002, 7).

The impetus given by a series of terrorist attacks has pushed the EU member states to act collectively in the field of counter-terrorism. It has enabled them to give impulse to old legislative texts sitting on EU official desks and to agree on some common structures and further coordination through, for instance, the institution of the office of EU counter-terrorism coordinator. Established in March 2004, in the wake of the Madrid attacks, the counter-terrorism coordinator is based in the Council Secretariat and coordinates the work of the latter when it comes to combating terrorism 'with due regard to the responsibilities of the Commission, [while] maintaining an overview of all the instruments at the Union's disposal with a view to regular reporting to the Council and effective follow-up of Council decisions' (European Council 2004a). The creation of this post went through a series of conflicts, reflecting past dependent patterns of EU policy making. Indeed, this role of enhancing cooperation between the Council and the Commission was regarded suspiciously by the services of the latter, who feared that the counter-terrorism coordinator will act as a Trojan Horse of national interests, which will try to counter the Commission efforts in the fight against terrorism (Keohane 2006, 19). These were unfounded concerns, since the EU's counter-terrorism coordinator has a very weak position: it does not have any budget, cannot propose legislation, cannot chair any meetings (Keohane 2006, 18). This example reflects some of the persisting patterns of policy making in the field of EU counter-terrorism, which are often counter-intuitive in a field, such as JHA — characterized by rapid developments.

The entry into force of the Lisbon Treaty, if ratified by all the member states on 1 January 2009, will render obsolete the pillar structure and it is hoped that the extension of the co-decision and the qualified majority voting procedure will bring more efficiency to the EU's counter-terrorism. One may hope that the involvement of the European Parliament on some aspects of this policy will improve accountability and democratic scrutiny (Carrera and Geyer 2007, 2). It is not totally clear, though, to what extent the member states will be able to retain influence. Indeed, compared to the Constitutional Treaty, the Commission will need to share its right of initiative with at least a quarter of the member states, when it comes to judicial cooperation in criminal matters, police cooperation and cooperation between administrative departments (Carrera and Geyer 2007, 5). A lots of opt-outs and exceptions seem to prevail under the new structure and it is difficult to assess how they will affect the external dimension of counter-terrorism. The new consolidated treaties, indeed, remain vague, since article 68 under Title V stipulates that the European Council will 'define the strategic guidelines for legislative and operational planning within the area of freedom, security and justice' (European Council 2008).

Thus, 9/11 and other critical junctures have acted as catalysts for further integration, pushing forward old legislative proposals that were sitting on the desks of European policy officers (the historical institutionalist factor). The development of a new cultural frame also played a favourable role (the sociological factor). The next section of this article looks at the output dimension: the way this foreign policy dimension has developed over time with the Mediterranean neighbours.

Tackling Terrorism with the Mediterranean Neighbours: the Output Dimension

The emergence of new forms of terrorism in North Africa has intensified cooperation between European and Mediterranean governments. Terrorism from the Mediterranean region has become an internal security concern for the EU and, therefore, projects have blossomed at a multilateral level between the EU and its partners. Nonetheless, it appears that cooperation is occurring mainly at bilateral level, which remains the main preference for cooperation between partners.

From Remote Security Concern to the EU's Internal Security

Terrorism is not a new issue in the context of EU policy towards the Mediterranean and has been part of the EU's security concerns in the region since the 1970s. The development of JHA and police cooperation in Europe has, itself, been influenced significantly by terrorism coming from the Mediterranean region.

Traditionally, in Arab countries, terrorist acts have been perceived as a challenge to state legitimacy, intended to destabilize the authoritarian regimes in place. Therefore, the issue of terrorism was, for a long time, very sensitive within the context of the Barcelona Process. Notwithstanding the Israeli–Palestinian conflict, terrorism was 'an issue of misunderstanding and misperception among Europeans, between Europeans and Arabs and among Arabs' (Biad 2002, 34). Recently though, the region has been affected by the transnationalisation of terrorist groups, notably in the Maghreb. Although experts still disagree in their assessments of the reality of such a phenomenon,[3] it is difficult to deny that terrorist attacks on the Mediterranean partners' territories have multiplied. In parallel, both European and Mediterranean partners are facing terrorist techniques imported directly from the Iraq war, such as suicide bombings.[4] The novelty of this type of terrorism and, in particular, of Al-Qaeda, is probably the 'absence of specific demands and the fact that its command structure was not hierarchical, or exclusively cell-based, but predicated rather on voluntary emulation by disciples who were often not even specifically recruited' (Spence 2008, 5). This new visage of terrorism has some deep links with activists living in Europe who have imported those same new techniques into European territory. Hence, while in 1995 the Algerian events were perceived by the Europeans (and particularly the French) as a domestic issue, elements converge today to indicate a transnationalization of the activities in the Euro-Mediterranean region.

In recent years, terrorism in North Africa has undergone important changes, and is now harbouring some terrorists linked to Al-Qaeda. As rightly pointed out by counter-terrorism experts, because of its landscape of mountains and desert, the Sahara/Sahel region constitutes an ideal place to train terrorists and is much closer to Europe than Afghanistan or Pakistan (Smith 2007). Originally an ex-dissident group from the *Groupe Islamique Armé* (GIA) during the civil war in Algeria, the *Groupe Salafiste pour la Prédication du Combat* (GSPC), created in 1988, has established links with Al-Qaeda and, since January 2007, has been called *Al-Qaeda in the Islamic Maghreb* (*AQIM*) (Europol 2007, 26).[5] This connection with the wider movement of Al-Qaeda followed the efforts of the Algerian government to put into place a national reconciliation process with Islamist activists. This led to important losses for the GSPC, which was constituted only of a few thousand activists, as pointed out by Mohsen-Finan (2007, 43). Foreign companies and citizens have also been the target of AQIM's activities. For instance, in December 2006 a bus transporting employees from the Americano-Algerian society, Brown and Root Condor (BRC), was the object of a terrorist attack in Bouchaoui (Mohsen-Finan 2007, 42). Counter-terrorism officials have revealed that the GSPC was thought to be the origin of thwarted plans against the metro in Paris, the airport of Orly and the *Direction de la Surveillance du Territoire* (DST), the French intelligence agency. Similarly, it has been reported that a related cell was planning attacks in Italy (Smith 2007). Some observers have pointed to the difficulties of the relationship between Al-Qaeda and North Africa, given different perceptions on Islam. Hence, some tensions between the GSPC and Al-Qaeda arose when the Algerian group was willing to change the name of AQIM into 'Al-Qaeda in the Mediterranean', a proposal rejected by Bin Laden since the notion underlines the commonness of the region (Guidière 2007, 275).

Although the transnational nature of AQIM is put under question by some analysts, for whom some of the attacks in Morocco in April 2007 were the deed of independent activists (Mohsen-Finan 2007, 43), these recent transformations have caused concern for both the European intelligence services and the USA, and have turned the Maghreb into a key geographical zone for the fight against terrorism.

Terrorism Cooperation Between the Euro–Mediterranean Partners

The 'permissive consensus' beyond the EU. The permeability of counter-terrorism cooperation with the Mediterranean partners was made possible by the post-9/11 context, which was a critical juncture for the development of a new cultural frame: 'a permissible environment for the emergence of a European foreign minister post and the smartening of the EU's external and security "act"' (Spence 2008, 12), embodied by the 2003 European Security Strategy. Indeed, 9/11 inaugurated a new era for CFSP and European Security and Defence Policy (ESDP), which were considerably strengthened through a generation of new ESDP missions, the conclusion of new partnerships with third countries (the European Neighbourhood Policy Action Plans), and the development of the notion of neighbourhood. The new security cultural frame was underpinned by various opinion polls, which demonstrated that a majority of European citizens were concerned by terrorism. Despite important national differences regarding perception of terrorism, in the Eurobarometer of autumn 2001 (Directorate General Press and Communication 2002), 86 per cent of Europeans declared that they personally feared terrorism, a growth of only 12 points compared with 2000; terrorism having being a constant concern for Europeans since 1996 (Spence 2008, 21). Democracy and rule assistance and, more generally, cooperation in the Mediterranean and other regions of the world, were from that point onwards structured in a way that encouraged a comprehensive security approach to impede violence and terrorism reaching EU territory.

Similarly, this 'permissive consensus' was reinforced by the fact that, prior to the interest of the EU in terrorism from the region, Mediterranean countries had been interested in counter-terrorism for a long time; the Algerian situation being one dramatic instance of terrorism irruption in the North African domestic arena. The Council of Ministers of Justice of the Arab League adopted a Convention on Terrorism in 1998, well before 9/11,[6] which came into force in 1999. The weaknesses of this convention have been denounced by many human rights activists. Thus, terrorism is defined as the following:

> Any act or threat of violence, whatever its motives or purposes, that occurs in the advancement of an individual or collective criminal agenda and seeking to sow panic among people, causing fear by harming them, or placing their lives, liberty or security in danger, or seeking to cause damage to the environment or to public or private installations or property or to occupying or seizing them, or seeking to jeopardize national resources.

Vagueness in the definition renders a flexible interpretation of terrorism easier, and prompted Amnesty International (2002, 19) to question whether this might increase the risk of arbitrary arrests and detentions.

Later, in 2003, the interior ministers of Arab countries agreed on a strategy on the fight against terrorism, during their twentieth meeting in Tunis (Saudi Press Association 2003). This agreement was denounced by the United Nations Development Programme (UNDP) 2004 Arab Human Development Report, for contributing to the strengthening of restrictions with respect to the freedom of opinion and expression and the field of human rights (UNDP 2004, 9).

Thus, 9/11 rendered possible a *rapprochement* of previous security discourses between the North African elites. The past experience of North

African countries with terrorism, as well as domestic difficulties faced by Mediterranean partners internally with Islamic opposition, helped Arab leaders to legitimize cooperation with their European counterparts, even though both partners differ on the analysis of terrorism. The 9/11 critical juncture created a window of opportunity for the Mediterranean leaders to join in the international fight against terrorism, thus legitimizing internal domestic problems with political opponents, often of Islamic faction. This 'permissive consensus' enabled the 2002 Valencia conference to take place, and to ask the Euro–Mediterranean partners to commit themselves to the fight against terrorism.

The instruments of cooperation. One of the most important texts agreed amongst the Euro–Mediterranean partners is certainly the Euro-Mediterranean Code of Conduct on Countering Terrorism of 2005. Drafted by British diplomats, the document presents terrorism as a common threat for Euro–Mediterranean citizens and, despite not agreeing on any definition, pledges cooperation and coordination amongst the governments of the region (Euro-Mediterranean Conference 2005, 1). Seen by some observers as a unique political frame of reference in the region, the document is, indeed, the first of its kind, committing the partners to an international counter-terrorist legal framework, and establishing a dialogue on counter-terrorism in the region (Reinares 2006, 4). The partners have committed themselves to act within the framework of the Security Council resolutions on terrorism, in the framework of the Charter of the United Nations, international law and humanitarian law. The Code encourages the partners to ratify and implement the thirteen UN counter-terrorism conventions, to refuse asylum to terrorists and deny them safe haven in accordance with international law, to share expertise and best practices, to ensure respect for human rights in the fight against terrorism in accordance with international law, etc. However, when looking carefully at cooperation in the field of counter-terrorism amongst the Euro–Mediterranean partners, it seems that cooperation is 'a matter of mutual convenience between individual countries rather than part of a broader region-building project based on shared understandings' (Gillespie 2002, 10).

Alternatively, the external dimension of JHA in the field of terrorism has materialized through the adoption of clauses within the framework of association agreements with third countries, the so-called 'counter-terrorism clauses'. This instrument was foreseen by the 'Plan of action to combat terrorism', which insisted upon the external dimension of the EU's counter-terrorism policy, and was concretized with the 2002 Seville Summit. The European Declaration on Combating Terrorism, in the aftermath of the 2004 Madrid bombing, gave the mandate to the Council to 'include effective counterterrorism clauses in all agreements with third countries'. The 2004 Council document, which assesses these clauses, remains quite vague regarding the legal basis, and simply specifies that 'counter-terrorism clauses can take different forms in respect of their legal source, namely, they can be part of a formal agreement or they can make the subject of an exchange of letters or of a joint declaration' (European Council 2004b, 5). It is explained further that the counter-terrorism clauses are usually elaborated on a case-by-case basis and 'negotiated' with the third countries. The Council document recognizes such instruments as 'a useful tool, even as EU foreign policy extends its reach and develops a global scope' (European Council 2004b, 11). Counter-terrorism clauses are a cross-pillar instrument, since they concern the cooperation of the third country in the fight against the financing of terrorist activities (first pillar), and the dialogue and cooperation in the second pillar, as much as third pillar *per se* cooperation. The 2004 document also provides a sample of a standard counter-terrorism clause decided at the 2002 Seville Summit, which reads as follows:

> The Parties reaffirm the importance of the fight against terrorism, and in accordance with international conventions and with their respective legislation and regulations agree to cooperate in the prevention and suppression of terrorist acts. They shall do so in particular:
> - in the framework of the full implementation of Resolution 1373 of the UN Security Council and other relevant UN resolutions, international conventions and instruments;
> - by exchange of information on terrorist groups and their support networks in accordance with international and national law; and,
> - by exchanges of views on means and methods used to counter terrorism, including in technical fields and training, and by exchange of experiences in respect of terrorism prevention (European Council 2004b, 15).

Within the context of Euro–Mediterranean relations, such clauses have so far been concluded with Algeria and Egypt. The Euro-Mediterranean Association Agreement (EMAA) concluded with Algeria on 22 April 2002 at the Valencia conference includes a clause in article 90, which reads as the standard model counter-terrorism clause mentioned above (Council of the European Union 2005). Similarly, but in a slightly 'lighter' version, article 59 of the EMAA signed in June 2001 with Egypt includes a counter-terrorism clause.

The other instrument used by the EU is technical assistance. As a follow-up to the EU Plan of Action on Combating Terrorism, the EU provides technical assistance through a 2004 counter-terrorism capacity-building project with Algeria, Indonesia and Morocco, which tries to bring the aid projects financed by the European Commission and the EU member states under a single framework (EU Council Secretariat 2007, 6). It is, indeed, the first time ever, according to the ex counter-terrorism coordinator Gijs de Vries, that the national budgets and the EU budget have been synchronized as instruments of EU counter-terrorism policy. These projects are relatively sensitive and very little information has been released. A network of national contact points has been created to facilitate co-operation (De Vries 2006). These technical missions are pursued hand-in-hand with the UN counter-terrorism committee and, in March 2005, a mission was sent by the counter-terrorism executive directorate to further this counter-terrorism cooperation with Morocco (Fini 2006). Actions under the counter-terrorism technical assistance plan include, for instance, programmes to 'tackle radicalization in particular in key environments, for example prisons, universities, places of religious training or worship'. Border, airport and maritime security, and training on crisis management, appear as other elements of the technical assistance provided to Morocco and Algeria (Council of the European Union 2007b). Technical assistance usually is provided through the ENP Action Plans or the MEDA/JHA programmes, but also through the participation of the EU in the UN counter-terrorism committee external assistance programmes. Following the wide definition of UN counter-terrorism activities, the Directorate-General Justice, Liberty and Security, calculated that, in 2007, the Community was providing around 400 million of counter-terrorism-related assistance to approximately eighty third countries.[7]

This was completed by the adoption of the Instrument for Stability (European Parliament and European Council 2006), which enables the Community to cooperate with third countries either in the context of a 'crisis situation' or of 'stable conditions', those terms being defined very broadly.[8] This first pillar instrument is aimed at 'strengthening the capacity of law enforcement and judicial and civil authorities involved in the fight against terrorism and organized crime, including illicit trafficking of people, drugs, firearms and explosive materials and in the effective control of illegal trade and transit' (article 4). Assistance can thus be provided for 'supporting measures concerning the development and strengthening of counter-terrorism legislation, the implementation and practice of financial law, of customs law and of immigration law and the development of international procedures for law enforcement' (article 4).

One of the main innovations was introduced eventually in 2007, with the adoption of the first CFSP Joint Action in the field of terrorism, underpinning the argument that traditional foreign policy instruments are used to achieve internal security objectives. The CFSP Joint Action on terrorism of 16 July 2007 (Council of the European Union 2007a) shall provide some financial support to the African Centre for Study and Research on Terrorism (ACSRT), inaugurated in 2004 by the African Union in the context of its own 2002 Plan of Action on the Prevention and Combating of Terrorism in Africa. The choice of Algiers as the seat for the ACSRT is noteworthy, not only because it values the Algerian experience in the fight against terrorism, but also because it enables a link between the Mediterranean and the African continent in the fight (Fini 2006, 4). By deciding upon a joint action to support the ACSRT, the objective of the EU and its member states is also to further cooperation with the African Union in the field of counter-terrorism and, in particular, to foster the exchange of information.[9] With a budget of 665,000, the project assists in carrying out audit missions on national counter-terrorism arrangements, in agreement with the countries of the African Union.

Unfortunately, this project might well go unheeded, since contest between France, Morocco and Algeria might impede implementation of the joint action.[10] The insistence of the French to include Morocco as a partner of the ACSRT clashed significantly with the Algerian position, demonstrating that bilateral relations with EU member states were still crucial in the region. Likewise, in other areas, it appears that the 'external dimension of JHA' is often the result of contest over the policy space by the member states, which instrumentalizes the EU level to pursue its own interests.[11] In the case of counter-terrorism, classical bilateral relations are still the option favoured by Mediterranean partners.

The Preference for Bilateral Cooperation

Looking at counter-terrorism cooperation within the Euro–Mediterranean region, Guazzone and Bicchi (2002) pointed out a blatant reality: most cooperation takes place outside of the multilateral framework that is the Euro-Mediterranean Partnership (EMP). Rather, states prefer to cooperate at a bilateral level, such as between France, Spain and North African countries, notably Morocco and Algeria. Historical relationships and trust between the services have proved to be key elements of bilateral cooperation.

France, in particular, had early experience of Middle East-related terrorism. The first experience of terrorist attacks on French soil was actually linked to the decolonization process and the diffusion of the war in Algeria; against the *Front Islamique du Salut* (FIS), and the terrorist attacks of the *Organisation Armée Secrète* (OAS), whose main motto was 'l'Algérie restera française'. Until the 1980s, France had been exposed to domestic terrorism emblemized by extreme-left groups, such as *Action Directe* and Corsican nationalist claims for autonomy. Middle East and Islamic-related terrorism irrupted on to the French landscape in the 1980s, with a series of anti-Semitic attacks in Paris and, in particular, the attack of the rue Copernic in 1980 (Shapiro and Suzan 2003, 69). Later, France experienced a series of attacks in Paris in 1985 and 1986,[12] led by Iranian networks linked to the Hezbollah, due to their financial, technical and political support of Saddam Hussein's regime during the war against Iran (American Enterprise Institute for Public Policy Research 2007, 2). This series of attacks led to important changes in French counter-terrorism policy and, in particular, to the progressive abandonment of the 'sanctuary policy' which, in the 1970s, aimed to avoid terrorist attacks on French soil by providing a sanctuary for international terrorists and ensuring impunity to their activities (Shapiro and Suzan 2003, 69). This strategy led to tensions with the other European member states; notably with Spain, since some ETA members had been sheltered in France.

France has historically maintained close relations with the intelligence services of North African countries. As early as 1965, France played a role in the disappearance of the Moroccan nationalist leader Mehdi Ben Barka (Joffé 2008). Ben Barka was abducted on 29 October 1965 in Paris and given by the French services to Moroccan agents. Later, in the 1990s, the French services established quite early the connection between the terrorist attacks of the GIA and Al-Qaeda. The attacks perpetrated in France by the GIA, GSPC or the *Groupe de Roubaix* showed some organizational links with Al-Qaeda. Some of its members, sometimes French nationals of Algerian origin, had been trained in Al-Qaeda camps in Afghanistan and Sudan (Shaun 2003,

133). Those links were identified early on by the French intelligence services, and criminal investigations were open on these Afghan channels, thus creating important expertise on the topic (Pochon 2005, 66).

Spanish cooperation with Morocco has increased since the 2004 attacks in Madrid, which involved some Moroccan nationals. Spanish interests and citizens have, indeed, been the target of terrorist groups, and intelligence reports from both countries have identified the regions of Tarragona, Granada and Almería, but also Ceuta and Melilla, as 'hubs that link criminal organizations and mosques to various terror groups where the hashish trade, money laundering, and human smuggling provide huge profits to finance terror operations' (Celso 2006, 136). The two intelligence services are working hand in hand and, thanks to their collaboration, managed to unveil a plot to bomb the Madrid courthouse (Celso 2006, 138). Despite some diplomatic hiccups, and the recent polemical visit of the Spanish kings to Ceuta and Melilla, the cooperation in the field of counter-terrorism continues (Agence France Presse 2007).

Spain started to have an interest in the security situation in Morocco after the attacks of 2003 in Casablanca. Spain realized then that the king was not a guarantor of the immunity of the country against Islamic terrorism and, consequently, started to get involved in order to ensure the security of its own citizens. In 2007, the Spanish Interior Ministry declared its ambition to establish a permanent mixed group of experts in the fight against terrorism, similar to the one that already exists for migration issues (Ministerio del Interior Español 2007). Collaboration has also intensified in the field of the fight against financing of terrorism, between *la Fiscalia General del Estado de España* and *la Corte Suprema de Marruecos* (El Mundo 2007).[13] Relations also intensified following a series of attacks in both countries (Marrakech, 1994; Casablanca, 2003; Madrid, March 2004; Casablanca, March 2007). The two countries have also collaborated closely during the investigation of the 2004 Madrid bombings.[14] Eventually, cooperation between Spain, France and Morocco will be encouraged through, for instance, the signing of an agreement between the three public prosecutors' offices to exchange information on the three countries 'in real time and systematically'. As rightly underlined by Guidière (2007, 270), this initiative is very important; in the sense that it will enable the three police services to assist interrogation with their partners, for instance, and have immediate access to elements of proof.

Conclusion: the Challenges of the External Dimension of Counter-terrorism

From an *input perspective*, the case of the fight against terrorism is particularly instructive for shedding some light on the conditions of institutional creation and design. Our investigation reveals that EU counter-terrorism policy increasingly affects the relationship of the EU and its member states with the Mediterranean region. This externalization of EU counter-terrorism policy is not completely novel, and one needs to look at several 'critical junctures', such as the 1972 Munich Olympic Games, the 1999 Tampere Summit,

9/11 and the 2004 Madrid bombings, to understand the weight of history in current policy making dynamics. Such 'critical junctures' have reinforced the trend towards a mainstreaming of EU counter-terrorism policy into the EU's external relations with its Mediterranean neighbours, as well as some reforms which have not yet got rid of persistent patterns of EU counter-terrorism policy making, such as the fear of national sovereignty loss of the lack of coherence. This historical institutional reading needs to be combined with a wider sociological reading, which combines it with the apparition of 'cultural frames', such as the need to protect EU's internal security and to achieve the AFSJ.

An important external factor (*output perspective*) in explaining the EU's externalization of counter-terrorism policy to its Mediterranean neighbours has been the changing composition of the security landscape, particularly in North Africa and the Sahel region. The appearance of a new kind of transnational terrorism linked to Al-Qaeda has naturally pushed EU member states to address this issue together. In parallel, a 'permissive consensus' enabled Mediterranean partners to pursue a *rapprochement* of their security discourses with the EU, and to find a way to legitimize internal domestic action. Implementation is still slow and weak; and it appears that, in the field of terrorism, both EU and Mediterranean partners have a strong preference for bilateral cooperation. This is especially the case for France and Spain, where historical links and trust between intelligence services are at the heart of an efficient cooperation.

A last point that merits elaboration is that the emergence of a 'security *rapprochement*' between the EU, North African and Middle Eastern capitals (Volpi 2006, 120) poses a problem; in that the EU is running risks in externalizing JHA to partner countries where the rule of law is very weak. Because Mediterranean partners do not have independent judiciaries and police forces that respect human rights, it is of the utmost importance that the EMP institutions, if willing to pursue cooperation in the field of JHA, also put in place the necessary institutions to ensure that fundamental freedoms and the rule of law are respected. Having for many years pursued a policy of promotion of the rule of law, human rights and fundamental freedoms, the EU finds itself confronted with a dilemma, in which it seeks cooperation in the fight against terrorism with law enforcement agencies that do not enjoy full independence from executive power, and do not apply basic principles of justice.

Therefore, this article pledges the idea of a 'Euro–Mediterranean Ombudsman', which would be made accessible to the citizens, and who would be able to raise complaints about abuses and mismanagement of the EMP objectives by the national authorities (EuroMeSCo 2005, 43). In addition, it is believed that the EU must accompany JHA cooperation with a strengthening of the institutional capacities of the judiciaries; a process which is not only about training programmes, but also institutional twinnings or the establishment of policy networks of law enforcement agencies, which would engage in a true reflection of what is meant by the principle of justice, and its implementation in the Euro–Mediterranean space.[15] This will then enable possible sustainable links to be established between the internal and external security policies towards the Mediterranean.

Acknowledgement

This paper is complementary to a previous reflection developed in a paper prepared for the The EuroMeSCo Annual Conference 2006, October 2006 (Istanbul, Turkey) 'Paths to democracy and inclusion within diversity' — Working Group on 'The linkage between justice and terrorism in the Euro-Mediterranean area'. Some findings of this paper were also previously presented in 'The Mediterranean dimension of Justice and Home Affairs — The challenges of border management and the fight against terrorism' in CFSP Fornet, 6, no. 1 (January 2008).

Notes

The views expressed in this article are those of the author only.
1. Such as the agreement on a common definition of terrorism with Council framework decision on Combating Terrorism of 13 June 2002 and the adoption of the directive on the European Arrest Warrant on 13 June 2002.
2. The Police Chief Task Force (PCTF) was set up as an informal *ad hoc* committee in October 1999, and first met in April 2000 in Lisbon.
3. Some believe that the actual transnational movement is, in fact, dominated by ex-GSCP Algerian leaders.
4. While acknowledging that contemporary suicide bombing dates back to the Hezbollah attacks in the 1980s in Lebanon, this terrorist technique is relatively new in the Maghreb region.
5. According to French intelligence services, the links between Islamist Algerians and Bin Laden's organization are longstanding ones, since when Bin Laden was in exile in Sudan, GIA members were his personal bodyguard (Rodier 2006).
6. This reflection on the 'security *rapprochement*' has already been exposed in Wolff (2006).
7. Official number provided by DG JLS retrieved from http://ec.europa.eu/justice_home/fsj/terrorism/international/fsj_terrorism_international_en.htm.
8. See article 3 of the Instrument for Stability.
9. See article 1 of Council Joint Action 2007/501/CFSP.
10. Confidential interview — European Commission official, 17 April 2008, Brussels.
11. See, in the case of border management, the influence of France and Spain (Wolff 2008).
12. For a detailed analysis of the attacks, see Bigo (1991).
13. Some ideas on Spain have already been published in Wolff (2007a).
14. For more details on Spain and the external dimension of JHA, refer to Wolff (2007b).
15. Ideas from this last paragraph have already been aired in Wolff (2006).

References

Agence France Presse. 2007. Le 'combat' hispano-marocain contre le terrorisme va se poursuivre. Paris: AFP (November 7).
American Enterprise Institute for Public Policy Research. 2007. France: Europe's counterterrorist powerhouse. Washington: States News Service (October 31).
Amnesty International. 2002. The Arab convention for the suppression of terrorism a serious threat to human rights, *IOR 51/001/2002*. London: Amnesty International (January 9).
Anderson, M., and J. Apap. 2002. Changing conceptions of security and their implications for EU Justice and Home Affairs cooperation. CEPS policy brief. Brussels: CEPS, October.
Biad, A. 2002. The political and security partnership and its influence on stability in the Mediterranean region. In Huldt, Engman and Davidson 2002, 29–39.

Bicchi, F. 2002. *From security to economy and back? Euro-Mediterranean relations in perspective.* Florence: European University Institute.

Bicchi, F. 2007. *European foreign policy making toward the Mediterranean.* New York: Palgrave MacMillan.

Bigo, D. 1991. Les attentats de 1986 en France: un cas de violence transnationale et ses implications. *Cultures & Conflits* (winter), no. 4: 147–73.

Bigo, D. 1996. *Polices en réseaux. L'expérience européenne.* Paris: Fondation Nationale des Sciences Politiques.

Carrera, S., and F. Geyer. 2007. The reform treaty & Justice and Home Affairs. Implications for the common Area of Freedom, Security & Justice. CEPS policy brief. Brussels: CEPS, August.

Celso, A. 2006. Spain's dual security dilemma: Strategic challenges of Basque and Islamist terror during the Aznar and Zapatero eras. *Mediterranean Quarterly* 17, no. 4: 121–41.

Coreper. 2000. A item note from the Coreper to the General Affairs Council/ European Council. European Union priorities and policy objectives for external relations in the field of justice and home affaires, 7653/00 JAI 35, June 6.

Cottey, A. 2007. *Security in the new Europe.* New York: Palgrave MacMillan.

Council of the European Union. 2004. Integrating the fight against terrorism into EU external relations policy, 14456/2/04 REV 2 EXT1, November 18.

Council of the European Union. 2005. Council Decision on the conclusion of the Euro-Mediterranean agreement establishing an association between the European Community and its member states, of the one part, and the People's Democratic Republic of Algeria, of the other part. *Official Journal of the EU* L265 10/10/2005 (July 18).

Council of the European Union. 2007a. Council Joint Action 2007/501/CFSP on cooperation with the African Centre for Study and Research on Terrorism in the framework of the implementation of the European Union counter-terrorism strategy. *Official Journal of the EU* L/185/31 (July 17).

Council of the European Union. 2007b. *EU Action Plan on combating terrorism*, 7233/07. Brussels, March 9.

De Vries, G. 2006. The European Union and the fight against terrorism. January 19.

Directorate General Press and Communication. 2002. Eurobarometer. Report Number 56. Fieldwork Oct–Nov 2001, April 2002.

El Mundo. 2007. Cooperar para prevenir. Junio 19.

EU Council Secretariat. 2007. Factsheet. The European Union and the fight against terrorism, March 9.

Euro–Mediterranean Conference. 2005. Euro–Mediterranean code of conduct on countering terrorism.

EuroMeSCo. 2005. Barcelona plus. Towards a Euro–Mediterranean community of democratic states, April.

European Council. 1999. Tampere Presidency conclusions, October 15 and 16.

European Council. 2001. Conclusions and plan of action of the extraordinary European Council meeting, September 21.

European Council. 2004a. Declaration on combating terrorism, March 25.

European Council. 2004b. EU counter-terrorism clauses: assessment, 14458/2/04, May 11.

European Council. 2008. Consolidated versions of the Treaty on European Union and the Treaty on the functioning of the European Union, 6655/08, April 15.

European Parliament and European Council. 2006. Regulation (EC) No 1717/2006 of November 15 2006 establishing an Instrument for Stability. *Official Journal of the EU* L327/1 (November 24).

Europol. 2007. TE-SAT 2007. EU terrorism situation and trend report 2007, March.

Fijnaut, C., J. Wouters, and F. Naert. 2004. *Legal instruments in the fight against international terrorism. A transatlantic dialogue.* Leiden and Boston: Martinus Nijhoff.

Fini, G. 2006. Italy's role in Mediterranean security and the fight against terrorism. *Mediterranean Quarterly* (winter): 1–15.

Fligstein, N., and I. Mara-Drita. 1996. How to make a market: Reflections on the attempt to create a single market in the European Union. *The American Journal of Sociology* 102, no. 1: 1–33.

Gillespie, R. 2002. Regionalism and globalism in the EMP: The limits to western Mediterranean co-operation, conference on 'The convergence of civilizations? Constructing a Mediterranean region' Lisboa, June 6–9.

Guazzone, L., and F. Bicchi. 2002. European security policies in the Mediterranean: From comprehensive to 'neo-hard'?. In Huldt, Engman and Davidson 2002, 237–53.

Guidière, M. 2007. *Al-Qaïda à la Conquête du Maghreb. Le terrorisme aux portes de l'Europe.* Monaco: Editions du Rocher.
Huldt, B., M. Engman, and E. Davidson, eds. 2002. *Euro–Mediterranean security and the Barcelona process.* Stockholm: Swedish National Defence College.
Joffé, G. 2008. The European Union, democracy and counter-terrorism in the Maghreb. *Journal of Common Market Studies* 46, no. 1: 147–71.
Kaunert, C. 2005. The Area of Freedom, Security and Justice: The construction of a 'European public order'. *European Security* 14, no. 4: 459–83.
Keohane, D. 2006. Implementing the EU's counter-terrorism strategy. Intelligence, emergencies and foreign policy. In Mahncke and Monar 2006, 63–72.
Lugna, L. 2006. Institutional framework of the European Union counter-terrorism policy setting. *Baltic Security and Defence Review* 8: 101–27.
Mahncke, D., and J. Monar, eds. 2006. *International terrorism — A European response to a global threat?.* Brussels: Peter Lang.
Ministerio del Interior Español. 2007. Camacho propone crear dispositivos europeos permanentes de control en los países de origen de la inmigración ilegal, Nota de Prensa, Mayo 21.
Mohsen-Finan, K. 2007. Le Maghreb serait-il devenu un terrain privilégié pour les 'jihadistes'?. *Afkar/ idées* (summer).
Monar, J. 2006. Conclusions. In Mahncke and Monar 2006, 151–8.
Monar, J. 2007. The EU's approach post-September 11: Global terrorism as a multidimensional law enforcement challenge. *Review of International Affairs* 20, no. 2: 267–83.
Mounier, G. 2007. Civilian crisis management and the external dimension of JHA: Inceptive, functional, and institutional similarities. Doctoral workshop 'The JHA external dimension', September 21.
Pastore, F., J. Friedrichs, and A. Politi. 2005. Is there a European strategy against terrorism? A brief assessment of supra-national and national responses. Working paper, February.
Pierson, P. 2000. Increasing returns, path dependence, and the study of politics. *The American Political Science Review* 94, no. 2: 251–67.
Pochon, J.-P. 2005. Counter-terrorism in France: taking stock of the situation. Paper presented at the conference 'One year after Madrid ... Europe face to face with terrorism'. Paris: IRIS.
Reinares, F. 2006. The Mediterranean region and international terrorism: A new framework for cooperation? Real Instituto Elcano: ARI no. 149, Madrid.
Rodier, A. 2006. Pourquoi la France est menacée par le GSPC?. Note d'Actualité no. 58.
Saudi Press Association. 2003. Arab Interior Ministers' consensus for confronting terrorism, January 15.
Shapiro, J., and B. Suzan. 2003. The French experience of counter-terrorism. *Survival* 45, no. 1: 67–98.
Shaun, G. 2003. France and the war on terrorism. *Terrorism and political violence* 15, no. 1: 124–47.
Smith, C.S. 2007. Tunisia is feared as new Islamist base; Qaeda-linked Algerian group suspected of using country in network. *International Herald Tribune*, February 20.
Spence, D. 2008. *The European Union and terrorism.* London: John Harper.
Stetter, S. 2000. Regulating migration: authority delegation in justice and home affairs. *Journal of European Public Policy* 7, no. 1: 80–103.
UNDP. 2004. Arab human development report. Towards freedom in the Arab world. New York: UNDP.
Volpi, F. 2006. Introduction: Strategies for regional cooperation in the Mediterranean. Rethinking the parameters of the debate. *Mediterranean Politics* 11, no. 2: 119–35.
Wolff, S. 2006. The externalisation of Justice and Home Affairs to the southern neighbours: the EU's dilemmas in the fight against terrorism. The EuroMeSCo annual conference 2006 'Paths to democracy and inclusion within diversity' — Working group on 'The linkage between justice and terrorism in the Euro–Mediterranean Area', October.
Wolff, S. 2007a. La dimension méditerranéenne de la politique Justice et Affaires intérieures. *Cultures & Conflits* (summer), no. 6: 77–99.
Wolff, S. 2007b. España y la Gobernanza de la Seguridad Mediterránea. Vecinos, Espacios y Actores. *Revista CIDOB d'Afers Internacionals*, Special issue on 'La Política Arabe y Mediterránea de España', no. 79/80: 107–23.

Wolff, S. 2008. Border management in the Mediterranean: internal, external and ethical challenges. *Cambridge Review of International Affairs* 21, no. 2: 254–70.

Wolff, S., N. Wichmann, and G. Mounier. 2009. The external dimension of Justice and Home Affairs: A different security agenda for the EU? *Journal of European Integration* 31, no. 1: 9–23.

Index

Page numbers in *Italics* represent tables.
n after the page number indicates endnotes

abolition: pillars 19
acquis 71, 72, 82, 87
Action Orientated Papers (AOP) 13
Action Plan on Terrorism 50
actors: power 15; role 5-7; supranational 52-5; transnational security 56-7
Advanced Passenger Information (API): norm mirroring 127
agreements 35
air travel: tool for radicalization 128
Al-Qaeda 142
Albania 70, 75
Algeria 146-7
All Association (AA) 92
Allison, G.T. 30; foreign policy 30
Amended Operation Plan (OPLAN) 54
Amnesty International 144
Amsterdam Treaty (1999) 2
Anastasakis, O.: and Bechev, D. 66-7
anti-corruption policy 93
anti-drugs transfer 92
anti-terrorism strategy 123
Area of Freedom, Security and Justice (AFSJ) 11-12, 15, 32, 44, 46, 106, 136, 138, 139
Area of Justice, Freedom and Liberty (AJFL) 102
Armenia 110
asylum 89
asymmetry of interest 88, 96-7
Azerbaijan 110

Balkans 12; national security network 56
bargaining: negotiation 124-6
Basque nationalism 137-8
Bechev, D.: and Anastasakis, O. 66-7
benchmarking: monitoring 71

Berenskoetter, F. 103
bilateral cooperation 148-9
Black Sea 110
border control 73, 91
border guards: judges 56
border management: Mediterranean 19
border security 118; implementation delays 123; norms 17-34; policy 123
borderlands 105, 106
Bosnia: EUPM 56-7
boundaries 105
Brower, E.: and Guild, E. 125
Brussels Council (2004) 20n
Budapest process 91
Bulgaria 74
bureaucratic politics 10
Butmir military camp 56

Canada 126
candidate status 69
CARDS programme 72
CEPOL 98n
Challenge 1
Chevenement Group 35
Christiansen, T. 38
civil-military coordination concept (CMCO) 54
civilian crisis management 45, 53, 57; functional frame 51-2
civilian cross-management activity 44
civilian police 55
civilian power 48
Common Foreign and Security Policy (CFSP) 103
Community Assistance for Reconstruction, Development and Stabilization (CARDS) 70-1

Community method 5
Concept for European Community 53
conditionality 17, 65, 67-8, 82, 90, 106; credibility 66; external governance 83; membership 65, 66-7, 77; policy-related 66-7, 73, 77; programme 68; project level 68
conflict 34, 38; Georgia resolution 109
consistency 18
cooperation: asylum 89; inter-pillar 53; third countries 50
coordination 33, 54; cross-pillar 25-6
Copenhagen Criteria 69
CORPER 25
corruption: drug trafficking 92; fight against 88
Council of Ministers 12
Council Working Group (COWEB) 74
counter-terrorism 35-6, 145-6; clause 146; cooperation 4, 131; development 136-42; external dimension 149-51; foreign policy 136-42; Mediterranean dimension 135-54; policy 50; US architecture 15
Counter-Terrorism Working Group (COTER) 140
Court of First Instance (CFI) 27
credibility: conditionality 66
crime *see* organized crime
criminal justice reform 112
crisis management 55-7; activity 44; civilian 45, 51-2, 53, 57
Crisis Response Coordination Teams (CRCTs) 54
critical juncture 17, 145, 150; cultural frames 137-9
Croatia 69, 70, 71, 73
cross-pillarization 23-42, 53, 54, 140; approach 25-6, 27; external 28, 38; instrument 146; internal 28, 38; legal and policy aspects 26-7; macro 27-8; micro 27-8; policy dimension 29; politics dimension 29-30
cultural characteristic: ideological differences 34-5
cultural frame 142, 143-4, 150; approach 138; concept 136

data protection 36: 132n
de Vries, G. 118, 146

decision-making: intergovernmental 86; processes 33
DG JHA 33-5
Diez, T. 111
Directorates: Commission conflict 31-2
Directorates General 30; for External Relations 31-2
domestication 105
drug trafficking 114; corruption 92
drugs 11; irregular migration 88
Duchéne, E. 105

Eastern enlargement 65, 72
Easton, D. 14
Eklund, P. 114
EUJUST (rule of law mission 2004) 108-9
Euro-Mediterranean Association Agreement (EMAA) 146
Euro-Mediterranean Ombudsman 150
Eurojust 83
European Commission 12, 34, 36, 39n
European Council (EC) 12; Brussels (2004) 20n; Feira (2000) 12, 32, 48; Multi-Presidency Work Programme 12; Tampere (1999) 138
European External Action Service (EEAS) 37
European Neighbourhood Policy (ENP) 82
European Parliament (EP) 33
European Partnerships 70
European Political Cooperation (EPC) 8-9
European Security and Defence Policy (ESDP) 144; civilian component 47-8; civilian crisis management 57; police missions 5
European Security Service 38
European Security Strategy 52, 90
European Union (EU) 36; -Georgia perspective rule of law 109; -US asymmetrical relationship 124-5; Border Assistance Mission (EUBAM) 93; Consent 1; Drugs Action Plan (2005-8) 50; enlargement 11; external governance 81-100; influence works 67-75; internal security 81-100; South Caucasus policy 107-11; Special Representative (EUSR) 108
Europeanization: mechanism 77; membership 65-6
Europol 50, 83; Organised Crime Threat Assessment (2006) 49

experts 95
external governance: conditionality 83; EU 81-100; models 85
external relations: governance 83-4
External Strategy (2005) 13
extraterritorial approach 125; USA 125

Feira Council (2000) 12, 32, 48
financial assistance: money 70-1
Foreign Minister 37
foreign policy 10-11, 12, 30, 32; counter-terrorism 136-42; dimension 140; interior policy 49
France 15, 148, 150
Frattini, F. 33-4, 75, 77, 126
freedom 110
Friends of Presidency Group 19
Front Islamique du Salut (FIS) 148
Frontex 83-4, 91
functional frame 49-52, 50; civilian crisis management 51-2
functional similarities 49-52
functional unity 49, 52, 54, 57

gate-keeping 68
geographical prioritization 13
Georgia 4, 18, 101-6, 107-11; conflict resolution 109; Russia 114
Ginsberg, R.H. 14-15
governance: capacity 95; external 95-6; external relations 83-4; hierarchical 91; internal security 84-7; network 4, 73, 86, 87, 88, 95, 96, 97
Grabbe, H. 65-6
GRECO (*Groupe d'Etats contre la Corruption*) 94, 95, 98n
Group de Roubaix 148
Guild, E.: and Brower, E. 125

Hague Programme 12-13
Hansen, A.S. 52
Herdina, A. 82
hierarchical governance 91
hierarchical policy transfer 4
High Representative of Union for Foreign Affairs and Security Policy 58
historical institutionalism 17; perspective 137-8
Hooghe, L.: and Marks, G. 39n
human rights standards 113
human security 51

ideological differences: cultural characteristic 34-5
immigration: asylum 89; global approach 92; illegal 68, 114, *see also* migration
implementation networks 84
incentive membership 72
informal networking 38
informalization strategy 90
information networks 84
input/output conceptualization 14-15
institutional discourses 50
institutional fragmentation 15
institutional politics 30-1
institutionalism 119; perspective 136; rational choice 102
Instrument for Pre-Accession Assistance (IPA) 70
Instrument for Stability 147
instruments of cooperation 145-8
Integrated Border Management: Border Police 71; project 110
integration 28; capacity 66
intelligence services 149
intensive transgovernmentalism 86
inter-administrative exchanges: technical assistance 96
inter-institutional politics 38
interdependence 82-3
intergovernmental bargaining 90
interior policy: foreign policy 49
internal security 98n; EU 81-100; governance 84-7; policies 32
international conventions: mobilization 97
International Criminal Tribunal for Former Yugoslavia 69
International Narcotics Board (INCB) 93
intra-institutional politics 25
intra-organizational competition 30
irregular migration 89, 90; drugs 88
Islamic terrorism 138

JHAE 31, 32, 33
judges: border guards 56
judiciary 112
Justice and Home Affairs (JHA) 44; definition 9-10; external dimension 14-16, 46-7, 87-95; security environment 45-8

Kaldor, M. 51

158 Index

Lavenex, S. 47, 51, 102, 103-4
legal boundary 103
legislation 96
Lisbon Treaty (2009) 2, 15, 19, 37, 57, 58, 141
logic of diversity 18-19
Lutterbeck, D. 55
Lynch, D. 109

Maastricht Treaty (1993) 6n, 24; third pillar 2
Macedonia 71
Madrid 149; bombings (2004) 149
Maghreb region 151n
mainstreaming 140
Manners, L. 119
Marks, G.: and Hooghe, L. 39n
mechanisms: Europeanization 77
Mediterranean: border management 19; counter-terrorism 135-54; countries 4, 94; ENP countries 90
migration: -development nexus 92; illegal 104-5, 114; irregular 88, 89, 90; policy 47, *see also* immigration
military camp: *Butmir* 56
military power 114
missions: border control 91
mobilization: international conventions 97
models 69-70; external governance 85
Moldova 92
Monar, J. 110
money: financial assistance 70-1
Morocco 9, 98n, 146, 147-8
Multi-Annual Indicative Financial Framework (MIFF) 70
Multi-Presidency Work Programme (EC) 12
Munich Olympic Games (1972): terrorism cooperation 137
Muslim youth: radicalization 123

narcotics prevention 110
national security network: Balkans 56
National Strategy for Homeland Security 124
negative visa list 73-4
negotiation: bargaining 124-6
neighbourhood policy 103
neighbouring countries 104
network: governance 4, 73, 86, 87, 88, 95, 96, 97; informal 38; information 84; organized crime 63-4, 109; project-based 91; regulation 86; top-down 87; transgovernmental 83-4, 90, 97; transnational security 52-7; vertical 87; vertical coordination 96
New Institutionalism 11, 16-8
norm: Advanced Passenger Information (API) 127; assimilation 129-30; internalization 118-29; mirroring 127-30
North Africa 142; Sahel region 150; terrorism 143

operational cooperation 86
Organisation Armeé Secrète (OAS) 148
organized crime 34; networks 63-4, 109
Organized Crime Threat Assessment (Europol 2006) 49
organized frame 50
OSCE (Organization for Security and Co-operation in Europe) 109
othering 105

Pantz, S. 112-13
paramilitary: police forces 55
partnership: approach 105; concept 50-1
Partnership and Cooperation Agreement (PCA 2004) 92-3, 107-8
Passenger Information Unit (PIU) 128
Passenger Name Record (PNR) Agreement (2007) 35-6, 38, 117-34, 121-2, 129, 132n
Passerelle provisions 39n
Pawlak, W.: institutional fragmentation 15
peace 8-9
penitentiary reforms 112
permissive consensus 136-8, 145
personal data 125
Petersberg Tasks 44, 58
pillar structure 24, 141
Police Action Plan (2001) 48
Police Chief Task Force (PCTF) 141: 151n
police forces 55-6; paramilitary 55
police missions 48, 51; ESDP 5
police operations: civilian 52
policy: conditionality 4; cross-pillarization 29; networks 17; space 14, 17; universe 9-10
policy transfer 89, 91; hierarchical 88, 92
policy-making: communitarized method 85-7; cross-pillar 15; security 9
Political and Security Committee (PSC) 54

politics dimension: cross-pillarization 29-30
Pre-Accession Pact: cooperation against crime (1998) 11
pre-accession strategy 72-3
privacy 36
Prodi, R. 103
project-based networks 91
protection: citizens 111; norms and standards 50
public security 110-11

radicalization 123; Muslim youth 123
rapprochement 44-5, 49, 57, 58, 144-5; process 68-9; security 150
rational choice 30-1, 119-20, 131; institutionalism 16-17, 65, 102; perspective 121
readmission agreements 67, 77, 91; Visa Facilitation 73-5
Regional Co-operation Council (RCC) 70
regional programmes 53
Regional Protection Programmes (RPP) 89
regulation networks 84, 86
RELEX Counsellors 25
roadmaps 75
Romania 74
routes of influence 63-80
rule of law: EU-Georgia perspective 109
Rules of Procedure 34
Russia 109, 114

Sahel region (North Africa) 150
sanctuary policy 148
Schroeder, U.C. 53
securitization strategy 105
security: agenda 17, 19; building institutions 46; environment 45-8; external 45-6; homeland 35; human 51; internal 9, 11, 45-6, 57, 104; norms 118; orientated institution 38; peace 8-9; policies 35, 46-8, 123; policy-making 9; politics 44-5; public 110-11; rapprochement 150; regime 47; sector 51-2; third country threats 51; threats 51, 101-7; transnational 45; transnational networks 55-7; transportation 35-6, *see also* border security; internal security
Security Sector Reform (SSR) 51-2
Sedelmeier, U. 66

Situation Centre (SitCen) 141
Slaughter, A.M. 84
Smith, K. 105
smuggling route 64
sociological institution 17, 65
sociological institutionalism 31, 49, 131; perspective 129-30
Söderköping Process (2001) 89
South Caucasus 101-2; EU policy 107-11; threat perceptions 103-7
Southern Caucasus Anti-Drug Programme (SCAD) 110
Spain 15, 150
Stability Instrument 54
Stability Pact for South-Eastern Europe (1999) 69-70
Stabilization and Association Agreement (SAA) 68
Stabilization and Association Process (SAP) 67-8
Standing Committee on Internal Security (COSI) 57-8
states: weak or failing 104
Stetter, S. 49
Stevens, A.: and Stevens, H. 32
Strategy on External Dimension of AFSJ 31, 34
structural politics 39n
suicide bombings 142

Tampere Summit (1999) 138
technical assistance 146-7; inter-administrative exchanges 96
Technical Assistance Information Exchange Office (TAIEX) 72, 98n
technocrats 95
terrorism 50, 123; Islamic 138; Munich Olympic Games (1972) 137; North Africa 143, *see also* counter-terrorism
Terrorism Working Group (TWG) 140
Thessaloniki Agenda for Western Balkans (2003) 67, 74
third countries 33, 82, 94, 106, 140
threats: perception in Caucasus 103-7; security 51, 101-7; transnationalization 45-6
training 113
transatlantic security relationship 118-19
transborder challenges 54
transgovernmental network 83-4, 90, 97
transgovernmentalism 96

transnational security networks 52-7
transnationalization: threats 45-6
transportation security 35-6
travellers privacy rights 119
Tunisia 89-90
turf war 36
twinning 98n; advice 71; light project 98n

Ukraine 89, 92
unilateral approach: USA 125
unilateral policy promotion 12-14
United Nations (UN) 140; Development Programme (UNDP) 144; Interim Administrative Mission in Kosovo (UNMIK) 47
United States of America (USA) 5, 18, 118; extraterritorial approach 125; unilateral approach 125; VISIT programme 132n

Valencia Action Plan (2002) 90
vertical coordination structures 87
Vienna Declaration on Security Partnership (2005) 50
visa: facilitation 66-7, 90; liberalization 66-7; readmission agreements 73-5; regime 77
Visa Waiver Programme (VWP) 126

Wessel, R. 49
Western Balkans 63-80; Europeanization 65-7; relations 76
Western NIS 89
Wichmann, L. 17

Youngs, R. 111
Yugoslavia 69

9780415851121